MOTOWN
FROM THE BACKGROUND

MOTOWN

FROM THE BACKGROUND

The Authorized Biography of

THE ANDANTES

Vickie Wright
with **Marlene Barrow-Tate**
Louvain Demps,
Jackie Hicks

Edited by **Jennifer Ullrich**
Featuring photography by **Lynette Turner**

MOTOWN FROM THE BACKGROUND

ISBN 10: 1-904408-29-X
ISBN 13: 978190440829X

First published 2007

Cover photography: Lynette Turner
Production design: Dave Randle

Designed and typeset in England by

BANK HOUSE BOOKS
PO Box 3
NEW ROMNEY
TN29 9WJ UK

BANK HOUSE BOOKS is a division of BANK HOUSE MEDIA Ltd

Dedications

From Marlene Barrow-Tate
To my grandchildren, Judith Marlene and Racing.

From Jackie Hicks
In loving memory of my sister and mother.

From Louvain Demps
I dedicate this book to my family, and in loving memory of my mother and to all of our colleagues who are no longer with us..

From Vickie Wright
I dedicate this book to the fans and a few very special people who are no longer with us. My father Gilbert Wright, I inherited your adventurous spirit. My nephew Johnny Paul "Pod" Rice, and our co-worker and friend Jenna Johnson who inspired many of us with her young life.

Contents

Acknowledgements

I wish to say a heartfelt and very special thank you to Marlene Barrow-Tate, Louvain Demps, and Jackie Hicks. Thank you for showing me love, support, and backbone.

I want to thank everyone who has supported me in doing this work. There are very special people who have been with me from the beginning: Rigo Ardon, Rob Renshaw, Dorian Jones, Chance DeLap, Ludie Montgomery, where it all started, Grace Wood, Denise Oliver, Serge Crawford, Mae E. Campbell, Keith Summers, Pat Washington, Mia and Jackie Moser, Vonnie and Bobby, Dave Randle, Harry Weinger, Talya Meldy, Heather McGinnis, and Judy Zaylor. To my life coaches Kristin Taliaferro in Hawaii and Ylva Cramfelt in Sweden: you helped me so much and I will never forget your guidance and wisdom. I could not have done this without you.

To Jennifer Ullrich, thank you for being a great editor and taking care of all those details that I'm not very good with. My cheerleading squad and personal drill team: Sylvia Jahshan, Lynette Turner, Cathy Jenman, Jennifer Stitz, and Stacia Davies. We are the "Kick Butt Club".

Every day I thank God for the angels he sends to me.

Foreword

You can count on one hand the outstanding groups specializing in background singing. The Sweet Inspirations, The Blossoms, and original Raelets come to mind. And so do three ladies from Detroit called The Andantes. Their contributions to the music of Motown Record Corporation are monumental.

Unfortunately, not much has been written about Jackie Hicks, Louvain Demps, and Marlene Barrow. They were heard, but seldom seen.

The Andantes first came to my attention on an early '60s album titled 'The Motortown Revue'. It was recorded live at the Fox Theater in downtown Detroit and featured the Miracles, Mary Wells, Little Stevie Wonder, Martha & the Vandellas, Kim Weston, The Marvelettes and the Temptations.

At one point, Weston informs the audience that The Andantes were going to help her out as she performed her latest single, 'Just Loving You'. I was deeply impressed with the beauty of their voices. The blend was perfect, and it was evident that much effort had gone into the creation of that sound.

Louvain, Jackie, and Marlene were born to sing together! In the ensuing years, I learned plenty about The Andantes and studied the hundreds of Motown recordings they were on, including virtually everything done by The Four Tops. To say these ladies enhanced Motown's records would be an understatement. Among my favorites are 'My Baby Must Be a Magician' and 'This Night Was Made For Love', both by the Marvelettes, and Brenda Holloway's 'When I'm Gone'. A book such as this one is long overdue. It is a blessing for The Andantes and for the many people who have been blessed by their singing—even when they didn't know who they were hearing. The cream always rises to the top.

Steve Holsey
Entertainment Editor/Columnist
The Michigan Chronicle

Author's Notes and Introduction

This book began a long time ago; it just took some time for the components and people to come together and make it happen. I first met Louvain Demps several years ago over a telephone conversation we had regarding Tammi Terrell. I worked closely with Tammi's sister Ludie Montgomery and as I co-authored that biography, Louvain became one of my rocks.

Louvain would help fill in the many blanks for me, though some blanks should remain blank. Louvain and I had an instant chemistry and built a strong foundation on respect and truth. She asked me if I would help The Andantes write their memoirs. I was consumed with Tammi's and Ludie's lives, and all of the emotions that came with doing that work. It became clear to me that The Andantes were for me as well. They were an extension of the work I had already begun. I knew what had led me this far and my spirit was once more being summoned.

Through the music, Tammi, and now my lovely Andantes, I have begun to heal my own life. This has been history for music in telling these untold stories. I also feel that this process has been Part 1 and Part 2 of my own life and the conclusion is now up to me. After Tammi's book came out I read the book, *The Five People You Meet in Heaven* by Mitch Albom. I actually read it on a plane going to Detroit. The author is from Philadelphia and currently resides in Detroit. I picked up the book at the airport as a fluke, not knowing anything about Mr. Albom or his Philly and Detroit roots. I am a firm believer in "Synchronicity". I felt a powerful message from that book and I believe I know who one of my five people will be in heaven.

There is no way you can write books like these and not address the same issues for you. After Tammi's book was finished, I was not quite there with my own healing and forgiving. Now, I too have arrived where The Andantes and Ludie are. Louvain would tell me to remember who is walking beside me and never forget who I worked for. I enjoyed this work and these two books were true labors of love for me.

This is not the last you will hear from me. I feel complete

for now in writing biographies. I can honestly say that this is the hardest thing I have ever tackled. Lasting friendships form with this kind of work. I became intertwined with everyone to a point where I did not feel like a writer at times, but more like a friend who was seeking the same truth and results as they were. The only difference is that they were sorting their life stories for the book; through Tammi, Ludie, Marlene, Jackie, and Louvain, I began to sort mine for my future.

As Tammi's book was finishing up and we had our big celebration in Philadelphia, the mayor declared "Tammi Terrell Day". I had to get started right away for these ladies. Marlene and Jackie were not yet on board with the discussions Louvain and I were having. The first line of duty was to make certain they would be involved. We wanted it to be the official piece on what the grapevine truly had to say. Marlene and Jackie agreed it was time, and for the first time they began to share with me their stories and memories.

For several months I spoke with each of them weekly. Every Monday was with Jackie at 4AM my time. She would tease me because it was cold in California and I would have the heater on (after all it was 65 degrees) and she would laugh at me because she only had a robe on while it was in the 30's in Detroit. When Jackie and I first talked, she told me, "You better behave." Monday nights after work, I spoke with Marlene. We spent hours on the phone laughing and joking. She also opened up her life to me in a private way in which she had never spoken before. Saturdays would be with Louvain. My friend Heather McGinnis would be on the phone with Louvain and me taking notes (thank you Heather, for helping).

I sought out many of their friends, family, and colleagues to help tell the important elements of their history. At times this will read like a diary, a yearbook, and a most important life and history lesson. I wanted to bring The Andantes to their public and show the fans who they are. Once I began the work, it was blowing my mind that I was writing a book about the voices I have loved my entire life. They sing on an estimated 20,000 songs. The untold story here is filled with injustices. In recent years people like Martha Wash have come to the front of the line to claim her credit. Other times, Milli Vanilli would lose their Grammy for not having actually sung on the records.

One of my favorite quotes is by Harry S. Truman: "It is amazing what you can accomplish if you do not care who gets the credit." This is the essence of these ladies. Their place in history is more solidified than many singers who had one hit or a few years of fame and success. The Andantes had little recognition for many years and slowly their truth has come to the surface. Their contribution to music is lasting and timeless and each of us has a story of what their voices mean to us. They have been silent for so many decades and for me that makes them even more legendary. They tell their truths here and they do it in a way that is their own.

Cal Street explained to me that Motown was like a puzzle and each person fits the picture and the story. I wanted my work to show a tiny piece of that puzzle, such as I told previously with Tammi's life, and now with The Andantes. There are more puzzle pieces to be added. This book is about these ladies, their roots, and who they are. They defined the Motown sound along with The Funk Brothers. They are "The Sound of Young America" along with everyone else. They are a little piece of everyone, either by friendship and family ties or karmic and musical strands.

I am honored to be part of their history in telling it. I hope you enjoy getting to know these legendary voices in history. Music is healing and it brings us together. I want to thank Marlene, Jackie, and Louvain for making this work available to the public. It is important that the music be preserved and the stories shared.

I have always been a person who supports the underdog and when I tackled Tammi's story that was the case with her. She was misunderstood and wrongfully documented in history. Tammi's friends and family secured her legacy. This time everyone is backing up the backups and it has been a wonderful thing to witness. If I had a dollar for every time I heard one of them or their friends say "Girl, let me tell you something", I would have a small fortune. I loved hearing all of the stories. I will hold them close to my heart, sharing some and keeping others.

We were in Marlene's basement on one of my trips to Detroit. We had spent hours listening to records and looking at old pictures and they shared some stories. One of my all time favorite moments on record is The Andantes singing behind Diana Ross on "Love Child". On that record Louvain has a solo operatic scream.

The song was playing and Louvain looked at Marlene and Jackie to say, "You guys forgot to come in on that part." Then Jackie says, "We forgot to come in?? Well perhaps you came in too soon." They are so funny when they recall stories and they have a wealth of good things to share and say. At the same time, you can hear melancholy as it all becomes one package when you get to know them. They spent a portion of their life making music that has lasted a lifetime for some people. Their legacy and music is older than I am.

In my own life during the times I have been down, I would get my yearbooks out and read them. Some things in this book are repeated because there are three people here, but also because their friends testify on their behalf. The mantra is the same all the way through: the people who know you best are the ones you should listen to. When life gets hard we often listen to that one idiot or circumstance that changes how we truly feel about ourselves. To read a yearbook and see the truth about yourself over and over from the ones who know you…it must sink in. I know it made me feel better to read what a few hundred people who knew me had to say about me. In the case of The Andantes there are millions of people who feel strongly about them. Ladies, this is your yearbook of memories for you and your families. Please never forget who you are. Your love and friendship has lifted me, "higher and higher". Thank you for being my family.

Louvain sent me the following email on November 21, 2005. I thought it was revealing, yet at the same time personal. You can see where she, Marlene, and Jackie had to heal something that was so dear to each of them; yet it was something painful that needed to come out in order for the good to be shared.

Hello Sugar Pie Honey Bunch,

Why has it has been so hard for me to listen to some of the music? Before things got better than they are now, when I would hear "our" music; I would cry all the time, so I just wouldn't listen. It hurt to know that after all of the hard work and many hours, after the dedication and love, it seemed to come to such an unfair end. No one seemed to even want to help. Perhaps they didn't really know how to or understand how much Motown meant to me. It was life. Jackie and Marlene, my family almost everyday. We spent so many hours and days together to the point we were given an office.

Each song had a different meaning for me. I was unhappy at home and these songs meant so much (I guess that's why I cried so much). Sometimes it seemed to others I might have tried to sing too loud, or even as one person said, as a "star" - but to sing brought me such freedom and joy. Mostly, I sang from my heart. I suppose that I cried when I would hear these songs, because my heart had truly been broken. Perhaps "shattered" would be a better word, for when something is broken there is a possibility it can be put back together, or at least mended in some fashion. To put together something that is shattered, like glass, is impossible. How can one find all those tiny pieces? It seems there are so many pieces to make one small glass, so what about a broken heart?

Many years later, like now, I still cry at times knowing some have suffered greatly because they trusted in words of promise so many years earlier, only to be so let down when the moment of truth kicked in. It seemed to be just that - words. When your family suffers because of you, it's such a bitter pill. It's so hard. I really don't think that there was any intent to hurt anyone. But when someone's life becomes so much better, and their desires, hopes, and wishes have been met, people sometimes forget that others are waiting for their own dreams, hopes, and desires to be met and they expect to be blessed as well. They trusted you to remember them as you said you would. I cry because The Andantes were good, but seemed to just be pushed aside like nothing and never were able to take credit (where it was due). No royalties, no paychecks, no job, and no one to give a helping hand.

Such deep sadness can cause such bitterness. It can lead to one thinking about taking one's life, and, if not careful, ending someone else's. It gets to the point where you come to realize you cannot continue to live in bitterness, if you care to live at all. You can't cry everyday, all day, about things you can't change. Life goes on and becomes what you make it. Life becomes great in new ways and new songs are born out of lessons in living. Understanding comes when you have learned to forgive (even though tears emerge still when you hear some songs). I think about all the wonderful people that I had the pleasure of working with. Some have long ago left us, some are on the way out now. We are leaving everyday. Who will be next? Have they learned to forgive themselves and others? Have they taken the lemons and made a wonderful, delicious beverage? Vickie, God has been the lifter of my head. He has dried my tears. All my hopes and desires are in Him. He has never let me down and I can and will trust in Him. Never has He forgotten the promises given to me. The Andantes to me are a sound that God gave - it will never and cannot be forgotten. It sounds something like angels singing...

Love, Louvain

It is important that you meet each Andante up close and candidly. Each of The Andantes has a rich background and foundation in the church and just as you can feel it when they are singing, you can feel it when they are speaking. Their uniqueness shines through and you learn that their talent comes from deep inside. They have an ear for sound and they have perfect pitch. They create their own harmonies and build their own structures in song. When it comes to music, they are talented, and their roots are a big part of that.

Individually, they are different in personality. Collectively, they are a strong musical team and are great support for one another in friendship. They are intuitive with their talents and can read each other, knowing what sounds they need to make so that the work they are doing turns out the very best. They are masters at blending pitches and tones that have helped to define a sound we all know and love today.

In personality Marlene is the balance, Jackie is fun, and Louvain is the reflector. They each add something amazing to this book. Marlene's insight about the music business comes from her years of living so close to it. She shares a lot of wisdom that will be very helpful to any person who is coming up through the business. Louvain shares a lot of heart and soul about the music. Jackie adds so much about the importance of family ties with either blood relatives or chosen family. I found the three of them unique and wise. Jackie could run the world and solve every problem, Marlene would make it a fair place for everyone to live, and Louvain would fill it with love overflowing into other galaxies.

The Andantes are a staple in the Motown sound. They are similar to other mediums in the entertainment field that we all see and hear everyday, but often do not think about as being actual people behind the scenes that made it possible. Imagine seeing a movie with no sound effects or watching certain commercials with no hand or foot models. How can there be action flicks without the body doubles and stunt actors?

Imagine listening to Motown with no Andantes. Something would truly be missing. I am so honored to share with you; The Andantes.

Enjoy!!

Vickie Wright
June 2007

My Friends, The Andantes

I once read that friendship is the purest form of love. As we get older, I understand this better. When I look at or think about these ladies, it often brings up such feelings of love, pride, joy, honor, and gratefulness that words often become difficult. To have survived with and loved them for all of these years is a blessing. To have the opportunity to exalt them in writing is something I have long anticipated.

One of my favorite axioms is that the Creator and the Universe places you where you are supposed to be. The Universe allowed me to be a very insignificant dot in the Motown music and recording history and live vicariously there, through and with my best girlfriends, is more than awesome. I bow to the greatness in them that forever placed them in music history and to the humility in them that allowed for our long friendship.

I need to pause for a moment to thank you Vickie Wright for telling their story. I am sure by now you know my friends as the talented, beautiful, wise, witty, creative, loving, funny, infuriating, care-taking, strong women they are. The Creator and the Universe could have only placed them as the female voices in the Motown sound. We all know that life happens. We all have made mistakes, thank goodness; we have made lemonade and can wake up in this quarter of life and still smell the roses.

I just want to take us back to a time and place on the near West side of Detroit, Michigan, mid-1950's. There was community, interconnectedness, interrelatedness and interdependence in the African American Community. It was a time in our culture when we valued children and education, respected our elders and embraced the concept of community. We knew well that negative and selfish behavior reflected first on the family, then the neighbors, the community and our race.

We had powerful role models, right on our block. There were teachers, photographers, factory and domestic workers, postal workers, grocers, future lawyers, union big-wigs, preachers, dancers, a college professor, retired veterans, music teachers and stay at home moms. If we traveled within a 10 block radius in any direction, we often encountered people and places that would ultimately be on the world stage. If we traveled ½ block to the corner of Milford and then west, we traded and interacted with many African American entrepreneurs. There were tailors, doctors, dentists, pharmacists, barbers, beauticians, restaurateurs and shoe repairmen.

We were surrounded by churches. We lived just ½ block from the historic Hartford Avenue Baptist Church. We were just around the corner from St. Stephens African Methodist Episcopal and down the block from the Hartford Seventh Day Adventist church. We could walk several blocks to New Light Baptist, Tabernacle Missionary Baptist or to Carter Metropolitan Christian Methodist Episcopal churches.

Church was a place of course for Sunday worship but also for community meetings, missionary work, bible study, church bizarres, recreational and social activities. Powerful preachers, orators, politicians, athletes and musical performers frequented all of the aforementioned churches. All of the churches had world class singers, organists and pianists.

Back in 1955, Reverend Charles A. Hill was the pastor of Hartford Baptist Church. Under his leadership, we got to see and hear such people as the Honorable Congressman, Charles Diggs, Senator Jackie Vaughn, John Conyers, Sr., the Honorable Coleman A. Young former Detroit mayor and Erma Henderson former Detroit City Council president.

Reverend Hill supported the African American business community as well as organized labor. After Reverend's Hill retirement, in 1968, Dr. Charles G. Adams, was later installed and Hartford moved to a new facility in 1977. Under the leadership of Reverend Adams, Hartford Memorial Baptist Church remains a place that is known worldwide. Dynamic orators, labor leaders, gospel singers, preachers and politicians are welcomed. We had the opportunity to commune with Reverend Martin Luther King, Jr. and his church family, the Reverend Jessie Jackson, and many others. Reverend Adams is the current minister at Hartford and is known worldwide for his Christian leadership, powerful preaching, praying and singing.

During the late 1950's into the 1970's in Detroit and nationwide, the spiritual, social, political and economic orientation of African Americans underwent a "psycho-cultural revolution."

This revolution refers to the complete change that took place in the way many Blacks perceived themselves and their culture vis-a-vis White America. I now realize that we were by and large living in a segregated community resisting the pressure to assimilate into the culture of the "larger society" and maintaining lifestyles and behaviors that were unique, viable and valuable. We stood on the shoulders of our ancestors and elders embracing long-established African traditions. Africans and African Americans are notoriously spiritual and religious. Although I did not fully understand it at the time, our upbringing and daily lives were based on age-old concepts of our African ancestors. There was a collective consciousness in which people in our community had a function and a responsibility to the larger group.

By the time we were teen-agers and young adults there were six of us girls who were constantly together: Marlene Barrow, Jackie Hicks, Yvonne Washington, Louise Walls-Rembert, Etolia White, and me, 'Rashida' Yvonne Harbin. Jackie was the first one of us to get a driver's license. We were often permitted to go the various dance clubs, the parks, over to Windsor, Canada to the festivals and to any fun activities in the city, with Emory as a chaperone. We loved to dance at the Twenty Grand, the Graystone, T.U.L.C. or skate at the Arcadia and at St. Stephens Recreation Center. We settled into adulthood with the understanding that we needed to do something productive with our lives. Our friendship continued. Marlene, Jackie, and Louvain worked at Motown and the rest of us girls worked at various jobs.

We in Detroit, like the rest of the nation mourned the deaths of President John F. Kennedy, Dr. Martin Luther King, Jr., Malcolm X and U.S. Attorney General, Robert Kennedy. The rise of the Black Power Movement, the Hippie revolution, protesting the Vietnam War supporting Mohammed Ali and even the "1967 riot" interconnected the African American community with the larger society.

Africans and African Americans intuitively understand and value that the most enduring sense of obligation is in the area of familial and social relations. We consciously or subconsciously adhere to the concept, "I am because we are, we are, therefore I am." In the Afro-centric world view put forth by Asanti, there is no separation of the material or spiritual, profane or sacred, form or substance. All realities are united in one grand manner. This is the world as I knew it that spawned my girlfriends, The Andantes and of course the Motown Recording Studios.

Motown Recording Studios, Inc. captured like few other entities, Asanti's world view of Afrocentricity. Berry Gordy, Jr. and the Motown family embodied the African proverb, "To go back to tradition is the first step forward." What Motown and Berry did unwittingly was to go back to a tradition of family, community, spiritual, cultural, economic and artistic development of African Americans. The spirituality can be seen in the singing and writing of love songs. The cultural is seen in the unique sounds, rhythms and beats (The Motown Sound). He captured the economic tradition in the business of making, producing and distributing Motown's music. The artistic development of Motown acts is unequaled to this day. Marlene often says that Berry always wanted a good product. Whoever was in the studio that could contribute was called upon to do so.

Berry's vitalistic thrust behind the people, activities and behaviors indeed united "all realities in one grand manner."

Suffice it to say, the sounds of Motown will forever resonate in my head and I know in the universe. I clearly understand that humans acting with personal power, i.e. singing, writing, dancing, just creating, can animate, activate and galvanize the material or the spiritual world. Earth, Wind and Fire, said it well; "Sounds, they never dissipate, they only recreate to another place and time." The resonance of Motown's Music continues to reverberate through out the world, nay the universe. It can never go away. I am humbled and grateful that my friends of fifty plus years still live and sing. Music is forever in the universe and so are The Andantes. How powerful is that? If you can substitute the words Motown music or combine them with the word, love in Stevie Wonder's song, "As" you will capture my feeling about my girlfriends and about Motown. I leave this acclaim to my sisters/ friends.

Stevie Wonder lyrics:

'As'

As around the sun, the earth knows she's revolving
And the rosebuds know to bloom in early May
Just as hate knows love's the cure
You can rest your mind assured
That I'll be loving you always
As now can't reveal the mystery of tomorrow
But in passing will grow older every day
Just as all is born is new
Do know what I say is true
That I'll be loving you always

Until the rainbow burns the stars out in the sky
Until the ocean covers every mountain high
Until dolphin flies and parrots live at sea
Until we dream of life and life becomes a dream

Did you know that true love asks for nothing
Her acceptance in the way we pay
Did you know that life has given love a guarantee
To last through forever and another day

Just as time knew to move on since the beginning
And the seasons know exactly when to change
Just as kindness knows no shame
Know through all your joy and pain
That I'll be loving you always
As today I know I'm living but tomorrow
Could make me the past but that I mustn't fear
For I'll know deep in my mind
The love of me I've left behind
Cause I'll be loving you always

Until the day is night and night becomes the day
Until the trees and seas just up and fly away
Until the day that 8 x 8x 8 is 4

Until the day that is the day that are no more
Did you know that you are loved by somebody
Until the day that the earth starts turning right to left
Until the earth just for the sun denies itself
I'll be loving you forever
Until dear Mother Nature says her work is through
Until the day that you are me and I am you
Until the rainbow burns the stars out in the sky

ALWAYS

We all know sometimes life's hates and troubles can make you wish you were born in another time and space.

But you can bet your life times that and twice its double, that God knew exactly where He wanted you to be placed.

Andantes, Jackie, Marlene, and Louvain, Motown is because you are, you are because Motown is and I'll be loving you always.

To be blessed with friends for fifty plus years who happen to be the dynamic and melodious female voices most often heard in the background for Motown Recording Studios, Inc. is and has been a very unique life experience.

Rashida Yvonne Harbin

Meeting The Andantes

Jackie Hicks

"I was born Jacqueline Coela Hicks in Detroit on November 4, 1939. Coela is supposed to be an Indian name. One of the women in the beauty shop my mother frequented had that name; my mother liked it and gave it to me. I have a goddaughter named Coela. I like the name; I have never met a Coela in my life. I have a few friends and a cousin who call me by that name. If I am out and I hear it, I know it is someone who really knows me.

My parents are Aaron Luvell Hicks and Clara Lyons. My father came to Detroit from Alabama and my mother from Atlanta. I am their youngest child. All of my siblings were born in Detroit. My brothers are Aaron and Emory and my only sister is Clara, though we always referred to her as Annette. We were a very close family.

My father worked at the Ford Motor Company in the Foundry. He was there for most of his life and retired from Ford. My mother was a homemaker and later began working for the Board of Education, where she retired. Both of my parents were musical and sang in our church choirs. I have a strong foundation in this area. I felt musical inspiration from my parents at an early age and for many years, we all sang in the choir together. Our whole family sang in the choir at Hartford Avenue Baptist Church, right here in Detroit. This is where I met Marlene Reid. I was about six years old and she was five.

As far as our home was concerned, when we were younger, any music that we sang or played had to do with church. My parents were just not into the rock and roll music or R&B music. They were grounded in church and the music was important to them. Everyone came to our house on Sunday after church to reflect and enjoy dinner. Fellowship was a big part of our lives and it seems as though there was always enough food to share. Someone would be here before and after choir practice.

Sometimes when the choir had outside engagements our

house was close to the church so this was the meeting location.

My brother Aaron was renown with his singing. He sang with The Dupre Victorian Choir, The Depaur Infantry Choir, and The Brazeal Dennard Chorale. He was also a music teacher and taught piano. I believe that the world can connect in unity through music. It brings us all together.

In our teen years, music and dancing was a big part of our lives and we always bought the latest records. I was a big fan of the Drifters and the Dells. Our house was the house to come hang out and listen to music and dance. We had a piano in the living room. Aaron would give my friends and me lessons on it. We would all be here practicing the dances, so we would be hip at parties on the weekends. Back then, we would have basement parties. My momma would always let our friends dance in the dining room. I think that was momma's way of eye-balling us. All of our friends loved her and called her Mother Hicks. It was better for us to have a mother watching over us when we were growing up. It built character for us.

One time we were listening to records and we had 'Work With Me Annie' by The Midnighters on the record player. Momma was always listening and watching us. She came in from the porch, walked over to the record player and said, 'I don't ever want to hear that record in my house again!' The lyrics were 'Work with me Annie, work with me Annie, every time she starts to work, she had to stop and walk the baby cross the floor'. My mother said 'WHAT!' She thought the 'work with me Annie' lyrics implied sex. Later, the same guys who released that came out with a record called 'Annie's Aunt Fannie'.

I just loved Gene Chandler's 'Duke of Earl'. My brother Aaron didn't like the R&B music style, although that was the music I ended up singing for a career. Aaron loved classical music. One time in the music class he was teaching, the kids had a talent show and they performed 'Duke of Earl'. Aaron was very touched by that and it made him begin to appreciate that style of music."

Jackie's brother Emory recalls the younger years of Marlene and Jackie. "I was the chaperone; they didn't go many places without me watching over them. Even after they were of age, I was still looking over them and their friends.

They never got into any trouble. They went to a lot of parties and dances and sock-hops. These were the years of innocent basement parties where they just snacked, danced, and hung out. I was in charge of getting them back home if they had a curfew. I made sure I got them back home to their parents. They never left my sight.

Jackie and Marlene and their friends had really great personalities when they were growing up. They had good mothers that demanded they be good people and good young women. They have a solid church foundation and come from good families who were close. Their mothers were church-going women and they inherited those qualities. Marlene's mother was the music director of our choir and I sang under her direction. Her mother was an excellent musician and I imagine that is why Marlene is so excellent in her musical skills. We are a close-knit group of people; we were then and still are. I think we have had an excellent life together and it continues to be that way. All you have to do is make one phone call and everyone is back together again."

Jackie reiterates, "When we were growing up, we saw all of our family on a regular basis. I give my parents credit for giving me balance. I take my walk with God seriously because of my parents giving me that foundation. My parents taught us to do the right thing even when it was easy to do the wrong thing or when other people were being negative. The wrong choices did not make you happier just because they were easier. You have to learn to move on when negative circumstances happen to you rather than lash out at the people who harm you. If you cannot correct the wrong, then let it go.

My parents were older parents and my friends thought they were my grandparents because their parents were younger. I was the youngest child, so I got a lot from them. To have both of them in my life gave my siblings and me a solid foundation. My mother's brothers came to our house everyday. Either we saw our uncles every single day at our home, or they came by the playground to give us a quarter. Our house was on the way to and from the factory; they all worked in the auto factory together.

Our grandparents came from Alabama and Georgia. They visited often in the summers. This was grounding for us to have strong, stable adults around us all the time. Because of the women role models in my family, I was taught to depend solely on myself. I am thankful for this.

When Marlene and I were teenagers, we were singing in the choir at Hartford Avenue Baptist Church. Mildred Dobey was the choir director and piano teacher. We sang with our friends Emily and Edith Phillips who had a quartet with their cousins Barbara and Dorothy. Mildred helped to name us The Andantes. The Andantes of Hartford Avenue Baptist Church were Marlene, Edith, and me."

Mildred Dobey remembers, "I met them when they were children-literally, before they were born. I have known their families for years. When they were children, Jackie was a bubbly child and still is a bubbly person. She was the baby in her family. She was so loved. Marlene was more quiet than Jackie, but when they were together they were both bubbly, happy girls. Jackie brings that quality out in others. It was clear at an early age both Marlene and Jackie could sing. They sang very, very well and in tune. I started out with them in the church. We went around to different churches singing. Both of the girls were great with solos. Marlene didn't do as much solo work as Jackie did. I tried to choose songs that highlighted them together because they blended so beautifully.

Marlene's mother was my mentor. Her mother started me in the church when I was about ten years old and mentored me as a church musician. I played music in Sunday school and in church. Marlene's mother was my eldest daughter's godmother. Marlene was very special to me because of that connection with her mother. Marlene and Jackie had musical backgrounds from their parents. Both of Jackie's parents sang in the church choir. Both families lived close to the church. Everyone would go over to Jackie's house to get her mother's famous homemade rolls.

Being a musician myself, I had an ensemble group at the high school where I worked. I would put names of musical terms on the board and the young people would choose a musical term to give their group. I did the same thing at Hartford. The girls chose Andante as a name. I gave them the names to choose from and they chose that name for themselves. When they became teenagers, they left after they had an audition at Motown. They began a singing career there that lasted a very long time. I was very happy for them when they began singing at Motown. I would tell everyone that those were my girls."

Jackie continues, "In high school I was voted 'Most Popular Girl', 'Class Clown', 'Best Personality', and I was '12th Grade Celebrity'. We went to high school with our fellow Motowners James Jamerson and Richard 'Popcorn' Wylie. Richard Street grew up with us too. I actually would help James with his homework. At a young age, he was a very talented bass player. I helped him with homework when he had gigs, so it ended up that I helped him a lot. He was playing a lot of music at the time and he was phenomenal in his craft.

It was after graduation around 1959 when Popcorn Wylie asked us to go over to Motown with him. He had the opportunity to audition so we went with him on his project to sing background. He was trying to get his career off the ground. We sang as a favor for Popcorn and they were impressed with our sound. They asked us to come back and sing on other things for them. Popcorn became a songwriter there even though his band audition didn't work out. He has a lot of history with Motown as a songwriter and he recorded as Popcorn and The Mohawks.

Someone at Motown asked what we called ourselves and we said, 'The Andantes.' Emily Phillips joined us at our Motown audition. She didn't continue further with Marlene and me. Emily was married and Edith was going to get married after graduation, so they weren't in positions to continue singing as Marlene and I were.

Soon the powers that be at Motown would introduce us to Louvain Demps and she would become our new singing partner. We became the trio known to everyone as The Andantes. Even though my parents were involved in church and loved church music, they were supportive when I began to sing at Motown. It was a job that I went to and enjoyed very much. We would go to the studio and literally spend the night there recording. I know my parents were proud of me, but this was not a super big deal to them at the time. It was a way of making money and they saw that it made me happy.

Everyone started so young at Motown. Most of us were in our twenties. I think we are a little older than The Supremes and The Temptations. When it comes to Motown, I don't have the best mental recall with actual dates. I remember the things that happened, just not the actual dates that they occurred. We sang on so many recordings that there are too many to count. I wish I had kept a journal from that period of my life. Louvain is fantastic with her memory and has a lot to share about what happened with us."

Louvain Demps

"I was born in New York on April 7, 1938. I was named after my beautiful mother, Louvain Ameroux. My parents met in New York and then migrated to Ann Arbor, Michigan where we had family. They eventually settled in Detroit. I have a sister who is three years older than me. Her name is San Carmen. I lived on Arlington Street all of my life until I married; the area was predominantly Polish.

My father's name is Alfred Moor. He came from Philadelphia and my mother from O'Fallon, Missouri. When my father was a young man, he studied for the priesthood. I am not sure why he left the monastery but he had a change of heart and married my mother. He worked as a postman in Detroit. Music was important in our house. My father loved opera and classical music and he played it all the time. That is what I heard in my home. We didn't hear rock and roll or the other stuff. I love operatic voices and strings. I played the violin when I was a young girl. San Carmen played the violin very well at the time. I could play better on the rug than on the violin. Neither of us stuck with the violin.

I have many memories of my childhood. San Carmen and I shared a bike that we named Blue Bird. My favorite cartoon was *Mighty Mouse* and I loved Brenda Star. I loved Red Skelton, Lucille Ball, and all of the Bobby Breen series (he was a child actor and sang with a soprano voice). Old movies were my favorite and I absolutely loved Imogene Coca, Sid Caesar, Cary Grant, William Holden, and Joseph Cotton was IT! One of my favorite movies is *Picnic* and when they dance, I dance with them. I must have seen that movie fifteen times. My all-time-favorite movie is *The King and I.*

I must have seen that film more than thirty times. I had to

have the DVD when it came out. One of my favorite actresses is Margaret O'Brien and I love the movie *Little Women*. Some of my favorite singers are: Billie Holiday, Teresa Brewer, Ella Fitzgerald, and Sarah Vaughan.

I remember my kindergarten teacher was Ms. Lillian. We played this game called Hoops; it was not Hula-Hoop. I was little and we played this game on the playground; she would call me Butterfingers. I didn't have any favorite teachers back then and I don't think they had a favorite Louvain either. San Carmen and I went to the same school until I was suspended. I went to Courville Elementary School until I was expelled for fighting. The first day I got back into school, I threw a pencil across the room and I was expelled again. People would tell me that I would be cute if I had smiled more. I wanted to fight everyone. I was short with a bad temper. My arms would swell up when I got mad. I was thrown out of so many schools, the next option my parents had was to send me to an all-girl school. That's when I wanted to fight the nuns. I wanted to get at Sister James. My father said I was a hellish child.

My mother was a homemaker and she could sew and crochet. She also worked at The Tam O'Shanter Country Club, a Jewish country club. She managed the Deli Department. She made all of the salads, watermelon baskets, and cold-food baskets. She was very talented in this craft and made a dynamite salad. For a brief time I worked there with my mother. My mother told me to slice the tomatoes and I ended up smashing them, from there she moved me to the dishwashing department. My cousin Ruth Satterfield had come from Milwaukee to help my mother raise us girls when my grandmother Ella Mae Ameroux died. Ruthie and my mother worked there for John Szegedi who was the head chef. John will take the story from here. He knew my mother and Ruthie very well and I am happy that he shares his memories of them for this book."

"I was the head chef for eighteen years and we worked all the time, all year-round and on holidays too, except at Easter and Christmas. I worked with Ruthie and Louvain's mother; her name was also Louvain. We worked together for about twenty-five years. I made many friends there, but these ladies are like family. They really busted their butts for me and they have big hearts. That quality just runs in their family. They were good to my children and I helped them with their children. I would give them apples, cheese, turkey, and help their families. They really loved my sons and were close to them. Ruthie and Louvain worked in the pantry on the deli side of the golf course. Louvain hadn't known me very long when I got married and my wife and I were expecting our first child. She crocheted a gorgeous blanket to bring the baby home in from the hospital. This blanket was beautiful and she made it for us even though she didn't know us very well at all. Sometimes you don't know how big someone's heart is. The elder Louvain and Ruthie are simply beautiful people.

I would pick Louvain and Ruthie up when I was picking up my bread at 11 Mile Road. They took the bus to work. One Sunday, I was bringing them home from work and there was a truckload of arrogant white folks and they hollered out the 'N' word to me. They called me an 'N-lover' and I wanted to run them off the road. They said it was because I was white and helping them and giving them a ride. I loved these ladies and it didn't bother me. In fact, Louvain said to me, 'Don't let them bother you. They don't bother me, so don't let them bother you.' She held her head high. That was the kind of person she was. She had a lot of class and she didn't let those small things get to her.

Louvain's husband was a mail carrier. He was a quiet person and he just went about his business. They were a hard-working family. Ruthie has been a life-long friend of mine. I see them for the holidays and they are like family to me still to this day. Alice Carter was another one of their friends who worked for me. She was very neat and a very smart and wonderful person. She was a hard worker too. Alice Carter was a dishwasher for me and Louvain said she needed another pantry girl because we were getting too busy and the hours were getting longer. I asked her if she wanted me to look for someone or if she had someone in Detroit in mind. She said to me, 'You see that young lady over there washing dishes? I'll take her.' We were a family, all of us together, and we all stuck together like family and still do.

When Ruthie was pregnant, no one knew about it and then she had Ella. Ella is like family too. She is a young woman now with her own child, but my friendship with that family has lasted for many decades. My sons came to work for me and my boys just loved Ruthie. They would want to see her down at the club and she would make them a club sandwich, hot dog, or a root-beer float. I would tell them not to bug her because she was busy. I only have great thoughts and feelings to share about their entire family."

Cousin Ruthie has some things to share about Louvain's younger years. "Louvain and her sister San Carmen grew up in a predominantly Polish neighborhood in Detroit. Everyone was migrating to Detroit because the factories were going strong. The family found a nice place where the landlady had one requirement: quietness. If you found a nice place to live, you did as you were requested. Little Vainy and San Carmen came home from school and had to tiptoe up the stairs. Their house slippers were waiting; one had a little red pair and the other pair was blue. They had to slip into the house and put those house slippers on at the door.

When they lived there, the radio had to be played softly. You walked on tiptoes and everything was quiet. The family soon bought a big house and that is when they sang all the time. Their father had a large record collection. He was a very quiet man, conservative, and loved classical music. He played classical and opera all of the time. He loved the barbershop quartets and sang those songs for the children. He taught them all of those songs. Every night you would hear Louvain and Carmen singing while they were doing the dishes. They had a big house now, and they could really raise up their voices and they could sing. Both girls joined the choirs and both of them sang quite a bit. Another thing that I remember was they had violins and played them. Girl, when it was time for the violin practices, I used to hate that creaking sound when they were first learning. I still have the violins in my basement. Vainy and San Carmen were different as night and day. Carmen would always be in front of the mirror with all of the lipstick and she would be combing and arranging her hair, then fixing and ironing and fussing. She would fix her clothes so all of the little ruffles would stand out. All the little buttons would be in place too. She was busy picking with herself. Vainy was more the tomboy. She would be rushing and running over stuff and running and jumping and playing with the dog.

I do remember when Vainy was in her teenage years she

went somewhere and had a record made for her mother. Her mom was so happy and every time I looked into her mother's face, I knew it was her favorite record. I think she had it made for a dollar."

Louvain continues, "We grew up Catholic and I eventually went to Sacred Heart Catholic School around age ten. Our family attended Holy Ghost Roman Catholic Church on Binder and 7 Mile Road. I attended Cleveland Elementary and went to Pershing High School. In school, I had fellow classmates who I would work with later on at Motown. The Holland Brothers went to my elementary school, but I didn't know them then. I went to school with Richard Morris who would later be a Motown producer and also my friend, Sylvia Moy. I went to high school with Duke Fakir of The Four Tops. We all came up together from an area called Conant Gardens. I attended elementary, junior high, and high school with Little Willie John, whose sister was Mable John. I also went to school with his brother Haywood John. Little Willie was a cute little boy. Some of the boys were mischievous and naughty. They would put mirrors on the floor to look up the girls' dresses. I would beat them up when they did that to me. I would make sure Willie wasn't around when I was wearing a dress at the drinking fountain.

I also went to school with Donald Goines, who lived in the Dequindre area. He wrote novels from prison and has since passed away. The thing about Detroit was its diversity and it was much safer back then. Most of the kids I knew came from the 6 Mile area, Nevada area, and Dequindre. I had to go to school outside of my school district because I was a troublemaker, so I knew kids from the other neighborhoods.

I was a strange little kid and my dad would tell me I was a bit odd. I wasn't happy sometimes and if you asked me why I was unhappy I would be unable to tell you. I am able to relate to children now. When children cry and are unhappy and you ask them what is wrong they say, 'Nothing.' I am able to hone in on that and get to them. I was a loner in childhood and my friends were usually the underdogs that other kids didn't want to befriend. I didn't like many people either. I was an intuitive child and saw through people. I kept to myself and away from people. I was mostly by myself unless I was in school or church. It had nothing to do with anyone, I just liked being alone and I would go off by myself on the playground.

I was a tomboy and I liked to wrestle, climb fences, and run races. I didn't like playing with girls because when you wrestled with them they got hurt and cried. I didn't like girly things either because I thought they were boring. I always had little boyfriends to wrestle. My mother would dress San Carmen and me as twins and I did not like that at all. You had one that looked girly, dainty, and cute and the other was jumping over fences, ripping the dress, and tearing the pockets like the Hulk. In school, they wouldn't let girls run track and I was the fast one. I raced in the street with neighbors, and my friend Harold Stone would come to our street and other kids from surrounding neighborhoods too. We had drag races on our feet because there weren't a lot of cars. I was athletic and had no outlet in school to get the aggression out."

Harold Stone grew up in Detroit and recalls, "We would race and run in the street. She wanted to race me and I was a pretty good runner in track. She had a very competitive and courageous spirit. Louvain lived a block over from my friend Kenny Harrington. I was always over at Kenny's house. Louvain and I were in elementary and high school together. As a girl she was just as she is now; she was a comical, funny, funny person. She was an all-around very nice person and a giving person. Her personality is 'what you see is what you get.' She cares about people, sometimes to a fault, and listens to people. She's there for people. Sometimes I have talks with her to tell her, 'You cannot always help everyone. You have to let some things go.'

When we were coming up Detroit had some gangs. Gangs at that time were more bark than bite. The kids just hung out and some Motowners were in The Gigolos. There were The Gigolos for boys and girls were in The Gigolettes. There were The Shakers too. The gangs back then were not violent as they are today. It was more to just hang out and belong. There was a book published about Conant Gardens. A friend of mine wrote it and I sent Louvain a copy. It was an historical place because it was one of the first places where blacks could buy homes. The interesting thing is where we lived in the 11th Precinct of Conant Gardens. At one time it was documented in the newspaper that we had the lowest crime rate in the entire city of Detroit. Detroit when we were growing up was great and was a lot of fun."

Louvain continues, "I had big dreams as a child. I told my parents I wanted to be a comedian and they said 'okay', and then I told them I wanted to be a singer and they said 'okay, okay'. Then at one point, I told them I wanted to be a nun and they said, 'What the heck are you going to do, beat the hell out of everyone?' After that, I thought about being a nurse. Then I thought I wanted to be an actress. I was a dreamer and a fighter and all I knew is that I could sing, run fast, and wrestle any boy. Music was always in me and soon became my passion. My father had a great singing voice and my cousin Ruth had a great voice too. I always sang in church choirs and glee clubs and my father sang in the choir too. He sang during the mass and he sang the Gregorian Chants. I always loved the Gregorian Chants.

By the time I was a preteen I wanted to be in the music business. I credit Little Willie John for this and I am forever indebted to him. He was an extremely talented young man. He was the one who got me my very first audition and interview for singing. After he finished doing some of his first records, he told many people about me and my singing. He laid down a foundation for my reputation as a singer at a very young age. When I would go to a new school they already knew I could sing before I came there.

Coincidentally, I had two godsisters from childhood who sang with me in the choir at Holy Ghost Roman Catholic Church. Their names were Marlene and Jackie Harper (they were sisters) and they were the children of my godparents. We had a great choirmaster. His name was Oreal Taylor and he had a wonderful tenor voice. I liked to jazz it up when we were performing and cut up a bit for the people. Mr. Taylor didn't know when we would do this. We would really cut loose at Midnight Mass. We would sing so well that the people would turn around to watch us. In Catholic Church, the choir is behind the parishioners so that the focus would always be on the altar. It would be a beautiful mass. I would like for my godsister Jackie Harper to tell you about some of our times together."

"I met Louvain when we were children. I was about six years old. We went to the same church and we received

Communion together. She was in my first Holy Communion class and my mother is her godmother. Ironically, my sister's name is Marlene and we sang with her and her sister San Carmen in the choir at Holy Ghost Catholic Church, long before she began to sing at Motown with Jackie Hicks and Marlene Barrow. Midnight Mass was *the* event of the year. It took place on Christmas Eve and was always so very special. The priest would come down the center of the aisle and an altar boy would carry baby Jesus and put him in a manger. The whole entire gospel would be including the Christmas theme where Mary and Joseph were in the stable. It was a beautiful event. We would sing traditional songs like 'Silent Night' and 'Away In A Manger'. I remember it was a candlelight service and how I felt special to be a part of that. Holy Ghost Church was built in our community so black Catholics could have the opportunity to attend church. Some churches did not allow blacks to attend mass so we had to get on the bus to go to church. Sacred Hearts is where we went to school and Holy Ghost is where we went to church.

Louvain and her sister San Carmen always came to our house for dinner after mass on Sundays. It was a Sunday tradition. They came for dinner and we played together after church. It would be dark when we took them home. In the summer, they would stay later because it got dark later. They spent every Sunday with our family. My mother mentored Louvain and San Carmen. We loved it because we had someone to play with. It gave us sisterhood that we still share today.

Louvain wanted the best for everyone and was caring and giving, and is still like that today. She never lost her traits. We were like sisters because my mother was their godmother. San Carmen was a jovial child. She was a very good singer too. I still sing in the choir at Sacred Heart Catholic Church in the city of Detroit. If I hear Louvain's voice, I can pick it out because she has a unique operatic voice. She is a soprano and when she hits the high notes, her voice is so distinct. I think she and her colleagues, Jackie and Marlene, are unsung heroines. God blessed her with a great gift and talent."

Louvain says her childhood was happy at times and unhappy at times. "What made me the happiest was when I could run with my dogs, be free, and sing. Music gave me joy. I loved to perform, imitate people, and escape in music. We had a neighbor named Mrs. Lula Potter. We called her 'Sugar Potter'. One day my mother told me to go over to her house. Mrs. Potter knew a singer and she told me one day she would introduce me to her. The singer was Maxine Sullivan who was famous for the swing version of a Scottish folk song called 'Loch Lomond'. I was about fourteen and Maxine told me if I really wanted to sing then I should just do it and pursue it. Meeting her was encouragement for me since she was someone who sang as a professional and traveled all over the world. I saw her as a success and took her words to heart. I was very serious about what she had told me. She also was an actress in several movies. In recent years, I saw a documentary about her life and I realized she was the person I met as a young girl. While in her seventies, she was performing in the UK. She died on my birthday in 1987.

San Carmen and I were in competition musically and she actually had more potential than I did, but I think I had more drive. My sister had other interests so her musical talents did not have an avenue to grow. At age sixteen San Carmen was so good that she was the only one from our parish who made it to the big city choir. She could read music very well."

San Carmen remembers growing up in Detroit. "Louvain and I grew up on Arlington Street. It was a very nice little neighborhood street lined with trees. We played a lot outside and no one bothered us. If people did try to bother us, we would fight and stick up for each other. We had to stay close to home. I was not allowed to go on to the next block. I sang a lot when I was a child. Louvain and I sang in choirs. She has an operatic voice and I have a voice similar to Nancy Wilson. I sang with The Detroit Symphony Orchestra once. I didn't keep up with the singing and I wished I had."

Louvain continues, "Perhaps San Carmen needed a shove to pursue music. After I met Maxine Sullivan, she was the motivation I needed. The music I was hearing at the time, besides the opera that my father played, was on the radio and in the skating rinks, and I loved it. I remember a really great skating song was 'Bad, Bad, Whiskey' by Amos Milburn. Years later I would work with him at Motown. You never know what direction life is going to take and how you cross paths with someone; you may be intertwined with them and not even know it.

In Jr. High, I cut the record for my mother that Ruthie spoke about and it was called, ‘Waiting For The Sunrise’. It was previously recorded by Les Paul and Mary Ford, the guitar players. I loved this song. I was the singer and a girl named Errone Connelly played the piano on the song we cut for a dollar. They only printed a few copies for the families. We also did a concert together on Woodward Avenue and that was when the record came out. Music was making its way into my life more and more. The first time I saw Levi Stubbs was when he came to our school to sing at a record hop with all of the guys from The Four Tops, but they were not named that yet.

I knew what I wanted to see happen with music. It had to manifest itself in my life and it took some hard work on my part. I married Max Demps in June of 1956. The singing fell into place slowly over the years for me. I met Max through a girlfriend of mine from high school. Her name was Rachel Lewis-Chapman. Max was visiting his aunt who lived on Arlington Street, five doors down from the house that I grew up in. He moved here and then we married. I ended up living on Arlington with Max in his aunt’s house. I thought our marriage was wonderful at first and I was just as nutty as I could be over him. We didn’t have furniture and I had never lived on my own before. We had little material things but we had each other and were so in love. He worked two jobs when we first married. He worked at a grocery store and at Cunningham’s Drug Store. Being married was more fun than being at home. It was new and exciting and I was so in love. After I had little Max, I would soon begin singing at Motown.

Though Max worked hard and we had little savings, we traded toilet paper and soap with Charles and Anita Russ, they were Max’s friends from Kansas. They were our babysitters for little Max. We found out early on that little Max was having trouble hearing. It was hard to detect because he only heard some tones from an early age. He was reading our lips and we did not know this. The reason why some people cannot tell their child is deaf, is because some children hear in lower tones and some high. Max’s hearing was in the lower tones.

Everything seemed normal, but you had to try and get his attention to communicate with him. When children are that young they cannot tell you what is wrong. A friend encouraged me to have him tested and a teacher named Mrs. Kursh was the one who discovered this. She had another student with the same situation as Max and the boys turned out to be good friends in school.

I had a best friend named Rhoda Collins who grew up around the corner from me. Rhoda was the one who found out about Motown. She saw an advertisement in a paper and she met Raynoma Gordy. At the time, Marv Johnson was about to release the song, 'Come To Me'. Rhoda came to tell me all about Ms. Ray. Rhoda was writing songs and was trying to get them published and recorded. I went to Motown to demo her song and they told her if she wanted it recorded, they would charge her $100 dollars. I paid the money but nothing ever happened with the song.

It turned out that I ended up with an audition from this. They were located in a duplex building on Dexter. It was before Motown and Hitsville's Studio A existed. Everyone came out when I sang at the audition. Brian Holland, Marv Johnson, and Berry Gordy took turns playing the piano as I sang for them. They were excited and they let me do different things with my voice. I sang several songs like 'Over The Rainbow'. They played impromptu songs and I sang along with the piano. The more I sang and hit different notes, they could see I had a lot of range.

I was nineteen when I began singing at Motown with The Rayber Voices, which included: Raynoma Gordy, Brian Holland, Robert Bateman, Eugene Remus, and Sonny Sanders. Some of the early recordings I sang on were 'Money' by Barrett Strong and 'Because I Love Her' by Eddie Holland. I was supposed to have a solo on that, but I was so nervous it didn't turn out so good. They all would tease me in the studio and tell me to go sing at The Metropolitan Opera because of my high operatic voice. I was at Motown for a little while doing background before Marlene and Jackie arrived there. I wasn't working there everyday. I was also singing outside of Motown. I had my first airplane ride in these very early times. It was with Berry, The Miracles, and Raynoma, and we were going to Chicago to record because there was no Hitsville studio yet. My parents and Max were supportive of my singing at Motown. My parents did not think it would last and did not take it too serious. After it was clear that it would last they realized it was a solid job for me, they were happy for me. They felt if I was going to be a singer, they had wished I had sung in the opera.

Someone told me that Harry Balk was looking for singers to be The Dream Girls. I began singing with Bobbie Smith and The Dream Girls. I went to Raynoma and told her we had a record coming out and I asked her if I was secure with the studio work. She told me not to quit working for Motown, to wait and see if the record was a smash. She wanted me to stay with Motown. The record we had was called, 'The Duchess of Earl'; it was the answer song to Gene Chandler's 'Duke of Earl'. I was one of The Dream Girls with Sheena and Bobbie Smith (they were sisters), and another young woman named Thelma. We had two records called, 'Mr. Fine' and 'Wanted'.

Back at Motown, Raynoma was aspiring to do other things within the company, so she began to sing less and less. I began to sing her part and then they put me with Marlene and Jackie. The Andantes became the in-house voices for everything. We were working more than I did with The Rayber Voices.

I was doing record hops as The Dream Girls with Robin Seymour and other DJ's in Detroit and Canada. Marvin Gaye and Anna Gordy were at one of the record hops when I sang with The Dream Girls. He was doing hops at the same time I was because 'Mr. Sandman', which the Andantes sing on had come out. The Dream Girls gig didn't turn out for me and was short-lived. Motown would become my home for several years and Marlene, Jackie, and I worked together from this point on.

Motown became more solid work and the other jobs I had just gave me the chance to perform. We were young and The Funk Brothers were young. Joe Hunter was the first professional musician I ever worked with on a session. No book is complete without hearing from legendary Joe Hunter. He was a dear friend to me all the way up until his death."

Joe says, "It didn't take The Andantes long to learn their parts and do the tracks. They were very talented and were excellent singers. They were so smart."

<u>Panis Angelicus</u>
from The Gregorian Chants

Bread of Angels,
made the bread of men;
The Bread of heaven
puts an end to all symbols:
A thing wonderful!
The Lord becomes our food:
poor, a servant, and humble.
We beseech Thee,
Godhead One in Three
That Thou wilt visit us,
as we worship Thee,
lead us through Thy ways,
We who wish to reach the light
in which Thou dwellest.
Amen.

Latin Translation:

Panis angelicus
fit panis hominum;
Dat panis caelicus
figuris terminum:
O res mirabilis!
manducat Dominum
Pauper, servus, et humilis.
Te trina Deitas
unaque poscimus:
Sic nos tu visita,
sicut te colimus;
Per tuas semitas
duc nos quo tendimus,
Ad lucem quam inhabitas.
Amen.

This is taken from 'Sacris Solemniis', written by St. Thomas Aquinas before the year 1274.

Marlene Barrow-Tate

"I was born Judith Marlene in Detroit on September 25, 1941. My parents Victor and Johnnie Reid raised me. As far back as I can remember, I was called by my middle name, Marlene. Later in life, I learned that I was adopted when I was three months old and that I had several siblings. My dad and his brother, who was my biological father, came to Detroit from Mt. Bayou Mississippi to seek job opportunities in the auto industry. My dad worked at Dodge Main in Hamtramck, Michigan for thirty-three years.

My Mom, an only child, came here from Hawkinsville Georgia and my dad's five brothers settled in Chicago to work on the railroad. My mother was a church musician who directed our youth choir. She also played piano and organ at Hartford Baptist Church. She taught piano lessons and worked for some of our local funeral homes. She gave our pastor, Rev. Dr. Charles G. Adams his first piano lesson. I grew up on Stanford Street, which is one street over from Hartford Street.

My mother being a church musician was not a great fan of rock and roll music. She was more interested in classical music, opera, and church hymns. I liked a cross section of music because that is what I was exposed to all of my life. I studied piano for a while and learned to read music because of my mother. I was inspired at a young age to sing. I loved singing in the church choir. My father sang in the adult choir.

Growing up in Detroit was basic and my parents were very grounded in the church. No matter what happened we went to church and Sunday school every Sunday. It was a strong foundation since my mother worked at the church. That foundation and those values never leave you and they remain in you all through your life. Pastor Charles Hill is who baptized me. Music started for me very early in life. As a child I loved hymns like 'Jesus Loves Me', and as I got older I loved 'I Surrender All'.

When I was a young girl, I was able to read music and I attended ballet and tap-dancing classes with my childhood friend Elaine Horn. She later married Willie Tyler. I enjoyed little girly things like playing with dolls. I remember that I wanted to be a nurse. I was a good student for the most part and my favorite topic at school was English and Spelling because I loved to read. In the sixth grade, I won a Spelling Bee at Weingart Elementary School and I went to the finals in the state championship. I was in a few little plays where I had small parts, but no singing roles.

Because we had a large family, we took many car trips to visit them. My aunts and uncles were in Chicago so we went there all of the time. We also traveled to Akron, Ohio to see relatives on my mother's side of the family. Our grandmother Dolly came from Georgia to be with us when I was in my teen years. When I was growing up the neighborhood was very close. Neighbors and friends stuck together. Our neighbors were who we knew as extended family; we were in each other's company every day. We had barbecues and picnics together. You would be in each other's homes all of the time. After we did our homework, we went outside to play. We did a lot of playing and went to summer camp.

Jackie and I met when we were very young. Our parents knew each other and our families were friends. We lived around the corner from each other and we met at Hartford Baptist Church. We went to the same schools our entire life: Weingart Elementary, McMichael Jr. High, and Northwestern High School. I'd describe Jackie as a playful child-yet she was bossy. She was an assertive child and still is an assertive person. I was a passive person so we always got along very well. One of our best friends was Yvonne Rashida Harbin. Yvonne grew up on Hartford Street. She was also part of our lives as children and at Hartford Baptist Church.

We grew up knowing a few of our Motown colleagues: Melvin Franklin, Richard Street, and Richard 'Popcorn' Wylie. Popcorn went to Northwestern High School with us. He had a little band and we would go over to his house and sing. We worried his poor mother to death singing there every night in their basement. We would sing and practice songs that he wrote. They had a big ol' upright piano and we would gather around it and sing. We would come up with different things. He was writing and trying to put together a demo for Motown. I lived about ten minutes from Hitsville.

Popcorn finally had an appointment at Motown to audition and take his tracks to them. He took Jackie and me with him, along with Emily. I think I was about nineteen years old when we went with Popcorn to Motown. We already had the name The Andantes when we arrived there. We went just to help Popcorn, so it was a fluke that we went and that we stayed for so many years. Because of Popcorn we were so well-liked by them and they hired us. Louvain Demps was already there singing background with The Rayber Voices. Shortly after our audition, they put us together with her because we needed a high voice. I sang the middle, Louvain was the high, and Jackie was the lower voice. That's how we became connected to Motown.

Popcorn Wylie is one of our dearest friends still to this day and we want him mentioned in this work. If it had not been for Popcorn we would never have gone to Motown. Popcorn says, 'The song that got The Andantes noticed at the audition was a song called 'I'll Still Be Around'. I wrote it with Janie Bradford. I was the bandleader at the time and I told Motown they had to hear these ladies sing, so they came over with me when I was recording. They are wonderful ladies. The Andantes add so much to the Motown sound. They had perfect pitch, perfect harmonies, and were perfect ladies. I am proud of their legacy at Motown. I got my nickname 'Popcorn' when I was in high school with them and I played football. The players called me that and then the cheerleaders overheard it, so that was how it began."

Marlene continues, "Soon after the audition at Motown, I married Thomas Barrow. I met him through his cousin who lived across the street from me. We spent a lot of time together as young teens talking, playing, and riding bikes. Thomas eventually worked for the city of Detroit."

Jesus Loves Me

Jesus loves me! This I know,
for the Bible tells me so.
Little ones to him belong;
they are weak, but he is strong.

Refrain:

Yes, Jesus loves me! Yes, Jesus loves me!
Yes, Jesus loves me! The Bible tells me so.

Jesus loves me! This I know,
as he loved so long ago,
taking children on his knee,
saying, "Let them come to me."

Jesus loves me still today,
walking with me on my way,
wanting as a friend to give
light and love to all who live.

Words by: Anna B. Warner (st 1) and David Rutherford McGuire (sts 2, 3)
Music by: William B. Bradbury

<u>I Surrender All</u>

All to Jesus I surrender;
All to Him I freely give;
I will ever love and trust Him,
In His presence daily live.

Refrain:
I surrender all,
I surrender all;
All to Thee, my blessed Savior,
I surrender all.

All to Jesus I surrender;
Humbly at His feet I bow,
Worldly pleasures all forsaken;
Take me, Jesus, take me now.

All to Jesus I surrender;
Make me, Savior, wholly Thine;
Let me feel the Holy Spirit,
Truly know that Thou art mine.

All to Jesus I surrender;

Lord, I give myself to Thee;
Fill me with Thy love and power;
Let Thy blessing fall on me.

All to Jesus I surrender;
Now I feel the sacred flame.
Oh, the joy of full salvation!
Glory, glory, to His Name!

Words By: Judson W. Van DeVenter, 1896

Jackie's Parents, Aaron and Clara.

Photo credit Jackie Hicks Collection

Marlene's mother, Johnnie

Photo credit: Marlene Barrow-Tate Collection

Marlene's father, Victor

Photo credit: Marlene Barrow-Tate Collection

Louvain's father

Louvain Demps Collection

Louvain's mother as a young child, and Louvain's Grandmother Ella May (opposite)

Photo credit: The Louvain Demps Collection

Ella May Hunt
1906

Louvain's mother, Louvain Ameroux

Photo credit: Louvain Demps Collection

Two of Hartford Baptist Church's original Andantes, Edith Jackson-Fails and Emily Phillips-Helvey. They are The Phillips Sisters who were named The Andantes by Mildred Dobey along with Jackie and Marlene.

.

Photo credit: Marlene Barrow-Tate Collection

Marlene and Jackie with Mildred Dobey, the woman who named The Andantes at Hartford Baptist Church in Detroit.

Photo credit: Lynette Turner

Louvain during her early modeling years.

Photo credit The Louvain Demps Collection

A very young Louvain.

The Louvain Demps Collection

The early days....Jackie, Louvain, and Marlene.

Photo credit: Louvain Demps Collection

A young Louvain

Photo credit: Louvain Demps Collection

A very young Marlene in the early days of Motown

Photo credit: Marlene Barrow-Tate Collection

Jackie and Marlene in the engineer's booth at Motown.

Photo credit: The Louvain Demps Collection

These Things Will Keep Me Loving You

By 1962, Motown was a young company and The Andantes were steadily singing behind such artists as Marv Johnson, Barrett Strong, Henry Lumpkin, Popcorn Wylie and The Mohawks, Debbie Dean, Singin' Sammy Ward, The Satintones, The Isley Brothers, Eddie Holland, Eugene Remus, Amos Milburn, and LaBrenda Ben, just to name a few. The Funk Brothers were becoming a staple there and the roster also contained within it the future icons and legends we know today, including: The Supremes, Mary Wells, Martha Reeves, The Velvettes, The Miracles, The Marvelettes, and a young drummer named Marvin Gaye. The background voices in the early years of Motown were not as recognizable as they would become. The Funk Brothers would define their own sound and give birth to the recognizable beats we know today. Those years were learning processes for everyone and the early sessions were reflections of the times. The company was growing and the music of the era was reaching out far beyond Detroit. There was a distinct sound in sixties music. The famous "Sound of Young America" was a work in progress as The Rayber Voices faded into The Andantes and the background voices of Motown became a part of history.

Marlene remembers some of these early sessions. "The Funk Brothers and we would be in Studio A. It was very small. This was when they would put everyone in there together; we called it 'the pit'. Sometimes they would put us in a tiny booth and the band was in the pit. They would just tell us that we were singing this part and another would sing that part. It would be a group of voices thrown together. We sang background with The Supremes and The Rayber Voices on some of the early sessions. I remember rehearsing one time when I was pregnant, and recall it being so hot in there, because it was a small space with so many people, and I almost fainted. It was so small and cramped and they would tell people not to flush the toilet when we were recording. They would turn the air off too, that's why it was so hot.

"Those early sessions were collaborative voices, to tell you the truth. It was anyone and everyone who was around or had stopped by. Sometimes I would be out shopping and just stop in to say 'hi' and they would put me in a session with other voices besides Louvain and Jackie. One of the earliest sessions I remember was 'Jamie' by Eddie Holland; it was with The Rayber Voices on that one. The beginning years were a learning process for everyone. Eventually they began to record the voices separately from the band. Everyone was on their own track so that we didn't bleed into each other and so you didn't hear the drums where you should hear singing. Time was money in the studio, so to record separate was faster. I loved when they finally started putting everyone on separate tracks; you just came in and did your part and then you went home. When everyone was together there was a lot more starting over because there were too many things going on.

"Eventually, The Rayber Voices weren't singing on regular sessions because the individuals in the group became interested in other activities within the company. Raynoma Gordy is a very bright woman and is an important piece of this history and The Andantes' history, especially during those early years. She loved what she was doing and she really was instrumental in helping the company to grow. She did not get the credit she deserved for her hard work at that time. As The Rayber Voices were ending, we were beginning to sing more and more.

"The Andantes soon became the first choice for producers to use on their records and we worked all the time. They would schedule us on a regular basis and used us frequently because we were readily available at the last minute, and we made it a priority to be available like this. A producer would tell the secretary to call and ask us to be there at 2:00 and we would be there. Motown was a machine and an assembly line, so to speak, so having us there made it possible to record the songs quicker. They kept us quite busy in the early days but we never knew what our schedule might be. It was not like a normal nine-to-five job. Sessions could be at any time of the day or night and even on weekends depending on what artist they were recording and how many tracks they were doing. A week of work could be twenty hours or fifty hours, it just depended. They were flexible with us because they wanted us singing on the records. If one of us had an appointment, such as a doctor's appointment, they would work around us; they were good about that. We did not have a manager or agent. We communicated well amongst the three of us and we always kept each other informed when we had work. We discussed our business together as a group. It was always a group decision about what we were doing.

When it came to the sessions, most of the time the producers knew what they wanted in their head beforehand. They would let us give our input many times on tracks when we had ideas to share. Other times they'd just say to sing it this way or that way. When you get going with a track, more ideas come up and they begin to click. Sometimes it would just blend and flow and other times we'd have a few takes on a track. We'd be in the studio and realize we were singing every line. We would look at each other and say to the producer, 'Hey, we're singing every line here', so our part was more than background on some tracks. The producer hadn't realized it until we brought it to their attention. The Originals sang many of the background vocals with us, so it would be us with them and whatever group we were recording with at the time. We would do sessions and may not know who the track was meant for and may never hear it again, and then other times we would hear it on the radio just days after we did it. A song could be completed in the can and be on the radio pretty quickly.

"The choir effect you hear on the records is called 'stacking'. We would record a couple of different tracks with the three of us singing in different ranges so the after-effect sounds like six or nine voices instead of just three. They would do that with us and The Originals. That's the choir you hear on the records. Whether our vocals are just us or us singing with other people, I can pick us out. I know our sound. The Originals were Freddy Gorman, Walter Gaines, Henry Dixon, and Crathman Plato Spencer.

"More often than not, we heard the lead or the producer sing the lead as a guide. When Smokey Robinson produced records he gave us a guide to follow, but that was rare to have. Most of the time we used our intuition or we were improvising from what they told us to do. By the time The Andantes came in, there was music and sometimes a vocal guide to follow. We didn't do any demos. Producers and songwriters typically did the demos for the artists.

"I remember being in awe of meeting some of the people we were singing and working with, and a lot of them were just starting out too. To be there with them was exciting. Berry told The Supremes they had to finish school and it was exciting to meet Smokey Robinson for the first time. We did not have the insight or the intuition then to know that what we were doing, and what we were part of, was going to sustain all these decades later. For us it was our jobs and we loved it.

"When you first hear yourself on the radio, it is just overwhelming. It was exhilarating, I do remember that. We worked with so many wonderful producers and talented individuals. Everything that we did during that time was just fun moments and good memories and it did not seem like a job. It was very hard work and repetitive at times, but it was good times and great moments in my life. I am proud and honored to have been part of Motown and would not trade this experience for anything in the world. It was a family environment where everyone came together to make music. The hand-clapping and finger-snapping on the records could be from anyone who was there that day-someone's friend or girlfriend, and many times it was us. Producers were very creative when it came to sounds. We stomped our feet on boards to get certain sounds. If it worked and sounded good they would use it. Whatever came across their minds to use in the studio, the producers would use it to make sounds.

"My parents were proud of me for singing at Motown, the work I did in my life for the company, and the history I was a part of. Once my family heard me on the radio everyday, they were very happy and proud of me. I was the older sister who sang. I would hear my mother on the phone telling her friends about me, so I knew she was proud. Our neighbors and friends were tickled to death to hear us singing on the radio, you would have thought it was them singing, they were so elated about it. When you think about it, it really is something special to hear: the work you did then, being shared with everyone, and now some forty-five years later you can still hear it and know that people love it so much-still, all these years later."

Jackie adds that not only did they sing at Motown, but The Andantes worked extensively with other singers. "We went to Chicago and did quite a lot of work there with Jerry Butler and Gene Chandler. We sang on Vee Jay Records with The Dells. Others we sang with were John Lee Hooker and Bobby Blue Bland. I wish I had kept a journal because there were so many sessions. The Andantes did many favors for people too. I cannot tell you how many times we helped our buddies because they needed girls on their records. Sometimes they would give us ten or fifteen dollars and buy us dinner. Many sessions we sang on were not related to Motown. There is more out there than what we know. Our name isn't attached to our work because they didn't add us on the record sleeve. We didn't always know who the songs were for, as Marlene said.

"It's hard to remember so many sessions and some of them we never even heard the final product of. I was the one who handled the money for the outside sessions. When we sang at Motown they paid us individually by check. When we did outside work, we had regular people who hired us and they would want us to work as a favor. Sometimes they would try to pay only me and I would tell them that we all had to make money, equal pay. They wouldn't have enough money to pay us for all of the hours we worked, so they'd ask me to get the girls there and try to pay me more for doing that. I would tell them I couldn't do that to my friends. Either we all made the same amount or we all had to agree that this was a favor. If there was only seventy-five dollars to be made, it was a three-way split.

"The music business has crooked people in it. They would try to pay me more to get a favor, so they could get another favor later. Other singing groups would mess their own members over to make a little more money; con-artists were everywhere back then. You'd hear these stories about other groups and whoever was singing lead was making more money or whoever was setting up the session was getting paid more. That's what causes problems. You're in a relationship and a family when you sing together. I believe in comfort and it's nice to make money, but it's also nice to share money too. There was plenty of money to go around. Marlene, Louvain, and I had a good friendship. Singing was our livelihood and it was dependant on the three of us. We needed to be able to get along so we could work. We got along with each other the way the guy groups did. Why would you harm another member of your group and harm your livelihood by doing that? Why attack another member and make it harder to book jobs for yourselves? We would be puzzled with some of the girl groups who had bitterness and jealousies within the group. It bothered me that the girls had to act that way and I didn't understand it.

"When we first started at Motown, I recall that they didn't take anything out for taxes. My mother told me I better put money away for that when tax time rolls around. When tax time came, I was one of the few people there who had put money away for the IRS. It's good when your parents teach you about saving your money, structure, and responsibility. People didn't plan for things as simple as taxes. There were people who were big stars and making a lot more than us, plus royalties. They couldn't pay their taxes because they were so lavish during the year with their earnings. We made $2.50 per session. We finally got up to $25 a session and that was a bonus for us. Sometimes they paid us $25 for just a few hours. We earned a good living but we were not in the union when we first started. We were paid by the session, so it is impossible to guess what our yearly salary was.

We certainly didn't think to seek royalties for our work. I would imagine we would have a very good argument now. We were considered the session artists and we got paid for the session. There are so many songs that we are prevalent on, but we are not the ones who got the credit for them, nor the royalties. We can prove we were there and we sang. We know it's us singing and everyone knows we were there singing. In recent years background singers have more protection. It is one thing to do a session or two, but we are on literally *thousands* of sessions as the house singers, and the sound. If your voice is used in the media today, you get paid. We do not."

There were other voices thrown into the mix in the beginning. Etolia White is a childhood friend of Marlene and Jackie's. Etolia was there with them on some early sessions. "I met Jackie as a freshman in high school. I was coming down the stairs and she said, 'Hi, my name is Jackie, what's yours?' That was in 1956 and we've been friends ever since. I moved onto Hartford Street, just down the street from her family and near Marlene. I worked at Motown with Jackie and Louvain in the early years. At first during Marlene's pregnancy, and after she had her son Larry, I filled in for about a year and a half, off and on. I worked in Marlene's place and then after she returned from having Larry, the four of us sang together for a short time.

"Sometimes there were at least eight of us in there singing background. The Supremes would be in the booth with us singing background. I remember standing next to Florence Ballard singing. We would be paid $2.50 per record. Sometimes they would give us more. I remember the first check I got was for $7.50 for doing background on three songs. Whenever we did background, we could do five different songs that were for different groups; it wasn't necessarily just for a certain group. We also did some jingles together for the radio stations in Detroit.

"Jackie and Marlene were telling me about this girl they were singing with. They said that she could really sing great. We ended up going to the studio and I worked with her too; it was Kim Weston. I sang on 'Love Me All The Way' with them. I was singing with Marlene in her range and they told me to take the high voice on it, so Louvain and I sang the higher voices on that song.

"When I knew everyone at Motown, there were four Supremes and it was when they were just starting. Berry was so young and everything was up and coming. As many people who came into Motown, ten went out. There were people coming in and out so much. I was happy and excited to be at Motown. I was only nineteen. I sat there on the bench with Marvin Gaye and we prayed together; both our fathers were ministers. The first record I sang on was 'Mister Sandman'. I can't remember all of the song titles I sang on. It was too long ago. If I hear them, I can remember. I can tell The Andantes' voices on the radio. I hear Jackie's voice. It is very distinct to me. My favorite song is one I sing on, 'Love Me All The Way'.

I remember Stevie Wonder feeling my face and knowing who I was. We would be rehearsing on the steps and he would come up and we would hush up. He would say, 'I know you're all in here.' He would laugh and feel our faces and tell each of us who we were. He was about eleven and could tell who each one of us was by feeling our faces.

I was able to do the Motown Revues at The Fox Theatre and at The Gray Stone Ballroom. I did two of the shows. The Motown groups sang and danced on stage and we would be behind the curtain singing as well. What people don't understand is, when you are dancing and moving around, you can't sing as well. The Andantes were more behind the scenes than people really know.

"What I saw during my short time at Motown…I had to ask many questions because I was so green. I was naïve and green. They would call me 'The Golf Course' because I was so green. It was very interesting working at the studio and on the revues. Being a preacher's daughter, I was exposed to few more things than what the law allowed."

Mickey Stevenson came on-board early at Motown as well. He was A&R director, producer, and songwriter. Mickey was one of Berry Gordy's right-hand men. "When I would take the Motown Revues out, they would sound the best and sound just like the record. Our revues were hotter than the others because we sounded like our records. I would take The Andantes and put them off stage with microphones, behind the curtain. I intentionally did that so we sounded great as The Motown Revue. I came from a Broadway and theatrical background, so my point is to let the audience have the richest sound they can. I would even put The Vandellas behind Marvin Gaye. I would have everyone backing everyone and the audience would never see any of that. They were happy about what they heard because they spent their money on a ticket and they wanted to see and hear a good show. The show and the sound would be fantastic. I would use The Andantes and every format necessary to make the whole thing sound great. As long as you're dealing with the background voices and the music, and not the lead voice, all of that is just adding to the sound of the show.

"The big Broadway shows do this all the time. It is not only the orchestra behind them. It's hard to entertain an audience and still keep that perfect sound when you're dancing and moving around. You have to enhance what is happening on stage. When it came to producing records, it is a fact that The Andantes recorded on everyone's product, from The Four Tops to The Supremes; they did everything. They did it all and they were really unsung heroines. There should not be any controversy now over the ladies and what they did. The controversy would be if anyone said or claimed it was not them.

"I don't recall the first records I used them on and I will tell you why I do not remember: to me they were just there as part of the sound of Motown. They were like The Funk Brothers and they were part of the sound we were creating at the time. To not have them on the product was out of the question. If you wanted your records to be great, you had them singing on them.

As a producer you hear in your head what you want. When you listen to the product that they were on, they were never separated from the hook that the other artists would be singing. They were always combined in the major part of the song structure. You always hear them with the lead singer and the other members of groups. The Andantes coming on to the record made it richer and fuller. Their sound was unique and that gave the records a rich and positive sound. The other artists on the record gave it the individual sound, and they sounded great too and gave it freedom with the harmony, but The Andantes gave it the Motown sound and that 'on the note' sound.

"They were added to any record to enhance it and make anyone sound fuller and richer. You want your background to sound just as good as the lead. The whole idea was to make the record sound right. As a producer and A&R director of the company, my job was to make sure everything was right on the record. If the record didn't sound good, none of it would have worked. If I didn't like how a production sounded, I would bring the ladies in and fix it. When you produce records you want them to get airplay, sell, and sound the best. We wanted to have the best records and you cannot separate these elements. It has to sound right to get airplay, and it has to be good to get people to buy it. It is all the same. Little airplay means little sales.

"I don't have a favorite song. All of the songs we did at Motown are my favorites. It was my job to keep the hits coming so I loved them all. The Andantes are phenomenal. I would like for their fans to know that they were the sound of Motown. These ladies have good hearts. They have warm hearts. When there was something not right with a record or we were overdubbing, they did not just quit and walk away and take their paychecks. They wanted it right too and wanted it to sound great and they did the work to make it sound right. They had spiritual hearts and they wanted what they were doing to be great. Some people you would tell to do it again, The Andantes would say 'Let me do it again.' They were the 'let's do it again' people who wanted the record good. They cared about what they were doing and that made my job really easy. Throughout my career, I've looked for people like them to work with, as I do now.

"Some of the artists had no concept of what made the records work and get on the air, some did. Some were just singing. A few had a slight inkling in understanding the industry and what it took. Artists were artists, and the machine was behind them making them go. In my opinion, the key to a successful operation is the ability of the individuals in charge to pick the right people to do the right things, and that is a gift and a talent all by itself.

"In the beginning, Berry picked great people to help him do great things. I for one picked some other great people. He chose me to bring in the right people and make it work. I found people all over the country, not just Detroit. I found Gil Askey in Atlantic City conducting. I found Ron Miller, who wrote 'For Once In My Life', in Chicago selling pizzas. My eye was able to get talented people and bring their talents out even more. I was able to bring them and their talent together. You have to groom people."

The Andantes were used in the studio so much at Motown that they were given an office upstairs. Louvain says, "It would be 2:00AM and we would be in our office waiting for them to call us into the studio. We were there all of the time and it gave us a place to wait and to rest until they needed us. We were part of the family in the beginning. Raynoma Gordy did so much for everyone then. She was the backbone of Motown. She was a smart business woman too. We were paid more money because of her and she made sure the artists and musicians had food to eat. She and Berry lived upstairs and the artists were so young, some of them teenagers. Raynoma would make bologna sandwiches and gave them food when they came to work. She knew they did not have much money or food to eat. She added so much heart and soul to the company and it was her kind spirit that made it like a family. She invested herself in people and in the company.

"She would teach others to read music. It was Raynoma who convinced Berry to add strings to the Motown sound, her cousin Dale was the first violinist to join the Motown sound. She was the one who brought finesse to Motown and completed the package. She cared about people and Motown and I will always have the greatest respect for her.

"Raynoma was a dear friend to me and she would tell me that I needed to get out more to meet people. She'd say that I never did anything or went anywhere. She made sure I was included and invited me out with other people. It was touching to me that she cared enough about me to include me. She picked me up in her VW bus and took me to my first night club. She took me roller-skating too. I had never been to a club before. It was dark inside the club and I was so excited. I was trying to be cool, you know? We were sitting there and the show began; I told Raynoma that the dancer was really good but her feet were too big. She told me that it was a man. Raynoma knew I needed a friend at this time. She took me under her wing and we talked about things. I had never seen a female impersonator before.

"The voices you hear on the really early records are anyone and everyone. I remember many times a producer's girlfriend would be there and they would just throw her in to sing with us. I recall one woman couldn't sing, so they told her to move her lips so she could get paid. We were always there though. I did a record with The Supremes before they were *The Supremes*. They would use all of our voices in a session just to see how the voices sounded. They were experimenting a lot then. Once they fine-tuned the sound it was mainly us singing background on everything. Eventually, they began to pay us more money and we made a good living.

"We were the in-house voices. People think we sang with The Supremes only to fill in as Florence was leaving, but we were there in the very beginning. We are on just about all of The Supremes' songs and I know that will shock people, but we are singing. We did the first Supremes Christmas album with Harvey Fuqua. The Spinners sang on that too. Some of the first engineers were Robert Bateman and Brian Holland. I remember Mike McLean, he masterminded the sound and microphone equipment and the placement of the equipment. Mike and my husband became friendly because Mr. Demps enjoyed working with sound equipment and machines too. Mike was so brilliant and smart. He would clap his hands and then tell them where the instruments should be placed to get the best sound.

"Our early times were good. Our life as The Andantes was fun times and a moment in time that can never happen again. It was a dream and some people do not see their dreams happen. Our moment in time is everybody else's soundtrack to their lives. When you stop and think about it, what we did is sentimental to others for various reasons. We have been on their first date with them, so to speak, or maybe we are a wedding song or perhaps a sad memory. Our job was a dream for us and we enjoyed it. Our job touched so many people and we still hear them telling us all the time how much our singing means to them. You never know what you may be doing in your life and how it can touch another, if not in the moment perhaps later. A song we recorded in the early years could be the song that two people fell in love to just a few days ago, a first date, or a first dance. The songs have sentimental meaning to me on so many levels. Being in the studio was an escape for me and the lyrics for me fit my life many times.

"I think the formula for The Andantes was that we were friends, first and foremost. Marlene was the balance between Jackie and me. She's a Libra and kept us in rhythm, so to speak. We each knew the other loved one another. The three of us were content in our positions and there wasn't one of us trying to get ahead of the others to take over the group or be the star. We were a group and we knew we sounded great when we sang together. We loved what we were doing.

"One rule of thumb when you are singing in a group is you spend a lot of time together, and when you are in front of the microphone that often if one person eats onions, everyone should eat onions. One day I took the onions off my burger to be courteous and they didn't. It was a smelly situation. I still tease them about it to this day.

"Motown was young and vibrant. Many talented people came through those doors. Our beginnings were the company's beginnings. We were there literally from day one and mainly during the prime years of history-making music. People were happy to make music and sing. They would pay people up to $5.00 and eventually $7.00 to clap and sing and people were happy to clap on those records. We did not have a contract with Motown, but we had a verbal agreement. We never left Motown because there was no contract, but we did do outside sessions and moonlighted. We didn't tell anyone because they would try to find us."

Rita Lumpkin-Daily is another childhood friend of The Andantes. She spent a significant amount of time with them in social settings and at Motown. Her cousin is late Motown singer Henry Lumpkin who recorded several songs at Motown, including 'I Got a Notion'. Rita recalls, "I have known Jackie and Marlene since the 1940s. We all grew up together. I knew Louvain, but not as well. I was younger and I would use Marlene's ID to get into The 20 Grand. Tammi Terrell would be hanging out with us too. We went from one cabaret party to the next with Popcorn because he had so many gigs. The Temptations would hang out with us too. We partied together and it was fun times, but nothing naughty or bad, just fun, good times.

"One time we were at Marlene's mother's house hanging out all day playing cards and just singing and harmonizing. Someone said they could smell smoke. We went outside where we had been putting our cigarette butts in the trash can and it had caught fire. There was so much smoke. We lost track of time hanging out singing—those cigarettes were in there smoldering for hours.

"Our friend Julie Watkins and I would go to the shows at The 20 Grand. I even rode on the back of David Ruffin's motorcycle. He was fun and crazy. I remember Mary Wells' mother would drop her off. Now if my mother had caught me at that place, I would be in big trouble.

"I was at The Fox Theatre during a Motown Revue and Marlene, Jackie, and Louvain were behind the curtain singing. The girl group that was on stage ended up getting boo-d because the microphone for The Andantes went out. The girls on stage didn't sound so great and the audience let them know it. Back then, you wanted them to sound like the record. The audience got restless because the girls on stage weren't sounding like the record. Julie and I looked at each other and laughed; it was something! The Andantes sang in these situations too and people just don't know it, and this needs to be told now. The girl group onstage was surprised at the audience's reaction, but we knew what had happened because we knew The Andantes were behind the curtain.

On another occasion, Julie and I were down at the studio and we witnessed them turning the microphones off for the female group that was in the studio. We only heard The Andantes singing during the playback. We saw that happen. The thing is, everyone at the time knew that The Andantes were doing a lot of the singing. They knew what was going on. It just needs to be told now that their part is bigger than what people think.

"When they first started recording, I was the 'wannabe' Andante. I used to sit at home on the porch and wait for them to come back from the recording studios. I knew that Jackie was going to give us some parts to sing. Julie and I would wait for them to come back and they'd tell us the songs and sing to us the songs that they had just recorded. We'd learn them and sing them. We'd know the next songs that Marvin Gaye, Martha Reeves, or The Supremes were going to release.

"We would sit on the porch after they came in from work and sing. We were singing the songs before they were put on wax. Jackie came home one day and told us how bad (bad meaning awesome) Marvin Gaye's new record was. She told me, 'Rita, you sing this part' and I sang, 'How sweet it is to be loved by you.' Jackie and Marlene would sing it for us first and then we would all sing it together. Emory, Jackie's brother, would be with us too. We were younger than Marlene and Jackie and went to Northwestern High School. We would walk down the halls at Northwestern and sing the tunes before they actually came out on records. We would wear out a Mary Wells song before it even got on the radio.

"I used to wrestle with Diana Ross. Diana lived across the street from my aunt and we'd wrestle in the front yard. We were about fourteen. She would remember Mary Lumpkin. That's me-Mary Rita Lumpkin. Richard Street and I would play the dozens and talk about our mommas. We were around everyone from the era. We used to have such good times too. Since I was younger than they were, I had to sneak out of the house to go to Hitsville and hang out. I went there several times with The Andantes. Julie and I snuck down there and sometimes Jackie and them wouldn't know we were there. At times they would be in the sessions working and sometimes it would be secretive what they were singing. There were times when we couldn't go inside when we got there. They'd be strict sometimes about who was in there with them when they were singing. My cousin Henry would also get me in with no problems. People in the neighborhood would hang out at Motown too—on the lawn, in the lobby, on the curb, but we'd be inside with them.

"I grew up in the neighborhood. I moved to Beverly Court and Grand River. There was a studio around the corner called 'Correc-tone Recording Company'. I went in there one day and that's when I met Popcorn, Sonny Sanders, and William Witherspoon. They told me I could come in any time I wanted. I started playing the conga drums. They let me play on Teresa Lindsey's records, a song that Popcorn had written for her. They began to let me do different things. For instance, I sang on Gino Washington's record, 'Gino Is A Coward'.

"I was the look-out at Correc-tone. They were trying to get the Motown sound there. Berry didn't like The Funk Brothers or The Andantes to be working outside of Motown. They'd put me outside as a lookout because I knew everyone and I knew all of the cars that they drove. They would drive by to spy on them and look for The Funk Brothers and The Andantes to see if they were working there. I saw them drive by looking for them. Nobody could trust anyone back then not to spy on them.

"I too dabbled in music at that time. I became one of The Tonnettes with Sharon Hicks; she was bass player Rodney Hicks' sister. I played the drums and congas. Billie Jo Thomas was the piano player and we had a drummer and bass player. We toured and played all around Canada. Our manager was Carmen Murphy of the House of Beauty.

"I have the utmost respect for my friends The Andantes. Their singing never went to their heads. They never bragged about it and they didn't tell people what was really going on at Motown and on the Motown Revues. They were modest about what they did and I admire them for that. They were loyal and they stayed the same over the years. They never were haughty, but they deserve to be proud of what they accomplished. They do not want to take away from others, and that is why they are not telling all of it. They should share enough so they can get the recognition they deserve. They are older now and everyone knows what they did. I think it is time everyone is mature about it.

"You cannot tell on people, because when you tell

something and everyone was in it together, then you tell on yourself; you would end up telling something another does not want known. The secrets need to stay secret but the good needs to come forth. This is a Motown legacy that can fall away. The privacy people want to keep private, they can keep it private. What The Andantes did is part of history."

Lead singer of The Velvelettes is Caldin Gill-Street. She adds, "The Andantes sing on several Velvelettes tunes. In fact, they dubbed over and/or did background vocals on most of our records. They have beautiful voices. I can remember sitting in the control booth listening to them sing. The blend was just beautiful. I loved to just listen to them sing. I am pretty sure that they sing on some of my solo work as well. I would go to the studio at 2:00 or 3:00 in the morning and the next thing I knew, the song would be out on the radio. I would hear it in the next few days and hear the background vocals on it. It was them singing with me. I have always admired their skilled vocals.

"I came from a college town. My mother was a nurse and my father was a Baptist preacher. They raised seven children. I grew up in Kalamazoo, Michigan and I formed The Velvelettes when I was in the ninth grade. My sister Mildred and the oldest member of the group, Bertha, were co-founders. We created our name ourselves. We had smooth harmonies, so we started with the name Velvet and expanded on that. We went to Motown with that name. We came to Motown around 1962-1963 with five original members. Our older members started getting married. Songs subsequent to our first three years at Motown have The Andantes singing on them. Sandy Tilley and Annette Rogers replaced the original Velvelettes and traveled with me for the rest of our career. During my years at Motown I could relate to it being the family environment that people describe it to be. The Velvelettes came from homes where both parents were in the home, just as Berry did, so we could relate to him and what he was doing.

"I was still in high school and Berry told my parents that work would never interfere with my school. We didn't do many sock-hops and shows. We worked on weekends and not during the week. Betty Kelly sang with us and then she had the chance to become a Vandella with Martha Reeves. All five of The Velvelettes are still living.

"When we did shows together at Motown, we all rooted for each other and cheered each other on because Berry encouraged and promoted friendly competition. We were just as responsible for keeping ourselves out there in the public's eye as management was. Berry and Motown didn't have the resources to make everyone a star at the same time, and on the same level. Diana Ross had a hunger and I remember her telling me she was going to be a star.

"Johnny Bristol was another unsung hero of Motown. He co-wrote one of my favorite songs, 'These Things Will Keep Me Loving You'. The Andantes sing on our version. Norman Whitfield was one of our main producers, but we worked with Mickey Stevenson and Johnny Bristol also.

"What I would like people to know about The Andantes is that they are wonderful ladies, extremely talented, and skilled vocalists. They met the challenge of singing background for any and all of the groups. They deserve recognition for their work. They sing on so many songs. I imagine that on many records the fans and public think that the female voices they hear are that of the girls in the group. It was a blend and they were utilized on everyone's records. They enhanced the vocal qualities and kept the Motown sound at a level that was distinguishable to the public's ear.

"Their vocals are very distinct on any record, especially behind the male groups. The assumption with the female groups was that it was the girls in the group singing. They were combined with the other voices and a lot of time they were put in the forefront of a lot of songs. Their vocals enhanced the quality of the vocals and they made everyone sound better and made the whole record sound great. It was acceptable to have them because they gave the song a fuller sound and the producers wanted them. It was also more convenient to have them sing. In my situation with our group, I was the only one available in Detroit during the transitional period when the other Velvelettes were being homemakers and mothers. I was trying to sustain the group and find new members and audition singers. The company was still recording The Velvelettes, so they sang in that capacity. The Andantes were used on many of our recordings. It was never meant to take away anything from the original groups, but rather to enhance the quality of the sound and make it better. I feel Motown was blessed to have the quality of vocals in The Andantes to utilize in the recording sessions. To me, they are a very significant part of defining that Motown sound.

"In my mind, they are just as significant to the Motown sound as The Funk Brothers. Their voices were so heavenly, they sounded like angels. One of my favorites is 'Just Ask The Lonely' by The Four Tops and I really like 'It's Growing' by The Temptations. Every time I see them, I just love them and I have the utmost respect for them because they sing on many of our recordings. They have always been good to me and nice to me. I totally respect and love these ladies for the value their voices and personalities added to everyone's music at Motown. I have learned in recent years that they did not only lend their voices to Motown, but to other record companies as well. I look at Motown as a family and I don't look at the negative aspects of it. There are negative situations in every family and you still love your family. Motown is no different than any other family situation. In the last few years, say ten years or so, we all are realizing that it was a very important piece of history and how important it is to tell it. There are so many people who love Motown with a passion.

"There is so much to be told from that era. Everyone has a different take on it. Some were in the same experiences and felt, saw, and lived it completely opposite of others who lived it. The Velvelettes tried not to create any enemies or animosity and we strived to be good people. We did not like to make waves and worked hard to get along with others. Mrs. Powell would tell us not to be negative. She would tell us to always be pleasant and focus on the positive. We would be taught to say the good and share the good. A negative attitude can really ruin you and can be your downfall. There is a way to tell your hurts and pains without focusing on the negative. One also needs to take responsibility for being part of any problem, acknowledge it, and not always blame other people. Everyone from Motown has a story to tell, and each one of us adds a piece of the puzzle that makes up what Motown was and became."

How Sweet It Is

During the mid-sixties, Motown was largely successful with major hits on the charts. By this time The Andantes had sung on such hits as their signature classic, 'My Guy' by Mary Wells, The Supremes' 'Run, Run, Run', The Miracles' 'Mickey's Monkey', The Velvelettes' 'Needle in a Haystack', Martha and The Vandellas' 'Quicksand' and The Four Tops' 'Baby I Need Your Loving'. The Motown sound was labeled with the slogan 'The Sound of Young America', and that it was. Motown was everywhere and that promotional slogan still fits today when describing what Motown meant to music and young people in the 1960s.

As the hits of the 60s were climbing the charts, The Andantes were helping to create the sounds of Motown and steadily making history with everyone who was part of the hit-machine. Louvain remembers the day when 'My Guy' became a hit and went to #1. Management called all three ladies up to the office and gave them a bonus along with a nice letter signed by Smokey Robinson. The Four Tops would also give them a bonus and share the good fortune when a song of theirs was a hit. Norman Whitfield was another who gave them bonuses when a song was a smash.

There was a look to Motown at the time and a definite sound as well. The Motown acts that appeared on television shows were embedded forever in our memories and in musical history. They were polished and smooth. It is a known fact that the Motown artists moved and looked a certain way. The sounds that America was hearing at the time were also a big part of this phenomenon. The product that Motown was presenting to the world was similar in a way to the car factories of Detroit. The product rolled off the assembly line and it looked and performed beautifully, but you never met or heard of the factory workers who built the cars. Although The Andantes were busy and they were making history with the music, they were also leading normal lives hanging out with friends, going to church, and raising their children.

Keep in mind that The Andantes were a little older than most of their colleagues. Louvain and Marlene were young mothers during the time we were seeing the Motown artists on television. Marlene was a newly single mother having gone through a divorce just after a year of marriage. Jackie is Godmother to Marlene's son Lawrence. Marlene and Louvain often brought their young sons to the studio to see Stevie Wonder. Both boys were very fond of him. Stevie was their favorite. Louvain says, "No matter what Stevie Wonder was doing, he would stop and come out to play and spend a little time with little Max. I think because each had something in common (Stevie was blind and Max was hearing-impaired), they bonded and became close. I had taken Max to see a show where Stevie performed 'Fingertips' and he nearly jumped out of my arms. There was an age difference between them, but they bonded in friendship. Stevie started touring and getting busy so they were around each other less and less.

"On another occasion, Max was in my arms when we were recording, and they had to stop because they heard noises; it was Max humming along with us and they picked it up on the microphone. It sounded liked feedback or buzzing and we didn't realize he was humming along with us.

"Singin' Sammy Ward and Janie Bradford would baby-sit Max in the lobby while I was in sessions. In these early years only a few of us had children. You have to remember how young everyone was, most were just out of high school and barely twenty years old. Janie had her son Lance in the lobby and I was out there visiting with her as Ralph Seltzer was walking by, he leaned over to talk to him and Lance slapped him. Ralph's face turned bright red and you could see that he was upset. Janie looked at me and then said to Ralph, 'This is Louvain's little boy.' She was just devilish back then and was always a prankster and played jokes on everyone, but she was a very good songwriter"

Max was a little boy during this time and he has some memories to share. He says, "When I was little, I remember Janie Bradford and the fact that she was so tall and pretty. I also remember Pat Cosby and Janie and where they sat behind the glass and took phone calls. I recall everyone was so warm and friendly to me. Marlene and Jackie were so nice to me. Shorty Long used to always give me a hug. I remember The Supremes and how pretty all three of them were. Flo used to pick me up and smother me with kisses and hugs. Smokey was such a nice man and his wife Claudette was so pretty.

"I went upstairs where they played cards and I saw all of the money piled up on the table. It was so much money to me as a little boy. Stevie Wonder was my friend and playmate when I was visiting at the studio and he would always come out to talk with me and make time for me. I remember lots of hugs from everyone. Singin' Sammy Ward would hug me a lot too. I remember going to Paul Williams' barbershop. My brother Michael and I would get our haircuts there. My mother's friend Ed McQueen was a police officer and he would come by our house and patrol our area. Edwin Starr came over to our house to visit and I remember I really liked his bright purple shoes. My babysitters were Agnes and Beans and I had a playmate with Little Beans Bowles."

Motown being the family environment that it was, Jackie loved the fun times and the picnics. She says, "A real highlight for me was meeting some of the people we were working with. I loved Gladys Knight and The Pips and I loved watching them perform. They were so fun. They would dance and do their routines in the lobby. Gladys is such a nice and spiritual person. We went to see some of their shows out of the state. Prior to the performance they held a group prayer backstage and we prayed with them. I don't recall if we sang on their records. The Pips backed up Gladys. Gladys Knight and Claudette Robinson had a different environment working with the guys. Women sometimes added that catty element, but when you worked with the Motown guys, it was more like a brother and sister type environment. That's how we felt with the guy groups. When we sang with The Temptations there was always wise-cracking going on and joking around. Any of the guy groups were just fun times in the studio, whether it was The Contours, The Originals, The Four Tops, The Temptations, The Spinners, The Isley Brothers, or whoever. Working with the guys was just a lot of fun.

"The company picnic every year was extremely nice. That's when they went all out for everyone and it really felt like family. It was usually in the summer and they held it in Canada. I was a fanatic taking pictures back then. They treated us like royalty and they would even park your car when you arrived. There was everything in the world that you could possibly want to eat. It was the one rare time when everyone would be together. Normally we just saw certain people we had worked with, but this was everyone together and it was nice-like a family reunion atmosphere. It was something that we looked forward to every year. The Motown Christmas parties were very nice every year as well and they would decorate the studio so beautifully during the holidays. We sang on the Christmas songs with Marvin Gaye, The Supremes, and The Tempations.

"There were always gathering and parties during the Motown years and I went to a few. Marlene and I did a lot of ripping and running. I enjoyed hanging out with friends and I never did drink or smoke. Marlene hung out a lot with our childhood friends like Yvonne Harbin. Marlene likes to play cards. I think that with cards there is too much sitting around. There was a lot of card-playing at Motown because there was a lot of sitting around the studio. I would rather enjoy fellowship and talk to the other people who aren't playing cards."

Louvain remembers the card games and the fun everyone had in between the sessions, how there was a time for work and a time for play. "There was a room upstairs where everyone gathered to play cards. I really enjoyed watching the guys play. Not too many women went up in the office where they played, unless they were going to play with them. I would sneak up there and watch. There was always a big pile of money on the table. It was fun to see the artists and musicians in a different atmosphere. In the studio, they were artists and when they were creating that was one thing; but when they played cards they got slick with each other and conned each other. They would not look each other in the eye. They were literally different people. A different side of them came out when they played cards.

"Marv Johnson would play cards; Marvin Gaye, The Temptations, the producers, and the songwriters too. After we were done with work and sessions, most of the time I would go home because I was married. I observed a lot and listened. I kept to myself and I had a few friends. I was better one on one with people and that is how I bonded with everyone. I would not talk in large groups and I would just listen. Once in a blue moon, I would go to a party. I smoked cigarettes back then, but nothing more. I would sneak off and get into my own trouble. One of the producers took me to a party and showed me how to smoke marijuana. Everyone at this party was smoking pot and I had never done it before. I won't say who it was, but he had to teach me how to puff it. I was never into drugs and that was the first and last time I smoked marijuana. It put me in a fog and I didn't like it. The drug scene was not for me. It was a dark scene and people sink darker when they do drugs. Music was the escape I needed from any darkness going on in my life.

"Marlene and Jackie were much more sociable than I was. They had a really nice group of friends. One year for my birthday, Marlene and Jackie had been trying to get rid of me and I didn't understand why, so I went home. After I was home for about thirty minutes, they came and knocked on my door with a bunch of their friends. They had brought me presents and a cake. I was so surprised and so happy that they did that for me, but my husband didn't let them stay and he made them leave. I was so hurt and I felt horrible. I don't know if they ever knew how much that day meant to me and how much it hurt that I was unable to spend that time with them and their friends. I had never had a party before and Max ended it. I was devastated."

The 20 Grand and The Fox Theatre were two of the greatest places to be. The Andantes would frequent the night spots when they would have a night out with friends. The biggest artists of the era were performing at these locations, including all of the local Motown talent. They were *the* places to dress up and go out on the town to. Furs were politically correct then. The women were glamorous and the men were debonair. The artists on stage were dressed up to shine like new money. Marlene remembers some of the special times. "We would see everyone at these shows. We went to The 20 Grand and we hung out with everyone even though we had our own little group of friends. We kept a low profile and there were groups of friends within groups of friends. We sang in the background at Motown and we hung out in the background with our own friends even though we knew everyone. We would go to Motown Mondays at The Roostertail. That was just fabulous and the live shows were brilliant and incredible then.

There was really no show like The Temptations. I could watch them perform six nights a week, I loved them so. They never missed a beat and they never had an off night that I saw. There has never been a group since that can touch The Classic Five Temptations. Cholly Atkins had them together on everything. They were perfectly polished. The outfits were superb and sharp and every male group around was trying to emulate them. I would go to see them every chance I had.

"We sang with The Temptations and we're on several tracks of theirs. They were onstage one time when someone in the audience yelled out, 'Where are them girls singing?' The audiences knew how the songs sounded and they wanted it to sound that way when they saw them live. Although we sang and sounded great with them, Melvin went to Berry and asked that we not sing because they were unable to duplicate that sound on stage. They were such a polished ensemble of five guys who could sing and dance, so I understood their concerns. I know Jackie and Louvain did too. The Four Tops didn't mind us singing with them, they would just sing the songs onstage. The Temptations were a polished show, so it was a different kind of thing."

Louvain was pregnant with her second child when The Andantes were recording in the studio with The Temptations. She explains, "We were singing on their song 'It's Growing' and I was visibly pregnant and Melvin was teasing me. Every time we got to the part where we sang 'it's growing', he put a basketball under his shirt and pretended to be pregnant too, teasing and cutting up. I have to say, if you've never teased a pregnant woman, perhaps you should rethink it. We are moody and emotional at that time. I got so mad at him even though I knew he was joking with me. When I hear that song now I have a laugh remembering how much fun The Temptations were in the studio. We were friends and family in the studio and it was always fun and joking around like that. I understood Melvin not wanting us on the records because they couldn't duplicate that sound on stage. I was never upset about that, none of us were. We sing on 'Get Ready' and several other Temptations tracks."

Motown, Detroit, and the 60's were a magical time in history. There was change going on in The United States and in the world. Motown was front and center when it came to making a difference and having an influence. There was a sexual revolution going on, the Civil Rights and Women's Movements. Yvonne Rashida Harbin is a childhood friend of Marlene and Jackie's. She helps to describe some of what The Andantes and Motown meant in a world where music brought people together, both then and now. "I have been telling Marlene and Jackie for years that they should write a book about their lives and experiences at Motown. It is a unique, one of a kind story. I would prefer they tell the whole skullduggery of the era so people understood, but I know that no one wants to bring up old wounds or others' secrets. The privacy of others is something they have always respected. There are love affairs in the mix. Part of what made that music is the inner relationships that were going on at the time. I know they do not feel the need to tell that. I lived this life with them and they have an amazing story. They were part of the woodwork at Motown and, talk about being a fly on the wall! They were three flies on the wall and I was right there beside them the whole time.

"We lived on what they called the west side of town, and as a matter of fact, my folks had a store called Foster's Market on the east side of town. A half-block from my parents store was Warren Court. That's where Smokey, Claudette, Bobby, and their families grew up. It was a wonderful experience for me growing up on both sides of town. If you know anything about the regions here, there are distinct differences between a west-sider and an east-sider. I wouldn't trade my life for anything in the world. Being on both sides of town, as a west side person you had to fit in with the east side and not have people think you were uppity or a snob.

"I went with Marlene and Jackie many times to the studio. I interacted with not only The Andantes, but also the artists, musicians, engineers, producers, and everyone. What I witnessed, with The Andantes, was they were very easy going to work with. I saw how Marlene, Jackie, and Louvain worked with producers and how they dealt with them. They were intuitive and could pick up exactly what the producer wanted to hear. In fact they added more to it and that is what the producers loved about them. They did not do many takes of a track; they would get it down in the can very quickly. I sat on the sideline observing or reading. I knew that they were good at what they did and I was always impressed with the process. I saw how it came together. I was part of it too because they would tell me to get up and clap and snap on this record and I did.

"Sometimes I would even sit outside with Martha Reeves when she was the secretary or be in the booth with the engineers. Engineers James Green and Larry Horn were very good friends of ours. We had our own little group of friends and we had a blast during these years. Lamont Dozier was just a funny man to hang out with. We would go over to his house and he liked to cook for everyone. He cooked dinner for us and made fried chicken and mashed potatoes, when we sat down to the table, Popcorn said, 'Oh there's a little bit of potato in my salt.' Lamont had used too much salt.

"Oftentimes it was like a party in the studio. It was fun times and so much fun that it didn't seem like work for them. It was like a family but there were some jealous moments here and there. Some of the girl groups didn't want The Andantes singing with them. The Andantes had to work through these issues as individuals and as a group. It was painful for them at times, and I know it was hurtful for them. All through the process and while making the music they maintained a loyalty to the sound that they helped create. They were part of the biggest thing in music and the hottest thing of the day. There were history-making events all over the world because of the Motown sound.

"All of us knew that they were part of that and they didn't get their props for it. I know them well enough to know that they tucked that pain inside of them and dealt with it quietly. They were able to bounce back from that hurt because of solid friendships, families, and their solid foundation with each other. I thank God that I came through that era where I could see up close the amazing talented singers. The artists then could sing and dance. It was poetry in motion. It was just a powerful moment in time. The shows were absolute perfection. Berry was a genius to pull all of that together the way he did and present it to the world.

"For most of the artists, there were highs and some very low lows during that time. The music as the backdrop gives it a different meaning for the ones who were there when it was being created. I can appreciate that music so much more because I lived that life with them. Those were different times and everything that was happening was okay for the moment. There is a lot of loyalty among this group of people, whether they are in each other's lives, best friends, or just distant former co-workers. The Motown family members have been loyal to each other and have shown support for each other over the years.

"Motown was a complexity of many relationships, pertaining to the music and personal as well. I was so square at the time, but we were all having fun in our groups of friends and relationships. Everyone was blended together in one way or another and that made it a very personal experience for everyone. If you were there you knew, and you know today, the personalities at play and the lyrics and the moment of the sixties. The sexual freedom, artistry, and all of it together made Motown something special. Some of that great singing and writing comes from the hearts of troubles. Something happens when you are meshed with another musically. It is chemistry and a camaraderie that bonds you closer.

"My feeling is that great people and artists have great sexual appetites. Some of that music is based on love stories of the time. It is in fact sexual music and the lyrics are about some of the people at Motown. If you do not understand love, Motown music will help you. I get the true meaning of The Andantes and what Motown has meant in music history. I have always been impressed with who they are and the fact that they had an impact in music. They are certainly an intricate part of that operation at Motown, in addition to a lot of the Chicago groups and sounds that they contributed to."

"My Guy" #1 by Mary Wells

Written by
William "Smokey" Robinson

MARY WELLS
Nothing you could say
Can tear me away from My Guy
Nothing you could do
'Cause I'm stuck like glue to My Guy
I'm stickin' to My Guy
Like a stamp to a letter

Like the birds of a feather
We stick together
I'm tellin' you from the start
I can't be torn apart from My Guy
Nothing you can do
Could make me untrue to My Guy

THE ANDANTES
My Guy

MARY WELLS
Nothing you could buy
Could make me tell a lie to My Guy

JACKIE
My Guy

MARLENE
My Guy

LOUVAIN
My Guy

MARY WELLS
I gave My Guy my word of honor
To be faithful and I'm gonna
You best be believing
I won't be deceiving My Guy
As a matter of opinion I think he's tops
My opinion is he's the cream of the crop
As a matter of taste to be exact
He's my ideal as a matter of fact
No muscle bound man
Could take my hand from My Guy

THE ANDANTES
My Guy

MARY WELLS
No handsome face
Could ever take the place of My Guy
JACKIE
My Guy

MARLENE
My Guy

LOUVAIN
My Guy

MARY WELLS
He may not be a movie star
But when it comes to being happy we are
There's not a man today
Who could take me away from My Guy
No muscle bound man
Could take my hand from My Guy

THE ANDANTES
My Guy

MARY WELLS
No handsome face
Could ever take the place of My Guy

JACKIE
My Guy

MARLENE
My Guy

LOUVAIN
My Guy

MARY WELLS
He may not be a movie star
But when it comes to being happy we are

There's not a man today
Who could take me away from My Guy
THE ANDANTES
What you say?

MARY WELLS
There's not a man today
Who could take me away from My Guy

THE ANDANTES
Tell me more

MARY WELLS
There's not a man today
Who could take me away from My Guy

Introducing Pat Lewis

Within the framework of Motown are layers and layers of talent and creativity that helped to make the company grow. The songwriters, producers, artists, and musicians were all helping to carry out Berry Gordy's vision. Contained within the house on West Grand Boulevard are many stories of unsung heroes. Some stories may never be told because the persons are no longer here; others may fall away because people are getting older. The Andantes made it clear that they wanted to tell their truth and at the same time enlighten some of the other stories that are underneath the success of Motown. They wanted some of their friends and colleagues to be known for their part in the history. Although Motown was highly successful and the world had never really seen anything like it, the truth about some of it would come out many years later.

The early background vocals for Motown were The Rayber Voices and they merged into The Andantes with various voices thrown in the mix until it was fine-tuned. There was one woman who filled in more often than others. Pat Lewis could sing any part and fill in for Louvain, Jackie, or Marlene if needed. There were times when she was with all three of them recording. Pat has her own legendary status and her own personal musical history outside of The Andantes.

Marlene says, "Pat is a dear friend and we met her in the 60s shortly after we began working at Motown. She filled in at different times when we needed a high voice. We consider her an honorary Andante. Sonny Sanders organized most of our recording sessions outside of Motown and in Chicago. We met Pat at Golden World Studios. Pat joined us when we freelanced outside of Motown, so she is on some of the Chicago sessions with us, in addition to The Golden World sessions and other local sessions we did, such as The Fantastic Four.

"It was a similar environment at Golden World, meaning if you were there hanging out, someone would ask you to sing. The Andantes hung out and worked there and we saw our friends. One day they asked Jackie and me to sing and we said, 'But Louvain isn't here today.' Ed Wingate said, 'Well Pat Lewis is here.' Then Jackie asked Mr. Wingate, 'Can she sing well?' That's how we met Patsy.

"Patsy has a large body of work of her own and is legendary as a background vocalist. She has done so much it is unreal. Patsy was singing backup for Aretha Franklin and would later play a pivotal role in Isaac Hayes' body of work. Pat, along with Telma Hopkins, Joyce, and Pam Vincent are among the voices in the background at Motown. This was long before Joyce and Telma were singing with Tony Orlando. Pat can sing any vocal part; she blended with us very well. Louvain has a very distinctive voice and you can tell it on records. I can pick Louvain out of a thousand voices and I can hear a record and tell you if Louvain is singing. I know because I stood next to her for so many years in the studio. Patsy sounds similar to Louvain, so The Andantes' sound was there when it would be me, Jackie, and Pat. You can hear the difference though."

Pat Lewis recalls working with The Andantes and being an Andante. "Marlene and Jackie liked how I blended with them. I sang first soprano like Louvain, so we blended very well together. I started doing some sessions with them, especially the outside sessions because they weren't supposed to be moonlighting and freelancing. One of the first moonlighting sessions I sang on with them was 'Agent Double O Soul' by Edwin Starr. They took me over to Motown and I started working on Mondays. I did some sessions over there. I want to say the first session I did with them was 'Uptight' with Stevie Wonder. That was me, Marlene, and Jackie on that. Sylvia Moy was the producer. I was standing at the microphone and they were asking me to sing a little louder, stand a little closer, and move in. I was scared as hell, and a little paranoid, because it was Motown. Once I relaxed, I was alright. Every session for me was exciting. This experience was a learning tool for me. I learned so much at that time. The sessions I did with them were a great learning experience. When we were recording back in those days, we didn't always have a headset. You just had the microphone and you didn't hear the playback in your headset, because there was none. They taught me about sound and about blending with each other. They were brilliant when it came to that. They were really thinking back then when they laid the backing tracks. The background vocals are a major part of the song.

"While working at Motown I did some of The Four Tops sessions. Some of the products I sang on for them, I never heard again. It's in the vault, or in the can. I did sing on 'Seven Rooms of Gloom' and 'Standing In the Shadows of Love'. I sang on Kim Weston's 'Take Me In Your Arms'. I don't sing on any of Tammi Terrell's recordings or Marvin Gaye's. When David Ruffin left The Temptations, we did an album on him but I don't know the name of it. Don Davis was producing the album. I actually had to record it twice because I brought some other ladies in to sing. Don asked me why I didn't bring 'his singers'. So, I did it over again with The Andantes. He didn't like the first singers I did it with.

"I did sing on some of the Christmas album for The Supremes, but my sister Diane Lewis did most of that album with The Andantes, and none of The Supremes were in the studio when they did it either. My sister and I did a lot of background work during that time, thousands of sessions. I cannot begin to think of all of these artists, there are so many. My sister, Rose Edward, and I were working for Don Davis on all of Johnny Taylor's stuff like, 'Who's Making Love'. We did Mavis Staples' background vocals and were working extensively for Stax; plus artists like Ivy Hunter, Jr. Walker, gosh there are so many. There were some very popular girl groups backing everyone at that time. The Sweet Inspirations sang with Aretha for many years. That is them on 'Respect' and 'Ain't No Way'. The Waters Sisters are great singers too. They are very talented. They worked a lot at that time also. They can sing beautifully.

"I was in a group called The Adorables. Popcorn Wylie, Freddy Gorman, and Bob Hamilton named us that. There were four of us, two sets of sisters: Betty and Jackie Winston, and Pat and Diane Lewis. We were singing for Golden World and were like the competition with Motown. So when Martha and The Vandellas had 'Heat Wave' we came out with 'Deep Freeze'. We had several singles out. The label had JJ Barnes, who was the competition, so to speak, for Marvin Gaye. We had the Holidays who sang 'I Love You Forever'. They were the competition for the guy groups. It was very competitive back then. I worked with Gino Washington and sang on 'Gino Is A Coward'. Telma Hopkins and Joyce Vincent did sessions at Motown as well. Berry Gordy eventually bought Golden World.

"We sang for a lot of the local Detroit artists like Emanuel Laskey, Melvin Davis, JJ Barnes, and Steve Mancha. I worked for Golden World mostly and when I worked at Motown I sang with Marlene and Jackie mainly. If I couldn't make it to a session to fill in when they needed a voice, my sister would go. Sometimes things were shelved and you never heard them again. There are so many songs I sing on and that we sing on. You forget them after you walk out the door from the studio. During this time when we were all working and singing backup, the only thing I regret is that we never performed as The Andantes.

"I went to Chicago with The Andantes all of the time. We did Jackie Wilson tracks. We're on the whole album that 'Higher and Higher' is on, and 'Whispers Getting Louder'—we filled in the whole album. We went over on the bus to Chicago for those sessions and went twice to finish them. We stayed at Carl Davis' apartment in Marina City. He was a producer on Brunswick. Sonny Sanders got us the job and he brought some other musicians from Detroit for the sessions.

"I was on the road with Aretha Franklin around 1966-1967. Telma Hopkins basically took my place while I was gone. Telma has a very distinctive first soprano voice. Her vibrato is so recognizable. I did some studio work with Aretha. That is my arrangement on 'Call Me' and 'This Girl's In Love'. On that album it was I, Wylene Ivy, and Evelyn Green. We called ourselves 'The Sweethearts of Soul'.

"Jackie and Marlene were so creative because when we did the outside sessions, the producers often would have no idea of what they wanted. They would put the background together for them. They actually trained me how to do that. I am now a background vocal arranger.

"Another group is Hot Buttered Soul. That is me, my sister, and Rose Edward. I did background vocal arranging and it was Marlene and Jackie who taught me how to do that. I sang on everything Isaac did. 'Shaft', 'Walk On By', 'I Don't Know What to Do with Myself', I sang on all of those albums. I arranged all of Isaac Hayes' stuff and sang with him from 1969-1982. I didn't get the credit for arranging on the first album. The album was titled 'Hot Buttered Soul'. We named our group after that album. They needed another album from Isaac and he recorded it. He brought it here and I arranged the voices for it. The next thing we knew it had taken off and he called and wanted 'those girls' to go out on the road with him. I didn't get arranging credit on that album then either until later in the future, after it was a hit.

"We were out on the road and they hooked us up for *The Man and Woman Show* with Isaac Hayes and Dionne Warwick. I already knew Cissy Houston from when I had worked with Aretha. After we did our show as Hot Buttered Soul, we would back up Isaac on a microphone offstage. The Sweet Inspirations had come to our show. Isaac would have a choir and he would look around and think *where are all these voices coming from?* In later years we did the same thing at Madison Square Garden with The Pointer Sisters. They helped us backup Isaac offstage. There would be singers around and want to sing, and The Pointer Sisters backed him with us offstage. You had all these people wanting to sing and I would say, 'Yeah, come on and sing.'"

Joyce Vincent started in the music scene rather young in Detroit. "I grew up in Detroit. It was an exciting time and for me it was the only place to be. I was a kid and never really had been anywhere except maybe to Chicago. It was a happening place and there was music everywhere you went and studios everywhere. It was a happy time. We worked in so many studios and with so many producers. I had a girl group in Detroit called The Debonaires. We were a trio at first. It was me, Dorothy Garland, and Elsie Baker. Later a fourth member came in. Her name was Diane Hogan. We did sock-hops. I, Diane, and Elsie auditioned for Motown. It was Lamont Dozier, Eddie Holland, and Brian Holland who auditioned us. They probably don't remember that. They told us to come back after high school. We were disappointed and by the time we graduated, we heard about a record company by the name of Golden World that was looking for talent. We auditioned for Golden World and they accepted us. We recorded as The Debonaires for Golden World.

"Popcorn Wylie produced and recorded a song that actually got us some airplay. It was such a cute song. It was called 'Eeenie Meenie Gypsalini' and he wrote it. There was no lead vocal, it was just all of us girls singing on that record. I met The Andantes around 1966 or so. I knew who they were and I knew they sang at

Motown. We were all in the same circle. Those girls sang their hearts out. They were so good and were such great singers and they deserve their props. Back when people were making this music, the public wanted to actually see the people who were singing, or, who they thought were singing on the records. There is a big difference between singing on a stage and singing in a studio and doing the session work. The public wasn't informed of what happened in a studio and how the records were made. The background voices were a big part of the song and those girls worked hard. Those ladies sang on thousands of songs. They sang on just about everything that came out of Motown. They were that sound.

"My sister Pam and I sang quite a bit with everyone. There was so much work at the time that no one was ever really out of work. It wasn't like one girl group was going to do a session and another one didn't have work. There was enough work for everyone. We all had local girl groups and sang backup: Pat Lewis, The Andantes, my sister Pam and I, and a few others. We all used each other's groups to help one another. We all got along very well and supported what the other was doing. Many times Pat would call me for work and I would sing with her and her sister or she would call Telma Hopkins. I met Telma when I was about sixteen years old. Pat had several different ladies she could call and whoever was available would be on the session. Telma did more sessions at Motown than I did. I know she did some Marvin Gaye sessions. The Andantes called and we'd fill in. Some of the Detroit artists would caravan to Chicago to record and we went with them. I didn't record with any of the Chicago groups. I also recorded in Memphis with my sister Pam and Telma.

"When there was a session at Motown, the producers would run out to the lobby and see who was there to sing background and throw them in. I remember driving down Grand Boulevard, and at any given time when you drove past Motown, there would be a crowd outside hanging around; it was social hour. You could drive by and see a couple of The Temptations standing out there or members of some of the other groups. Telma sang there more than I did and she actually went to the Motown picnic. Everyone was there.

"We all had some really great times hanging out. I recall

being at Golden World preparing to head out to Chicago to record. We were in the studio and Pat had bought a Coke (when it came in a glass bottle). She poured half of it out and filled the rest with some alcohol. She asked me if I wanted a sip of her Coke and I said, 'Oh, yeah.' We had no business drinking at that age. We had a good laugh because that was the strongest Coke I had ever had. We had a lot of fun back then.

"It would be later that I became connected to Tony Orlando. Telma Hopkins was a sub-singer for the group Hot Buttered Soul, which was Pat Lewis' group. Hot Buttered Soul had a gig in New York and Tony Orlando was producing Barry Manilow at the same time. He wanted a different sound, so he asked a gentleman by the name of Tony Camillo about background singers. Mr. Camillo suggested that he try Isaac Hayes' girls because they were session singers and in town. Tony would eventually approach Telma to form a group. He had two hits out, 'Candida' and 'Knock Three Times', and they didn't know they were going to be as big of hits as they were. Telma and I don't sing on those two songs. Eventually, I was approached and we became Tony Orlando & Dawn. We sang lots of songs long before we ever had a hit. The first hit Telma and I sang on was 'Tie A Yellow Ribbon'. By 1977, Tony Orlando & Dawn was ending. Recently, our show came out on DVD and it is so nice to see that old footage from thirty years ago."

Like A Nightmare

The Andantes were so valuable to Motown that they were repeatedly denied the opportunity to record their own records and do their own shows. Marlene remembers how events occurred. "We talked to Berry about giving us a chance, and I hate to say it, but they just pacified us and kept us in the background. We stayed like good little children. They would tell us to just sit back and wait and we would get our chance. The truth is they wanted us in the background and that's where we stayed. We were secure in our position at Motown but it would have been nice to have the opportunity to grow as a group since we knew we had the ability to sing. We were confident in our singing and wanted the chance to develop it further.

"I don't know who to compare our singing to. I've heard some great singing over the years. The McGuire Sisters sang in harmony very well with perfectly blended vocals. I love group singing and harmonizing and in current time you no longer see that. If someone wants to be the star and sing lead, they shouldn't be in a group. The Philly Sound was really great harmonies and backing vocals. I wished I sung on some of that era of music. The Three Degrees and The Emotions do some very beautiful singing. I feel like that is group singing—where it is beautiful harmonizing and where all the voices blend so well together. I wish we could have had some solo work with us singing as a group. Not every voice in a group can sing lead and that's okay. The Temptations had five great singers. All could sing lead. There are background voices and there are lead voices.

"They didn't want us out on our own to make records or leave them. As you can see, we sing on just about everything in that catalog. If we had recorded as a group, there may have been an opportunity for us to travel and that would make us unavailable for studio work. They wanted us here, in town, and at their disposal when they were recording. Since we were only paid by the session and we didn't get royalties, we had to constantly look for work. Eventually they retained us on a salary and they discouraged us from taking the outside sessions. We eventually joined the union and being in the union made it easier to get other work outside of Motown. Our pay was decent and good and we didn't want for anything except to earn a living and have our own chance. It was a struggle at that time for women to find comparable pay in the real world, so that's why we stayed. Our agreement with Motown was a verbal one but they wanted us exclusively. We felt that if they wanted us to be exclusive, they should pay us exclusively and offer us an incentive to stay. And if we wanted to record as a group, they should have let us. If it was slow at Motown, we still had to feed our families. So you mean to tell me, because you think we're your sound, we can't work elsewhere if there's a slow week at Motown? If Motown artists weren't working, I couldn't feed my family. I sang, we sang, and we had the right to earn a living other places. It didn't seem fair to us that they discouraged us and tried to spy on us. We had to keep a low profile when we worked. We made certain that when we did outside sessions it never interfered with our work at Motown. We would take work at another studio because it was slow on a given week, but we made Motown the first priority always. If we needed money and were able to make a living off our voices, then we did what we had to do.

"Motown saw our voices as 'their sound' and Berry didn't like his sound out there unless it was on his products. When he heard Jackie Wilson's 'Higher and Higher', he was upset his sound was out there. That was me, Jackie, and Pat Lewis on that record. There's no doubt about it; there is a definite Motown sound. We're on a soundtrack with Jackie Wilson for the film *A Lovely Way To Die*, with Kirk Douglas. We're singing on the title song with Jackie during the opening credits of the film. We recorded that in the 60s. We have a little inside joke that the singing on 'Higher and Higher' was in the key of H because it was some very high singing.

"At one point we thought we were going to have a single come out with Ann Bogan. Harvey Fuqua was friends with Ann and he brought her from Cleveland to record in Detroit. We needed a lead voice and she was a strong lead singer. We had wished and hoped for a record. She sang lead on 'Like A Nightmare', but our dream never materialized. They had made a promise to record us on our own, but there was no real effort to put us out there or promote us. The song was recorded, but that was it. Nothing ever came of it. We were happy with it and it was a good sound that we had with Ann. It seemed a perfect fit but they wanted us to stay in the background."

"Sonny Sanders was instrumental in The Andantes working at other locations. He shares, "I think of them in the highest regard and esteem. The truth is that I've been attempting to track down titles of Brunswick recordings that they worked their vocal magic on. As you must know, we were cranking out recordings at a consistently fast pace. We employed the talents of numerous musicians, sound engineers, recording studios, singers, etcetera; many of whom were paid with cash, undocumented, and un-credited for one reason or another, making it rather impossible to retrieve specific information. Popcorn was instrumental and responsible in my getting into Brunswick Records and for my connection with Carl Davis. Popcorn is a very giving person. He has done so much for the music industry and he's a key ingredient to the success of that era. He didn't get a lot of the creative credit that was due to him.

"Even after speaking with Carl Davis and Marlene, the only recording we can recall, and perhaps the most important, is the Jackie Wilson mega-hit 'Higher and Higher'. It also included the talents of some of Motown's musicians-The Funk Brothers with Richard 'Pistol' Allen on drums, to whom I credit its ultimate success. He asked me during the recording of the rhythm section, which I was dissatisfied with, if he could try something. Drawing from my respect for the cat, I gave my permission. Pistol, to my delirious delight, simply doubled the drum beat and created a totally different, uplifting, driving beat-with the addition of the seemingly infallible, steadfast, crispy-clean, equally driving vocal performance of The Andantes (who were capable of delivering the total gamut from liltingly laid-back to hard-rock). Add a few butt-kickin' horn licks, all complimenting one of Jackie's best and greatest recorded performances. I've had the honor and pleasure of creating background parts and singing with The Andantes during my Motown affiliation, as well as later directing them as an arranger and producer. I remember them as being totally professional, diligent, and long-suffering, to a point at which Jackie Hicks seemed to be the first to protest the time element in the studio. I venture to rate The Andantes among the top three vocal and backup recording vocalists I have ever worked with."

Jackie adds, "We were told Berry was upset over 'Higher and Higher'. My thing about that is, how can you tell someone they can't make a living doing what they do? He was mad that 'his sound' was out there on another label. We felt strongly about the fact that these were our voices and our jobs, and if we could earn a living at another place, then we had that right. We had no contract to be exclusive, and if we could earn a living recording in Chicago then we did it. How can a person dictate to you that you can't go out and earn your living doing something you're good at, with the voice that is your own? We interacted little with Berry. There was no recognition from him and it was always business as usual, where he never really did say much to us. We were never punished for singing outside of Motown. He was more intertwined with the producers and songwriters and we knew about his disappointment when we were moonlighting."

Emory Hicks explains further, "They sang all the time. When they weren't recording in Detroit, they were recording in New York or Chicago. They could record anywhere they wanted to because they didn't have a contract. Those kids were underpaid for the amount of work that they did for Motown. People just loved them singing and enjoyed those girls' singing. When they told someone what they had sung on, they'd say 'Aw, we knew that sounded like you.' Their church background really came out in their singing. I was very proud of my sister singing at Motown and I talked about it all the time. As far as I'm concerned, she sang better than the majority of those that sang at Motown. She was a great singer. She had a very happy life doing that, and continues to. I loved everything that they did. They added so much to everyone they sang behind. I'm very proud of Jackie, Marlene, and Louvain as The Andantes. I feel good when I hear them on the radio. I brag about The Andantes every chance I get. They were just as great as any of those other groups that were being produced. They made the other groups sound even better by singing with them on the records. They helped so many groups."

"Kim Weston was one artist who was a fighter for The Andantes and she insisted that they perform with her onstage. Kim was the first Motown act to have them out front and onstage with her. Marlene recalls they did shows with Kim at The Fox Theatre and The 20 Grand, "Kim wanted the Motown sound on stage with her so she really fought hard to get us with her. Mickey Stevenson looked out for us too, most likely because of our closeness with Kim. They both were great supporters of ours. They were married at the time. To be honest, everyone had to look out for themselves at Motown."

Kim recorded several hits with The Andantes and she adds, "I feel honored and privileged to have shared my career with them. I was the only Motown artist at that time to take them out on the road with me. To me, they were the best voices at Motown. No one could sing like them or hold a candle to them. One of my favorite songs they sing on with me is 'Just Loving You'. I wrote that song, even though I didn't get the writing credit for it." Louvain adds, "The infamous photograph of us with Kim Weston—the one that hangs in The Motown Museum—that was taken when we performed with her at Brandywine."

Although The Andantes had the opportunity to go out with Kim Weston and were given a chance to record their own record with Ann Bogan, their experience at Motown was complex as time went on. Each of them wouldn't trade the experience for anything in the world because they loved what they were doing and they loved to sing. They had so much fun and simply enjoyed singing with everyone. There is heartbreak that comes with their story—the disappointment of not being recognized on the record labels and not getting the proper credits, the heartbreak of watching how things happened to their friends and colleagues. In addition, their presence at Motown made for some uncomfortable feelings and situations at times. The environment at Motown was a competitive one. Berry Gordy encouraged friendly competition with his artists. The producers and songwriters were also in competition to get product out and have big hits. In the everyday studio it was a much different story.

The Andantes, along with The Funk Brothers, really weren't in competition with any other entities at Motown. They didn't need to be. They stood alone as the house-band and the house-voices. They also spent a lot more time in the studio than the other artists did. The way things were handled in the studio made some situations uncomfortable. Jackie remembers some of those occasions. "Without naming names because it simply doesn't matter now, we saw some of the cutthroat tactics. We heard and knew what was going on. We saw firsthand the inner-workings and the results of what was happening to groups and/or individuals. When you're there as much as we were, you got hold of a lot of information. We were separate from everyone, yet we were right there hearing it—literally from the grapevine. We were in the background, but very much a part of the production.

"The inner-workings of a music group can be disrupted and we saw that happen. Many factors come into play and even management would or could contribute to the strife. There was nothing anyone could say to one of us to cause our group problems or pit us against one another. We felt close to each other, grounded, and we were solid. We saw that happen with other groups. They'd record us for a track and we'd hear the discussions about who they wanted the song for, and who was going to get it.

"Then they would say who was upset about not getting it. We didn't see the artists arguing and fighting with management or each other, but we knew the inner-workings and that this was going on. You could say we were very much in the know. It wasn't only us who didn't get the credit for our work, but many times songwriters, as well as producers, weren't given credit either. People worked on sessions and collaborated and got nothing. When the record came out their name wouldn't be on it anywhere. Popcorn did so much work on 'Please, Mr. Postman' and his name isn't on that song. Ivy Joe Hunter had the same thing happen to him. It blows my mind that they could work that hard and not get credit for their work, or any recognition. That's essentially our story. There were hours spent and so much time put in. There were so many things that went on behind the scenes and it really is just too much to unravel. You cannot put things in a book that are hurtful, that's for sure, but you can tell the truth so that the right people get some credit finally.

"I was at a party during our time at Motown and they were playing Motown music at this party. There was a guy bragging and he was telling everyone at the party that he sang on those songs. The host of the party came and got me and said to him, 'This is Jackie Hicks and she is singing on those records.' The host asked me if I knew him and I said 'No, I've never seen him before.' That guy disappeared from the party and never came back. You see, because our name wasn't on the records, anyone could say they did this or that. It was never told openly that there were in-house voices and the public certainly didn't know that information back then.

"The truth got twisted and worn down over the years. Other people stepped in and got credit or the credit was assumed by the public. They think they know who is singing. Our simple truth is that we sing on those songs, a lot of the #1 hits, and we want to tell it without the drama of the rumor mill. It doesn't matter who did what to whom, or this one said that to this one. It was a two-sided coin. Some people got what they wanted and some didn't. Some were bothered that we sang on their records and we were bothered that we didn't get credit for that singing. The point is, we were together on it and that is all we want to say now.

"We know what happened, and we are touching on it a little so you can see how our story could have easily fallen away, but also that there are others that were there beside us. There were many people who made Motown what it was. Most of what happened between people had nothing to do with the music and the legacy. There are certain things that one should take to their grave just for the sake of respecting others. It's been over forty years now, so a lot of what happened doesn't matter, and to be quite honest it shouldn't have mattered so much back then either. It's the music that matters. A lot of that negativity is only mistakes that people made when they were young and wished they hadn't made. We're talking over forty years ago. Who wants to be held accountable now for a mistake they made forty years ago? When you find people now, they don't want that stuff brought up because some of it was a bad experience for them and it was painful. Some were young and foolish. People do grow up. The body of work at Motown that we were a part of really means a lot to us; it means more to us than slandering some of the people who were doing the cutthroat things to not only us, but others. The cutthroat stuff has no place now.

"As far as our singing at Motown, we didn't understand why our name couldn't be on the record label and sleeve. We knew that singing with the groups was tricky-especially the girl groups. But with the solo artists, it could have said we were the voices behind Mary Wells, Marvin Gaye, Jimmy Ruffin, Tammi Terrell, or Brenda Holloway. Even just to say we were featured singing…there was a way to do it and it was hurtful that it was never done for us. You have The Magnificent Seven who are really ten people. We have people who have helped to tell it, such as Martha Reeves and Mary Wilson. Mary is a very honest person and our career with her goes through both 60's and 70's Supremes eras. We sang on 'River Deep, Mountain High' and when they recorded with The Temptations on 'I'm Going To Make You Love Me'.

"We were considered the session artists, so we only got paid for the session, but there are so many songs that we are prevalent on and it would have been nice to be compensated for that work as we were major contributors. We knew people were getting royalties and being in the background with no label credit made it impossible for us to seek royalties if and when they were due to us.

"We can prove we sang and that we were there. We know we are singing and everyone knows it. The labels aren't right and the ones who get royalties aren't correct either. There's no paper trail if we wanted to pursue this. Here it is, our voices all of these years later, and other people are getting the royalties for it. When I hear us singing in commercials and in movies today it just baffles me that we aren't paid for it. I feel we should have something to show for it being our voices. When it comes to the one record that we know we have the credit on, 'Like A Nightmare', I don't even own a copy of it. I would like to have a copy now. You're not anticipating that these things will be worth something one day, and I don't mean monetary-wise, I would just like to have a copy of that record for me. Popcorn called me a while back and asked me if I had a copy because a guy in England would pay $2,000 for it. If I had it now, I certainly wouldn't sell it. The music buffs over in England love us and they collect these things. I have found out, since we began working on this book, that The Andantes' name was on a few records and we never knew that until now."

Louvain maintains to this day that when the groups went out on television and made history on Ed Sullivan and various other TV shows, they looked great, but she adds that it was The Andantes that sounded great. "Marlene, Jackie, and I had to stand tall at times. Those were our voices coming through the TV set. We experienced what felt like alienation sometimes when it came to the girl groups. When things began to take off and there were so many big hits we noticed a change, towards us especially, in the studio. Although it was like family and it felt like it, I felt we were like the older children in the family. The older children tend to remain quiet. We ended up hurt with an inner struggle not to say anything about the fact it was us singing. You can be hurt in your emotions from what you witness as well as what happens to you directly. We never thought that not being recognized as being the ones singing and being the Motown sound would last over forty years. The Andantes didn't speak for a long time, just like The Funk Brothers said nothing for so long. As in a real family, you don't want to talk about your pain and then the moment passes where you just have to get over your pain. You really don't get over it until you get to speak the truth; then slowly you heal. When I would tell someone that I sang on a certain song they didn't believe me. The Andantes' name was not out there in history anywhere. In a real family, the older children suffer in a different way.

"The ways we were treated by some of the ladies, I never understood and still don't. This was our job to sing and we were met with animosity at times. Why did some of them have animosity towards us because we sang on their records? They had their name on the record, they received royalties, and they got to go out and perform. We didn't understand why they treated us the way they did. Unfortunately, women can be competitive and bitchy and catty. They didn't want us around. I think this came from insecurities and them being young and immature. We witnessed the jealousies within the groups themselves toward their own members.

"Petty seeds were planted, from that grew insecurities, and that created animosity. Some of this was unnecessary and it was cutthroat and just plain painful for us. We didn't understand how we could've been a threat, because we were on a completely different level than them. We had no records out and we didn't tour. They had what we wanted to see happen for us, but we were the step-children who had to stay home while Cinderella went to the ball. We simply did not understand why they created the animosity in the studio. Then they acted jealous of us singing on the records. After all was said and done, it was they who got mentioned in music history-not us.

"I was the one who encouraged Marlene and Jackie to talk to Berry and give us a contract that was more solid. He said 'No' and I should have challenged him on that, but I was too afraid. They told us that if we didn't like how things were done, we could go elsewhere. And so, it was never approached again. We were hurt that we couldn't have a real contract and be protected. At the time, I wished we would have been thanked. The producers thanked us with bonuses but people didn't just openly tell us 'Thank you for making the records sound great.' In recent years, everyone has grown up and they have acknowledged what we did.

"We were there to do a job and it was something we loved. We can't help that some producers turned off the microphones on the other girls or the fact the songs were recorded when they weren't there at all. I would've loved to trade places and wear the gowns, wigs, make-up, and perform. I was asked to be in a girl group and I declined because number one I felt dedicated to The Andantes and number two I did not want to take an offer that had strings attached. I would have loved for Marlene, Jackie, and I to go to Artist's Development. As far as being jealous of others myself, I'd say I was envious because I loved to sing, wanted to continue to, and wish we could have performed. A little unknown tidbit is that The Andantes also recorded as The Darnells.

"We were confined to studio work and I always felt there was enough room out there in the public for everyone—a Diana Ross, a Mary Wells, or a Tammi Terrell. The spotlight and the public were big enough and there were large amounts of people with various tastes. There was enough room for everyone to have a slice of the dream. I wasn't mad at anyone because I couldn't do what they were doing, so why were they angry at us for being there doing our job? We helped them to sound great. Our sound and legacy is important for us to preserve now and that's what we're doing. I think, honestly, they weren't grateful for our contribution and they wanted people to think it was just them on their records. I felt someone should have taken them aside and said to them, 'Hey, relax. They're just here to sing and make it sound better. They aren't taking over or taking your place.'

"They had the look and we had the sound. I'm so proud of what we did and very proud of what they did; it went together. I want to say, 'Guess what? We had feelings back then and everyone had their own set of problems.' Part of our problem was we never spoke our truth and we're doing that now. If you look beneath any person from Motown, you'll see there are layers and layers where they had to do their own repair work. I can't say why people did what they did; I can only speak what was true for us and how it affected us. Some people did a better job at covering up the hurt, while others seemed to heal completely. We didn't have coping tools back then, therapy, or Oprah. We each had to cope in our own ways and come to a peace with this history. Each and every one of us Motowners is proud of what we did, proud of the fact we all made it happen together. Some of the hurt comes from it being nearly impossible to share the story without someone's feelings getting hurt now. We were left out back then and we tucked that away, and even some of the closest friends who came into our lives after our Motown years—even some family members, don't really get to know about all the things we did because it's too painful to talk about it.

"You peel back the layers and you see that people were young. They're human beings and they made mistakes. All of us have grown up now, we are senior-citizens, and we deserve respect. We need to respect ourselves and each other. Nothing and no one can tell us that we cannot share our story now. If the band-aid gets ripped off in a disrespectful way, it can hurt everyone all over again. One layer at a time has to come off and this is our layer, to uncover and talk about our memories. I am glad we made it through.

"You can't go back in time and change things and you can't disrespect a person's life now. People have healed their various wounds and you have to leave them to remain healed. Any individual's Motown experience can never be erased. It was those inner-relationships, connections, and even the conflicts between people, that are part of that history. These things are personal and the participants of this history respect it enough not to divulge everything to the fans, because most of it has nothing to do with anything now. The music is what remains. You have to think of it as a mingling of laughter and tears all the way through. I wish some of our colleagues had lived to see how much people cared about them and how much Motown meant to people everywhere.

"I wish Benny Benjamin was here to see some of the stories that have made it to the public. He was one of the first ones we lost so he never had the chance to see that what we all did lasted so many years and how we made a difference in the world. Benny was wise and he had told me that one day the world would know about The Andantes as the voices. He had the foresight and predicted that for us. He was a brilliant drummer. They'd put marks on the wall where his foot was when he played. Robert Bateman marked the wall. Beans Bowles is another I wish was here to see the accolades come for him and his Funk Brother colleagues.

"Motown is the kind of moment that will never happen again. When you think about it there have been no duplications of this. There's only one Marvin, one Levi, one Diana, and so forth. My opening 'Pandora's Box' is not meant to hurt anyone but it is to give credit to those to whom it belongs and to the ones who did the work. It's like a deck of cards, if you take one out it's just a matter of time; one falls, two fall, then they all fall. No one should fall because the truth is told. The magic of Motown was like a passing note. You can feel it, you can hear it, but you cannot describe it.

"If I could put one memory in a time capsule from my time at Motown, I couldn't pick one. They were all special and meant a lot to me, even the trials. There were some very sad times because everyone was close and it was like family. I can't stress that enough. When people died young it was so hard on all of us. Happy and joyous and then very sad, it almost runs together for me when I have to pick out the moments. I try to answer the fans' questions now when I meet them or they email me. The truth gets very complicated and the fans themselves have convoluted in their minds what they think they hear on those records. Sometimes on the internet, they think they know what the truth is. The facts are the facts and you cannot change them. I can see where fans think things and then they actually make up what they think is someone singing, when it is actually The Andantes. We have to leave things unsaid out of respect and leave them where they are, but we are saying the truth and I do not feel that anything negative comes from speaking the truth.

"I met a fan who asked me what songs we sang on, so I named them. He seemed disappointed to find out that it wasn't who he thought it was singing. I broke the song down and told him where I was singing and he had thought in his mind for many years that it was someone else. I get hurt and angry because I want to say something more but it is better to be quiet and respect. I sleep better at night if I do that."

Marlene echoes Louvain and recalls some of the times in the studio. "Our singing on others' records made for hard feelings towards us. It was apparent some didn't want us in there. Besides Melvin going to management, I don't think they knew that some of the girls had issues with us singing. When artists and singers had complaints, we felt it directly from them. Our work was very much one on one with producers. Eventually they recorded us separately because the ladies would ask why we had to be there to sing on their records. This was our silent burden and when you think about it and factor in label credits, royalties, and us singing, it gets complicated.

"One occasion, the playback came on and it was clear that they had turned the microphones off for the other girls who were in there with us. We were hired to sing and we never meant to hurt anyone. As I have stated, we were confident with our singing abilities and we were enjoying what we were doing. After the playback, the girls said, 'We sound good!' Louvain, Jackie, and I looked at each other and wondered how they could've thought that it was them singing. We knew our sound and that it was us on the playback. Some records were a blend of us and them, some records it was just us with the lead. We knew where we sang. We didn't understand their feelings towards us at all. The Andantes' singing on their records didn't interfere at all with their careers or their money. We wished to be in their position but we were in our own position and remained content in our place. I don't think anyone will try to say our claims are false.

"They were there and they know we were there. You can listen and hear who is singing. If they didn't want us to sing, that really had nothing to do with us; the producers and management made that call. We weren't there to step on anyone's toes or hurt anyone. Our feelings were hurt by this and we had feelings about this then. We just want to tell our history. We sang on songs where the credits are wrong. I sang on songs where the credits are wrong. I don't need to tell the particulars out of respect for people and their families, but I feel it's important that my family know, and my grandchildren know, what I have done in my life. They never told us not to tell anyone what we did, it was just unspoken. Now it's time to tell it. There was no malice on our part then and we shouldn't feel bad to tell it now, this is the truth. They were able to have their name on their records. In my opinion, I feel that since we sing on the records that our name should have been on there too.

"We don't want to complain or make a fuss but we held this in for a long time—for many years. We respected other people's feelings while we tucked our own pain away. You shouldn't have to hide when you write a book and tell your biography. I want to say, 'What about our feelings?' It's pretty basic knowledge that The Andantes' history could fall away if we don't tell this. All we want is for it to be known that we were contributors and worked hard and that our voices are on many of those records. I couldn't tell you how many Gold Records, Top tens, or number ones we sing on. In fact, I'm not even sure I want to know that answer.

"The public and the fans often just see the glamour in show business and, unfortunately, they want to know the facts about a person's personal life and that is not for public consumption. Some of the facts aren't relevant at all to anyone outside of the three of us. For us to tell it some forty years later would just be gossip and disrespectful. I am not going to parade personal information about myself or any of my colleagues that could be harmful to them or their families. I know sometimes the fans want more of that, but I simply cannot give them the meat they wish for us to dish out. You pick up on quite a lot of tidbits when you are in the studio as much as we were. You learn who some of these songs are about. You can't have a front without a back so we went together with everyone and there's a loyalty to that. People have to remember that this is our lives and it involves our families and other people's lives. We want to have a respectful book here. At times the way things went down at Motown made for these hard feelings, but we don't blame anyone.

"There was tact that could have been used and, as my mother used to tell me, 'There's a right way to do wrong.' The powers that be were not sensitive as they should have been. I don't think it was intentional to be mean-spirited on purpose and we don't want to come across as mean-spirited by telling it now. Our way is to do things right by us and others. We were put in awkward situations back then and we don't want to do that to anyone now. When all of this happened they were just trying to get the best sound and make the best records and, of course, sell the most records. They wanted to get the product out fast to the public. They weren't thinking about people's feelings. They were doing the best they knew how to do. It was good for business but not good for the human spirit or the ones who were there. Everyone from Motown has a scar of some kind. Everyone has a different story and you can't change history."

Like A Nightmare

Ann Bogan sings lead
Written and Produced by Holland-Dozier-Holland

Went to a party
All by myself
Only to see you
With someone else
It hurt me so, I wanted to scream
To see you in the middle of a love scene
It was like a nightmare
To know my love you didn't share
Like a nightmare
To see you in a love affair
The nights were dimmed
Way down low
So you couldn't see me
Up in that glow
It was like a nightmare
Something I didn't want to believe
Like a nightmare
And how you made me grieve

I thought we would
Be left together
Remembering you vowed
To love me forever
I walked away that day
To scream
How could you ever be so mean
It was like a nightmare
To know my love you didn't share
Like a nightmare
To see you in a love affair

*Thank you Rick Bueche for finding these lyrics for us.

What Becomes Of The Brokenhearted?

When it comes to the brilliant songwriters and producers who worked at Motown, there's no argument that they were some of the most talented people in the music business. While some of the artists were produced by just a few of the talented writers and producers, The Andantes had the unique opportunity to learn, grow, and collaborate with the best of the best. They worked with nearly everyone who came through Motown's doors and their resumé is quite impressive. Within their story are more stories.

There were unsung heroes everywhere at Motown. There were the legendary production teams like Holland-Dozier-Holland who wrote and produced many artists, including major hits of The Supremes and The Four Tops. The Temptations had success with Smokey Robinson and Norman Whitefield, to name a few. Marvin Gaye and Tammi Terrell saw huge success with Ashford and Simpson along with Johnny Bristol and Harvey Fuqua.

With some pushing and prodding, The Andantes divulged some of their memorable moments with artists, songwriters, and producers. Honestly, they loved everyone and it was like pulling teeth to get them to talk about the songs and sessions. They didn't want to hurt anyone's feelings if by chance they didn't remember particulars about a colleague or song.

Jackie starts by saying, "I just would rather not say any names because I thoroughly enjoyed working with every last one of the producers that we worked with. Some moments and memories stand out with certain ones because we worked with them more often. Some sessions were easier than others. Everyone was different in style and technique. I loved all of the work that we did, so it's difficult to say who or what was the best. Holland-Dozier-Holland really had it together, as did Smokey. Smokey knew what he wanted before we ever got there. He was as business-like and appreciative as could be. As a producer, he had his stuff down to a science and ready to go. You could walk in and out in what seemed like twenty minutes. He was a great lyricist, just a genius at writing. His way with words and his play on words—the way he writes is phenomenal. 'What Is So Good About Goodbye' and 'If Leaving Causes Grieving'—the man can write. Of course, Popcorn was a great piano player, songwriter, and producer too.

"The sessions that do stand out for me are just the ones I seem to remember more clearly. I loved all of the sessions and we just had a lot of fun singing with everyone and working. The three of us enjoyed our work with The Four Tops. I loved how we sounded with them. They were just great fun in the studio and jokesters. Levi had an unforgettable voice in music, no one sounded like Levi.

"There were some unique voices at Motown. I really liked Gladys Horton and Wanda Rogers. I enjoyed the sessions we did with Wanda. That was a good era of songs, 'Don't Mess With Bill' and 'Hunter Gets Captured By The Game'. We sounded great with The Elgins; that's us singing on 'Heaven Must Have Sent You'. We sang with Syreeta; she had such a pretty voice too and was such a sincere person. Chris Clark was another we liked working with. She was very nice to us over the years.

"We were nice to everyone and it made us happy to see some of the great singers get leads on the songs. I think I can say good things about everyone we worked with really. Raynoma was a very sweet woman and Clay McMurray has always been nice to us. Annette and Rosalind of The Vandellas are very, very, nice ladies.

"I don't understand why negative reading is the best reading for some people. Some of the books that have come out were not complimentary to the artists. I don't understand why people want to read that and why it sells, it baffles me. Seems to me a good honest story should sell and rank higher than gossip and rumors. The things that aren't complimentary to you or your friends should stay out. You have to look yourself in the eye and live with yourself knowing you told their secrets. I cannot do that. People want to believe the negative even when it's not accurate. If someone has told you something in private or you just happen to know something very personal about another, you should have the good sense to be quiet and know that some things are not to be repeated. If it doesn't benefit anyone and there is no plus to reveal it, then do not tell it.

"I really loved all of the creative people we worked with. We didn't travel much on the road like the other groups did. We worked so much with the producers and songwriters directly. The groups would be out on the road or doing television spots. There was us and the Funks back home keeping the momentum going. They would fly Diana Ross, Marvin, or whoever into town to do the lead and then we would record the backing vocals; that happened often. There was constant music in production at home in Detroit. We'd be working beside a symphony orchestra at times singing our vocals, it was just amazing. I always enjoyed the strings. Most of the strings were arranged by Paul Riser. He was so young when he came and so very talented. He did an enormous amount of work for Motown. The strings are such an intricate part of the song.

"I recall 'What Becomes Of The Brokenhearted' was a very meticulous session. It was very long and one of the more difficult sessions we did. Paul was brilliant and he just amazed us with the arrangements he would do. To have that in his head, he was simply a genius. Paul is a very nice guy. We know him personally."

Paul Riser adds, "I worked at Motown for eleven years. I went into Motown when I was eighteen years old, right out of high school. It was January, 1962. You know how they treat the rookies on a major league team? That was how they treated me. They sent me through the gauntlet. It wasn't bad treatment, but just going through the learning process of the administration and management and coming up through the ranks of the company as a rookie was hard work. It was fun and I wouldn't trade my experience for anything, especially with The Andantes. The very first session I arranged was a Norman Whitfield session but I do not remember the song.

"My experience with The Andantes is that they'd take a song, and take ideas from a producer or a writer and they would tell them, 'Let us work with this.' They would come back, and it would be a masterpiece, a work of art. And I know this for a fact because I have seen them do it. I gave them ideas when we were working together on an LP called 'Strung Out' on Gordon Staples.

They sang on that with The Detroit Symphony and to tell you the truth, I don't think they've ever heard the finished product on that. Some of The Funk Brothers haven't heard the finished product on that either. They have so much stuff out there that they sing on that they've never heard the final product of.

"I enjoyed working with them and they did a fantastic job for me. They were just a pleasure to work with and had an excellence about them. They really sang. They could take a song that was mediocre and make it great with what they did in the background. The background vocals were never buried at Motown. I can tell you that they stuck The Andantes right out there. I would hear what I wanted in my head before I wrote it. I would get a track in without any vocals and I'd know where the verses were, and where the chorus was. Sometimes I'd get a hint from the producer and they might tell me what was going on vocally and what other instrumentals were involved and overdubs that were going to take place.

"They'd hint to me what they wanted, but most of the time they would just see what I'd come up with when they brought me a track. Then they'd weave a vocal around what I did, and The Andantes' vocals would be intertwined with the string arrangement I had put together. I and many other arrangers worked like this. The producers depended on them to make those songs great. The girls would make a song right on the spot. They didn't have to study it. They could do it right there and they fed off one another. They knew what the other was thinking and were intuitive musically when they sang. The voices blended perfectly. My general feeling of The Andantes is they were a lot of fun and they're my family. I love them to death.

"My journey at Motown was such that until 1965 we had to fight to get our label credits. They didn't start putting our names on the records until that time. This was a tragedy because there was a lot of product before that time that I worked on as an arranger. I did all of the music for 'What Becomes of The Brokenhearted'. I wrote it, produced it, arranged it, conducted it, and another person has the production credit. That was one of the biggest losses I had at Motown. After that happened, I began to shut down my creative juices.

"The chord structures were intricate on that song with

the harmonies. The girls had great ears. They have what you call 'big ears' when you're in the business. It was like one big family during those early years and it started changing when we moved down on Woodward Avenue. When we stayed in the house on Grand Boulevard, it was like family, but the big building was very corporate. We didn't do the work to get paid for a long stretch of time. We were all doing it for the love of the music and the love of being around family and good people. That was really why I participated. But then you start growing up and you begin to have obligations and families and you see that there is money to be made, because your other counterparts are making money. I think it's tragic that the credit wasn't given to the people who created the music. Everyone has families of children, grandchildren and even great grandchildren. They don't know all of the things that we did because it isn't documented and where are our names? All you can say is that you did it; there's no proof that you did it.

"As you grow older, you don't go ten steps forward to go ten steps back. The positive sides of the stories need to come out. The music has survived and will survive. There are so many great stories that have yet to be told. There are many fun things to be told about Motown, the music, and that era. I wasn't sophisticated in the business of production when I first started. I didn't know about percentages or points on a record. I had to learn all of that, and I learned it the hard way. I was having fun and making a few dollars and I was happy. I didn't know about the details of how people were paid. William Witherspoon told me about how my part of the song went to someone else.

"I tell you what the whole thing was. I figured it out over the years. The powers that be at Motown didn't want the rest of the country, especially the west coast to know who did what in Detroit on those records and who was setting the foundation at Motown (such as The Andantes, The Funk Brothers, and the arrangers). I too didn't get my proper credit on the records. If it was known what you did on the records, then someone could come along and maybe persuade you away from the company. Someone could offer you more money if they knew what you were doing on the records and you'd be gone. People who were contracted weren't allowed to venture outside the walled city of Motown. I was contracted as a writer, producer, and arranger. If my name was on the records, another label could try to get me to do the strings on their records. So, I didn't get the credit.

"I was dedicated to Motown, but as I grew in so many ways and as I got older I thought *wait a minute*. I thought I was in prison and couldn't grow any further until Ashford and Simpson came in and gave me a shot of adrenaline. I did so much work for them and I loved their songwriting."

Marlene shares more about working with Paul and Witherspoon. "One session that really stands out for me as far as how long we were there working is, 'What Becomes of The Brokenhearted'. It was a tedious session with a lot of takes. I recall we did it over and over. Those vocals are an example of stacking, which I explained before. We recorded that song with The Originals. William Witherspoon was a perfectionist. We'd be thinking it couldn't get any better than the previous take. He wanted it perfect though and of course, when you listen to those vocals now, they're very intricate on that record. He'd hear something we didn't hear and he'd say 'Let's do it one more time, just one more line.' Jimmy's tracks were already done and the musicians had their part done. He was a meticulous producer when it came to the background vocals. He was a lovely man to work with."

Louvain recalls working with Mr. Witherspoon. "I really liked working with him. He was a very nice man. I thought he was talented. He was meticulous in the studio and did many takes to get the right sound and feel. His work stands on its own. Another producer-songwriter I loved to work with was my dear friend from childhood, Sylvia Moy. I was thrilled when I saw she had made it to Motown. She's one in a million and so pretty. The Andantes were not the only ones at Motown who went without recognition for their work. All of these years later it should be known she produced many of the great songs that she wrote, but they wouldn't give her label credit for producing. She was the first female producer we had and she was warm and had it together."

Sylvia Moy shares her memories. "I arrived at Motown in 1964 and I didn't know Louvain was there. I had lost track of her after high school. We went to elementary and high school together. I was so happy when we ran into each other again. She really loved music as a young girl. She and I were in advanced music classes and she was a heck of a singer even then. Louvain sang beautiful soprano. We both loved music and I was singing with her in choir at Courville. We had the same teacher. Her name was Stephanie Riesner. Louvain had innocence about her as a child and she had a sweet personality, just as she does now.

"I wanted to get into Wayne State's Music Department after I was out of high school. I studied there under Kenneth Jewel. He was fabulous. I was told I couldn't get in because I didn't take instruments classes. I played piano and guitar by ear. The head of The Music Department didn't accept me because I didn't have musical training with an instrument. I played instruments by ear and in my family we were poor, so we made musical instruments out of anything and everything: sticks, pots, pans, anything that made a sound.

"After high school, I performed with a vocal instrumental group and I sang and played cocktail drums. I was trying to earn money to pay for my music classes. I had also been a guest soloist for The Detroit Symphony Orchestra. The conductor of The Symphony sent a letter to Wayne State University to recommend me for The Music Department. All I wanted to do was music and art. I took the academic classes at a Jr. College and I took music classes at Detroit Institute of Musical Art. I auditioned as a singer at Motown and I went in and sang two songs that I had written. They were all there: Smokey Robinson, Norman Whitfield, Mickey Stevenson, and The Holland Brothers. I didn't have anyone to play for me. I sang my two songs and they all joined in keeping the rhythm and beat on the table. Afterwards, Mickey talked to me about a contract.

I was one of the first female producers at Motown. For a while there it was about seventeen men producing and one woman—me. I had to produce under the guys' names. I didn't get my producing credit, the label credit. I eventually got the producer royalties for two of the songs, but not the label credit. I did get the writing credit. It was the label credit that would allow you to go on in your career and they knew that. If you had a track record in producing you could get more work. How could you get another job if your name wasn't on the label? I like to believe that I laid some of the groundwork for the women producers who came after me. I hope I paved the way for them to get their credit. The artists at Motown pioneered so many things. They laid the groundwork for a lot of the stars of today.

"The Andantes and people like Paul Riser, the other songwriters, and the musicians all helped to make those songs hits. Ivy Joe Hunter was another very talented and creative person. I'd sing the demos for the singers who were going to record the songs I wrote and co-wrote. I'd eventually get with the producers and watch them on the piano working out chords and chord progressions. I began teaming up with them to help them more and more and I was doing more work. I was writing the background parts, the bass parts, and I was basically producing. Then they started having me come to the producers' meetings and they would give out assignments, but they never called my name. I had to produce under the other names. I was paid as a writer and got the writer's royalties. I approached them and asked them 'I'm doing the same thing that the guys are doing, can I get what they're getting?' They told me that I couldn't have that because I didn't have a producer contract. I said, 'Give me one and I will sign it.' So it continued like that. I kept going to the producers' meetings and I kept praying that one day I would get my propers. I was working on a lot of hits. If you look at the body of work that I wrote, I did more than write them.

"I finally got a break with Stevie Wonder. I took an opportunity that came up. I had been waiting for my chance. They wanted new material on him because his voice was changing. In the producers' meeting they brought this up and said if anyone wanted to come up with some product for Stevie, they would consider it. No one volunteered. I walked out of the meeting and told management that I could come up with the material. I asked them to please let Stevie Wonder be my first assignment in my own name and they told me I had my first production assignment under my own name. I asked Stevie to play for me all of the songs he had written. He played every little ditty he had. I had a whole bunch of songs too, and then he said 'Wait a minute, I got one more.' He played for me, 'Baby, everything is alright, uptight.' He only had that much of it. I taped it and took it home and worked with it. I added to it and wrote more lyrics and the vocal melody for it. At this time over in Europe they were putting more words in a phrase. I used that style for this. That hit was 'Uptight'. It turned out I didn't get the production credit and I was so upset. I talked with my parents and they told me to stick it out at Motown.

"Some producers were strictly musicians who came up with the chord progressions. They would team with another who could hear a vocal melody and lyric to go with that. Most of the vocal melodies and lyrics came from songwriters who were also singers. The strong lyric writers such as Eddie Holland, Johnny Bristol, Ivy Joe Hunter, myself, and Smokey Robinson, that is where you see those songs with strong lyrics; a singer wrote them. A musician comes up with chord progressions and singers usually come up with vocal melodies. We hear that when we write; we hear and think lyrically.

"When I produced, I could step in to sing if one of The Andantes was unable to be there. I would step in and sing with the other two, or sometimes I would have Pat Lewis come in. I was paid only $7 when I filled in to sing backup. I just love The Andantes. I think they are fabulous. I like their spirit. All of them could sing their little butts off. There wasn't one of them that were trying to take the spotlight away from the other. They were equal in each other's eyes and major assets to their own group and their own sound. No one was trying to be a star or out-sing the other. They could sing anything you gave them. They were wonderful in the studio, never any hassle with them. They got it so fast and gave you what you wanted. They got along with everyone. The songwriters and producers just loved them on the records and loved working with them.

"As a producer, you make up the vocal parts and write the background parts. Sometimes The Andantes would come up with it. They were masters at the craft. You could just hum to them just a little bit of your idea of what you wanted and they could pick that up and run with it. They had it and were right on it every single time. They were masters, and talk about professionals. If you asked me what songs I like the most, I'd have to say all of them. I love all of the songs that they sing on. They're just excellent singers, and their blend is wonderful to the ear. They were the best of the best. They enhanced everyone's product. I believe they were more valuable as a group for Motown in the studio to sing on all of the products.

"They did the polishing on all of the products rather than

them just being a girl group singing just their own records. They were that special piece of Motown, just as the musicians were. They were what made it Motown. You would never have to fix anything you recorded on them. They never took the studio into overtime to do a track. Time was money in the studio and you wanted to get finished quickly if you were the producer."

The amount of work that The Andantes did under Holland-Dozier-Holland includes a large body of Four Tops and Supremes songs. They all agree that some of the best times they had were with Holland-Dozier-Holland.

Louvain has this to say: "I especially love a lot of The Four Tops work because it reminds me of The Gregorian Chants. I particularly loved working with Eddie, Brian, and Lamont as there were countless fun sessions with them. One of my very favorites is 'Bernadette'. The amazing thing that happened when they did the playback for that song, we knew it was a hit. We sounded great on that, the guys sounded great, and the production was amazing. The playback was so exciting to hear that first time. After all of the elements were on the record it was like, WOW! There are some other favorites I have. Mary Wells' 'You Do Something To Me', man we sing great on that. That song stands out for me as exceptional greatness. One of my favorite Marvelettes songs is 'Hunter Gets Captured By The Game'. I sang on 'Someday We'll Be Together' but Marlene and Jackie didn't. I was on that with some other ladies and I remember hearing the playback and thinking how great Johnny Bristol sounded in the mix. Some music I am very proud to sing on and I have the memory in my minds eye of Maurice King at the piano is during The Supremes session. We sang on the album of old standards. One of the songs was 'Funny Girl'. When the album was released, I was so thrilled that we sang that beautiful music.

"There was a song we sang on that Ron Miller wrote, 'McCurdy Park'. We recorded it with Soupy Sales. I loved that song. It was so funny and I wanted it to be a hit. It was a spoof of 'MacArthur's Park'. It was hilarious and it seems to me The Originals sang on that with us. I really liked Soupy on television but we didn't get to meet him. I love our singing with Brenda Holloway also. I love 'When I'm Gone'. I love that song and I had a good old time at Christmas with that song—me, and a bottle of wine. We worked with Bobby Taylor also and we sing on 'Does Your Momma Know About Me', he was wonderful back then and still is. He introduced me to Michael Jackson. He was a cute little boy and a very, very, talented child. I sing with Ashford and Simpson on Diana's version of 'Ain't No Mountain High Enough'.

"We recorded the album with Jimmy and David Ruffin. Jackie called me when she heard the song 'Didn't I Blow Your Mind' on the radio and she said, 'Girl if you were ever singing, you are singing on that record.' That's also us on 'Turn Back The Hands Of Time'. Another song that stands out for me is 'I Only Have Eyes For You' by Mary Wells. We shine on that with Mary. There was one time where our session overlapped and we were hanging out in the studio with The Contours while they were recording 'Do You Love Me'. We don't sing on that but we were there. They'd have to tell the guys to get back to the microphones because they would get carried away and forget to sing and dance all over the place. They were having a good ol' time. They were so excited when they heard the playback at that part where the music goes down low and comes back up.

"I also remember one of the last sessions we did with Shorty Long. Shorty was always happy go lucky and he would make you laugh. Those last times I saw him, he was the producer and the artist. He was more tedious and serious-almost moody, and he was more difficult than normal. The session was hard and people left it because he was being hard and difficult so they left him in there alone. I walked back in to get something I forgot and he thought I was coming back in to work and he said he was sorry. He said to me, 'I don't know what's wrong with me.' He asked me to go outside and round everyone up and ask them to come back in and he promised to be nicer. Most of the people had not left so we all forgave him and came back in to finish the session. Shortly after this session, he invited me and my sons out on his boat. Not long after the invitation was when he drowned off that same boat. Meatloaf was another singer that came through Motown that I thought had a great voice. I don't remember the songs but he had an operatic voice and I sang on those sessions with other singers, but not Jackie and Marlene. I can remember hearing them talk about Meatloaf all through the session, not realizing that was the gentleman's name. The session was kind of wild and it was years later when he made it big I knew that was the same guy."

Marlene's input about some sessions and colleagues: "Holland-Dozier-Holland are the nicest people you could ever know. One of my personal favorites is 'Baby I Need Your Loving'. I too loved how we sounded with The Four Tops. I knew when we heard that playback it was a hit. It felt so good when we were recording it, so we knew. I loved their writing style and their material. Eddie wrote for women very well. Lamont and Brian were brilliant with the music and Eddie with the lyrics. I also loved how we sounded with Marvin Gaye on the sessions Smokey produced. I liked Smokey's work too. He was the greatest lyricist ever. We didn't do many Miracles tracks but worked with Smokey quite a bit, especially Mary Wells' and Marvin's songs. There was magic in the air and a warm feeling in the studio when you heard the playback on a song you knew was a hit. That was the case with 'My Guy'. You're almost in awe that the magic was created in that small little place. Smokey was and is still one of the nicest people from Motown. He has never changed and he's still nice and sweet. He's the same old Smokey. Claudette Robinson was respectful and has a lot of class. She was never out of place in her appearance. Everyone looked up to her. She cared about people and was a first class lady all the way.

"If I had to put one record into a treasure chest I would have to pick 'Bernadette'. The production of that song is so amazing. The way it was put together, I thought we sounded beautiful with the guys and I love that. Lawrence Payton contributed to the organizing of the background vocals. He was very, very, talented with harmonies and he had perfect pitch. We would be looking at him, listening to him and thinking *how is that going to work?* He would play the track and tell us where he wanted us to do our part and we interjected it into the song. We practiced it a few times and then recorded it. He already heard it in his head. He pulled it right out of the air and after he put it all together, it was beautiful and the harmonies blended perfectly. That was really a nice session to work on. Jackie stands out exceptionally on Jr. Walker's 'What Does It Take'. That song was the perfect range for her.

"Producers would ask us what we thought and our input was always welcome. They hummed or sang to us what they wanted or wrote it on a sheet of paper. Berry would pop his head in once in a while but we really had little contact with him. We would ask for a re-take if we thought our performance wasn't perfect. On rare occasions, they would say it was fine the way it was and not give us a second take, most of the time they trusted our judgment. If we thought we could do it better they allowed us to do it better. A singer knows when they have a better performance in them. We goofed around and had fun and if we hit a sour note we were really hard on ourselves.

"We acted so silly at times and just had fun in the studio. Producers never gave us sheet music. James Jamerson would tear up the sheet music if they handed it to him. Time in the studio varied. If we were able to rehearse it before we went in, we weren't in there very long. We cut records in twenty minutes back then. There were so many producers that we learned from and they helped us with our singing. Being in the studio with Harvey Fuqua and Johnny Bristol was a phenomenal experience when they were backing others or singing on their own productions. Harvey, Johnny, and Marvin Gaye were like The Three Musketeers. They were so brilliant and talented. Harvey and Johnny were especially nice to us and gave us advice and pointers. Harvey was like a father-figure that you could trust. He'd been out there for a long time and he knew who to trust. They were just beautiful people and good guys.

"They were friends and fed off one another. You can hear in their music that they had a great partnership. If I was going to produce a record now, I would emulate all of the skills and techniques of those we worked with. Norman Whitfield was a genius in the studio and he had a lot of insight and was very wise. He used two microphones in the studio to get a fuller sound when we recorded with the groups. When it was just the three of us there was one microphone. I was usually in the center, Jackie to my right, and Louvain to my left. He was a sweet man and gave us a bonus when 'I Heard It Through The Grapevine' was a hit. Jackie and I went to California with some of our friends on that bonus.

"Ashford and Simpson were consummate professionals in my mind. They came in prepared and knew 100% what they wanted. Their work is just fabulous to me. There was no fooling around and they didn't spend a lot of time on something because they had it ready and mapped out beforehand. It was professionalism with them all the way and it was great working with them.

"There were some very memorable voices at Motown that we enjoyed singing with. Wanda Rogers was just as cute as a button and, oh my God, what a voice. Brenda Holloway, now *that* is a singing woman. I just loved her voice. Because of the family environment, there was support from people like Raynoma, who was a mother-figure for a lot of us. She would help the girls before Maxine Powell came onboard and she helped the guys too. She kept people in line and on their toes. Maxine was a wonderful mother-figure for many as well.

"It took many years for The Funk Brothers to finally receive their recognition. I wish that Robert White and Earl Van Dyke were alive to see that. Beans Bowles was another hero among us. He didn't get enough props and he was the genius behind the sax on so many of those songs. He was very wise and knew the pitfalls of show business. He'd been out on the road and played many clubs. He was father-like to many of us and at the same time he was able to be a friend to so many. If you went to him for advice he would tell you the truth and tell it like it is. He knew you'd have the wisdom inside yourself and he would make you see that. When he told you something, you listened. He was honest and he knew how slick the people out on the road were and how they operated. He was a great mentor to many. He almost died in a car accident and there were so many sad people because he meant a lot to everyone, but he made it through that."

Richard Dean Taylor, also known as 'R. Dean', was a Canadian singer who worked at Motown more than ten years; another unsung hero of the times. "I was recording in Canada before I came to Detroit. I had a few songs on the radio. After I had heard my songs on the radio that was all I wanted. I was working at an advertising agency and they'd always be looking for me and I would be in the car turning the dials listening for my records to play. There was a guy who worked there named Charles Dick who was an executive and he was from Detroit. I had an opportunity from him where he made the offer to help me out through his contacts in Detroit. He got me an audition at Motown so I went out there. I came to Motown in 1963. Luckily, it was

Lamont Dozier and Brian Holland who were the ones that listened to me audition.

"I played them the materials I had and it went from there. I was first signed on as a writer. I began working with Eddie, Brian, and Lamont. I hung out in their office all the time. Lamont was the best background vocal arranger. I used to just sit and watch him work. His background arrangements were like horn arrangements. I learned everything from him about background voices. Some people didn't know how to arrange background voices. When I first heard The Andantes singing, I thought *oh my God.* I hung around the studio all the time just to be around the music. Holland-Dozier-Holland were my mentors and I stayed around them a lot.

"I played tambourine on some sessions. I'd be in the studio fiddling around with the tambourine and Lawrence Horn, the engineer, would set up a microphone for me thinking I was going to play for a session, and so I played it. Lamont didn't tell me no or to get out. That's me playing the tambourine on The Four Tops' 'Reach Out'. I'd play it on my hip. Jack Ashford did the fancy stuff on his hands and made different sounds. I played on a lot of the Four Tops sessions so I could make an extra few bucks and stay there. Holland-Dozier-Holland was a machine. They would cut tracks with no titles and they just had a groove going on the piano. They were masters. They would name their songs later. They were the backbone of the company. They helped to put the company on the map and were the machine behind a lot of those songs being hits.

"You could put a good singer on a good track and put The Andantes behind them, and you had a hit record along with The Funk Brothers. Then there was Mike McLean who was a genius with the sound in Detroit. He mastered so many things in that studio that helped to create the sound. Eventually I told Motown that I wanted to be an artist, so then I started recording. 'Indiana Wants Me' was a big hit for me, I wrote and produced it. Most of my work was bigger in England. Thank God for the English people who embraced me. There are people over there who really have researched this stuff and they know the details and love the music. I started off overdubbing everything myself. I dubbed in Bob Babbitt and Dave Van DePitte put the strings on. They didn't put the arrangers' names on the records. I went to A&R at the time and I asked to have a gold record for Dave Van DePitte. I understand it was the first time anyone had asked for that. When the song went to #1, I got my gold record and Dave got his.

"I think they should have done that for everyone. He got a gold record for arranging. He was delighted. You know what that must have meant to him? Everyone should've gotten their credit for the work they did. Paul Riser was another who did not get his label credit. Ivy Joe Hunter was another who didn't get proper credit for 'Dancing In The Street'. I don't know what they were thinking to not give people credit. Eventually they did do it on some records.

"One of my first records was a song called 'Lets Go Somewhere'. I wrote and produced it. It sounded good and I had a vague idea of what I wanted, but once The Andantes came on the record their voices carried the whole thing. I still get feedback today from that record. There was a group called 'Rick Robin and Him'. Sally Thurman sang with them. Sally sang harmony with me on the bridge for 'Lets Go Somewhere' and The Andantes were the background. The Andantes are just as much a part of the Motown sound as James Jamerson, Earl Van Dyke, or any of them. They are just the Motown sound. They'd knock me out when The Four Tops would record; after, they put The Andantes on the track and it would fill up the song. Songs like 'Baby I Need Your Loving'. I'd hear the tracks before they were on them and they just really filled in those songs. They are long overdue for their recognition.

"The Andantes were so quick in the studio. They were very good at what they did. Some producers didn't know what they wanted and The Andantes would come up with it for them. They were the nicest ladies to work with, and just the nicest people you could ever meet. They were always on time. They had such a good spirit, all three of them and they were always up and wanting to make it better and say 'Lets do this again and make it the best we can.' They were never impatient when you had to do more takes. They hung in there and did the work and I cannot say enough good things about them.

"They loved what they were doing and it radiated from them. You felt so comfortable to be in their presence. The producers who didn't have a clue about background voices had nothing to worry about because The Andantes could take care of it and come up with it for them. They were very much in the background of everything, but a very important part. So much a part of it, and they were taken for granted. They were such an intricate part of the music. All of the people who were at Motown know they were there and sang on those records. Their sound is distinct and I don't know how anyone could ever say it isn't them or not tell it is them. When you hear a Motown record with The Andantes on it, they help to make it an identifiable record or product of Motown.

"I was a writer on 'Love Child'. It was Pam Sawyer who came up with the concept of it. Then we built a story around it. Of course, The Andantes sing great on that record. I recall Frank Wilson was in the studio and the background voices were not gelling; he and Berry were in the control room. I came in kind of late and saw everyone was a little impatient and I came up with the part in my head, 'Love Child wait, wait, won't you wait love, hold on just a little bit longer'. They sang that in there and Frank had them do it and the ladies got it in two takes. I actually had that phrase in my head because of another song I was working on called 'Hold On', but it fit in exactly where they were trying to make it come together.

"The Andantes heard it sung to them once and they sang it and had it down in two takes. I felt wonderful that I could contribute to that part of it and everyone thought it was great. It was a magic place and time being at Motown. As the years go by, you take for granted that you were there and you look back at it as wonderful times. It was exciting and when you tell people you worked at Motown, their eyes light up. It's the biggest thing in England, and to know that people appreciate it now means so much. I don't think any of us realized it would be around as long as it has. I'm writing my own book and I never knew writing a book would be this hard."

Frances Nero was at Motown for a short time. "I got to Motown by way of winning the first live performance contest at the Fox Theatre in 1965. I stayed at Motown until 1966. I never recorded an album for Motown but I did record the singles 'Keep On Loving Me' and 'Fight Fire with Fire'. The girls sing the backing vocals along with the Originals. The Andantes sing on everything and I mean *everything*. People fail to realize that The Andantes and The Funk Brothers are the Motown sound. Sometimes it would be The Andantes and the lead singer only and people thought it was the other girls in the groups singing."

Gloria R. Jones was one of the first women to get producer credits at Motown. Gloria adds, "I can recall working with The Andantes and Mary Wilson singing background on the song titled 'Oh My Poor Baby'. Pam Sawyer, Valerie Simpson, and I were among the first female producers at Motown. I also remember using the group on a Supremes session in Detroit during a winter month. Their smiles and attitudes beamed as being very professional. You'll have to remember Pam Sawyer and I were the girls from the west coast and were the new sound for Motown. I had the pleasure to work with the girls and I thought it was so special to be able to work with the voices that gave us so much joy and perfect harmonies. Brenda Holloway, the late Patrice Holloway, and I were the new sound for Motown on the west coast working with late and great Hal Davis.

"When we asked the girls to sing, I wanted their hearts because their sound was so pure and I never wanted to intimidate any artist in Motown, especially not ones who had given us so much joy with their sound. I remember their looks after meeting me. I was from the rock and roll world and camping out in the soul land of Motown with my British blond-haired writing partner Pam Sawyer. We all realized that Motown was changing and moving on with a harder feel and more gospel influences."

Pat Cosby, who was a friend to everyone, sums it all up for us. "You could say I was a fixture at Motown. I came by way of Mary Wells in 1962. She convinced me to apply for a job as a receptionist. I was reluctant at the time because I was going on to other things in life. I was hired as the receptionist and at the same time, I was the assistant to The Tape Librarian. I would supervise the receptionists and I did the scheduling for the switchboard. At one point, Florence Ballard's brother was one of our switchboard operators. I met my husband Hank Cosby during my years at Motown. I would eventually work in the tape library full-time. That was where I gained the history on the songs as they were being made. We didn't have computers so I was recording everything by hand on index cards. I would start with one index card for a song and then I could end up with five index cards for that particular song. Handwritten notes were made for every measure of that song. There were more songs that were put on the shelf than were released.

"In the period of time I was there, I can't tell you the number of songs that were recorded, but the material that was released is just the pinpoint. When the company moved to the Woodward Building, I was given the position of Album Coordinator. When I look back now, it just amazes me the volume of work we turned out with what we had. I never had the desire to sing and I would rather listen to music than make it. Hank took a couple of my ideas and wrote songs, but that is about it for me.

"Prior to Motown, I knew Marlene and Jackie from a distance because we went to the same high school. I would see them at the sock-hops, dances, The 20 Grand, and places around town where the teenagers went on the weekends. I knew Mary Wells, Florence Ballard, and Barbara Martin very well. There were little cliques of friends and Rita Lumpkin was part of our little clique, and also in Marlene and Jackie's little clique. I don't think that people, meaning the public, realize how intertwined we were and still are, all of us. I knew Norman Whitfield before Motown and who would have thought some of these people would become world renowned?

"Everyone has the same questions when they meet someone from Motown. What do you think happened back in those days? How did it all happen? My favorite answer is that everyone who passed through the walls of Motown (whether they were a janitor, a mail person, administrative assistant, artist, right on up to Mr. Berry Gordy Jr. himself), we all were the chosen few. I have no doubt it was a moment in time where we were all brought together. It has never happened since and it will never happen again.

"Each individual, regardless of how large or small his or her role happened to be, was a link in that chain. We didn't know what we were creating and doing when it was happening; had we known it would've been a lot different. I don't think it could have happened the way it did if we were really aware of the history and legacy that was being made at the time. I think the innocence of it all made it so huge. Most of the things I know about Motown I will never tell because I feel they are sacred. Until the end of time, Motown family will remain family. It doesn't matter who has had what experience since they left there, or where you are located. It doesn't matter if you left with a bitter feeling, or you left with a good feeling. We are all still Motown family. We know it and we respect it.

"This is a bond that cannot be broken. The older we each get, the more we realize how special that time was and how special we are. If any of the artists were going out to lunch, it was the norm to ask the receptionist and the switchboard what they wanted to eat. You would have David Ruffin, Smokey, Eddie Kendricks, or whoever bringing your lunch back because it was so much like family. When you look at that picture now you wonder why we were not going out to get the artists' lunches. It was ordinary and surreal at the same time.

"For a long time I didn't put myself in the same category as the legends. I thought the legends were the artists, writers, and producers. Fans view each one of us as legends. I feel if you mowed the lawn at Motown, you are a legend now. The beginning of my realization of what we all did was when I was working in television for Norman Lear and he had all of the top shows on television at the time. There was a Christmas party and all of the big actors and actresses were there. They were coming up to me in awe, asking 'Wow, did you really work for Motown?' They were looking at me like I had walked on water.

"We were caught up in the change that was happening in America and the music made the change better. There was a lot going on in our country. When you think of the Civil Rights Movement, there were many barriers brought down because people came together over the music. It was Mr. Gordy's intention to make music for everyone. Some of the early album covers didn't show who the artists were so the public didn't see that it was black artists. The appearance of the artists was a source of pride when presented to the public. The image of Motown didn't last as long as the music did. The image was classy and it was all one package. The music remained and stayed out front.

"The 20 Grand was a phenomenal place. It's a shame that there aren't more pictures of it because it was quite a place. The lower level was a restaurant and bowling alley. The upstairs area was where the Gold Room was. This was the place that they held the dances for the teenagers. Also, upstairs was The Driftwood Lounge where the top artists would perform. They knew they had made it when they played at The Driftwood Lounge. It was *the* place to be.

"I grew up about two blocks from it, so there were very few people that I didn't know; I was there all of the time. I snuck in just like everyone else did because I was underage. We had a system where everybody shared an ID and the security guys only looked at the date. When one of us went inside, we headed for the bathroom and then dropped the ID out the window to the next person so another one could come in.

"Hank passed away in 2002, and he never denied that Motown was a place and time that couldn't have happened anywhere else and he was happy to be there. Hank truly thought that The Andantes were stellar, in the sense that they were just so easy to work with. He never had to see if the girls could do something. He and the other producers walked in knowing they would get what they wanted from The Andantes because they delivered every time. They were absolutely part of the woodwork and if you wanted a hit, you had them singing on your records. It was assumed that The Andantes would be who you recorded for the background if you wanted a hit record.

"People in England know and love The Andantes. They really look this info up. The fans know that they sang, but not to what extent. They're just as important to the history as anyone else. Motown was all one motion for me and I know people want you to remember particulars, but it all meshes together. I know who was there with me but can't pick out any one memory over another. Our world and our jobs didn't stop and we didn't realize we were working among superstars. And when I say superstars, I mean everyone who sang, wrote, or played a note. I can't pick out a favorite song because I love all of it. If I was going to pinpoint a favorite Andantes moment on a record, I would have to say 'Just Ask The Lonely' by the Four Tops."

Louvain's mentor, Maxine Sullivan.

Photo credit: The Louvain Demps Collection

A very young Berry Gordy. The autograph reads, 'The wonderful girl, with the wonderful voice'.

Photo credit: The Louvain Demps Collection

An early publicity picture of The Temptations

Photo credit: Louvain Demps Collection

Louvain Demps Collection

Louvain Demps Collection

Louvain Demps Collection

The Miracles

Louvain Demps Collection

Louvain Demps Collection

Louvain Demps Collection

Louvain Demps Collection

S.20565 STRAND PALACE HOTEL. LONDON. W.C.2

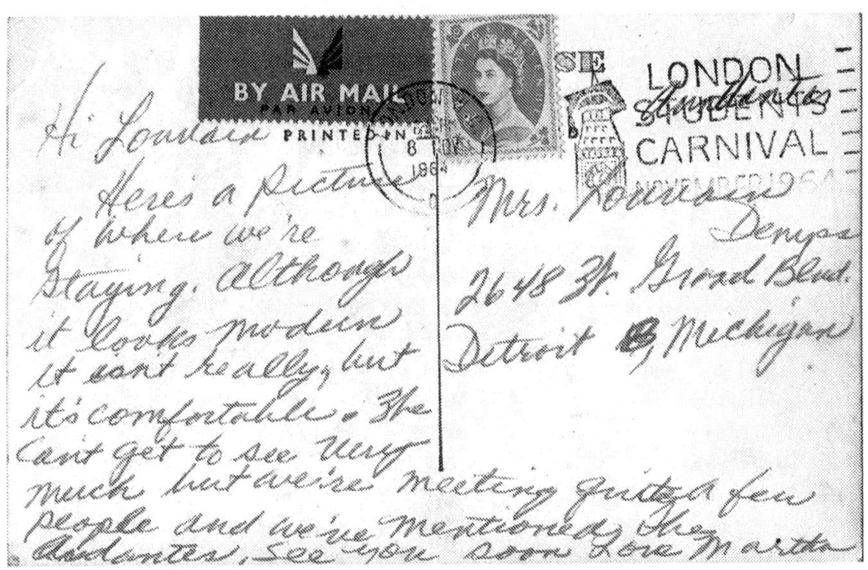
BY AIR MAIL
PAR AVION
PRINTED IN

LONDON STUDENTS CARNIVAL

Hi Louvain
Here's a picture
of where we're
staying. although
it looks modern
it isn't really, but
it's comfortable. We
can't get to see very
much but we're meeting quite a few
people and we've mentioned the
Andantes, See you soon Love Martha

Andantes
Mrs. Louvain
Demps
2648 W. Grand Blvd.
Detroit 8, Michigan

A postcard to Louvain from Martha Reeves, in London in 1964

Louvain Demps Collection

The Andantes with Kim Weston.
(Kim's in black)

The Louvain Demps Collection

JOE HUNTER & BAND
Motown Record Artists

Personal Management
BERRY GORDY, JR. ENTERPRISES, INC.
2648 W. Grand Blvd.
Detroit 8, Mich.

Louvain Demps Collection

"Can't Help Myself"

—★—

CONGRATULATIONS

TO ONE OF OURS

Louvain Demps

Lawrence Payton
—★—
Obie Benson

Duke Fakir
—★—
Levi Stubbs

the

FOUR TOPS

MOTOWN Records

Louvain Demps Collection

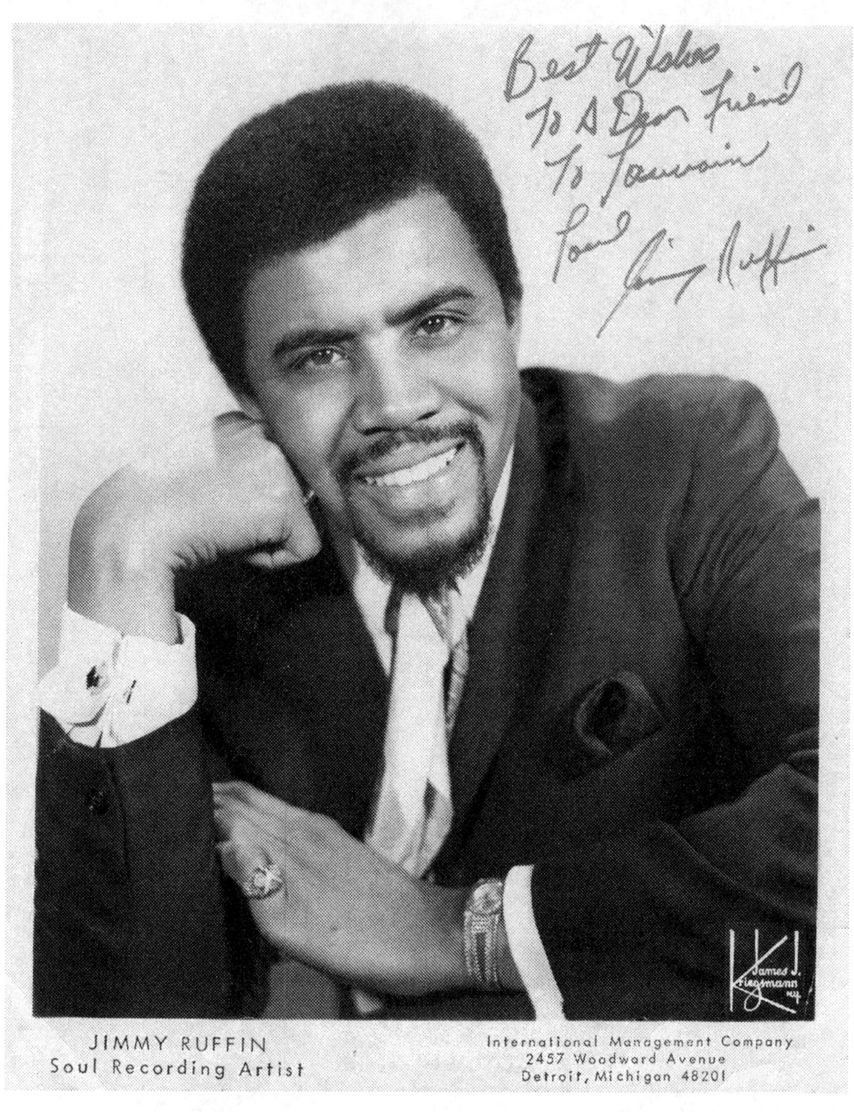

Louvain Demps Collection

JOE HINTON

Louvain Demps Collection

Louvain Demps Collection

Louvain Demps Collection

Louvain Demps Collection

CAROLE & HANK DIAMOND
Motown Recording Artists

Personal Mgmt.
BERRY GORDY JR., ENTERPRISES, INC.
Detroit 8, Michigan

Louvain Demps Collection

‘Money’ by Barrett Strong was one of Louvain's earliest recordings at Motown.

Scan courtesy of Ian Melia

‘Jamie’ by Eddie Holland was one of the early songs Marlene recalls singing on at Motown.

Scan courtesy of Ian Melia

Louvain Demps Collection

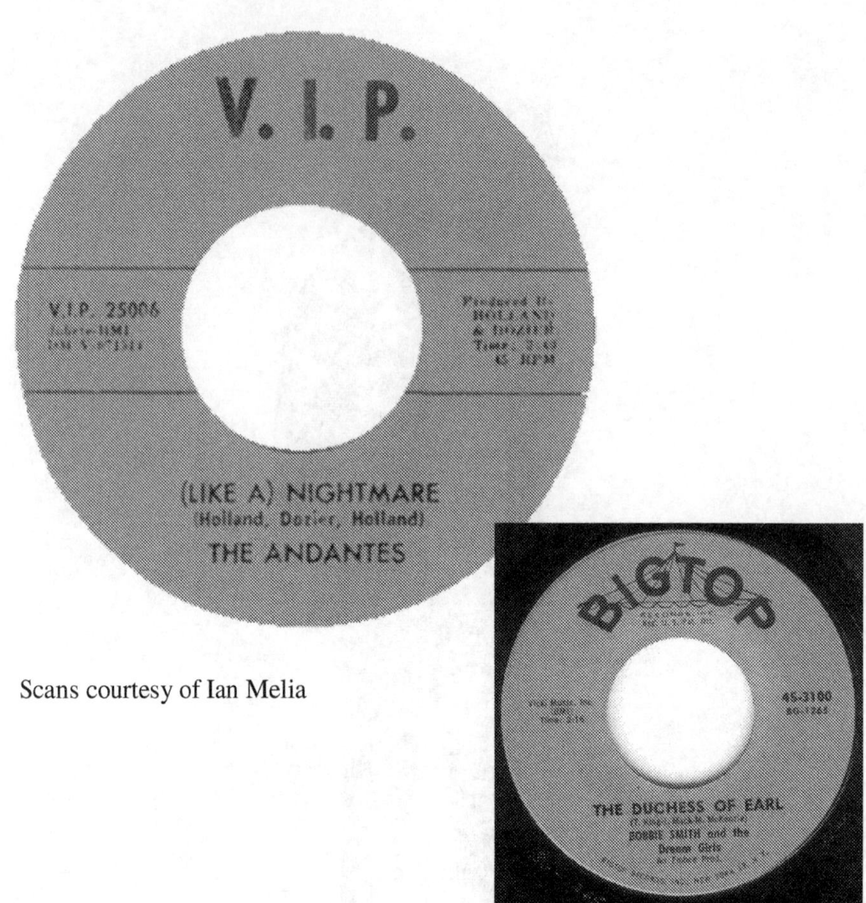

Scans courtesy of Ian Melia

DAWN featuring TONY ORLANDO

CMA

marc gordon productions
1022 N. Palm Ave.
Los Angeles, Calif. 90069
(213) 659-0055
(Personal Management)

ROGERS, COWAN & BRENNER, INC.
(213) CR 5-4581 (212) PL 9-6272
(Public Relations)

Tony Orlando, Joyce Vincent, (left) and Telma Hopkins (right)

photo credit: The Louvain Demps Collection

Our dearest friend Popcorn, dancing with his wife Gloria.

Photo credit: Marlene Barrow-Tate Collection

The Andantes backstage at Marvin Gaye Day in Washington DC. They performed with Marvin on stage on this special day.

Photo credit The Louvain Demps Collection

Marlene, Pat Lewis, Jackie, Herman Griffin, and Louvain. This was in the studio during The Motorcity recordings.

Photo credit: Marlene Barrow-Tate Collection

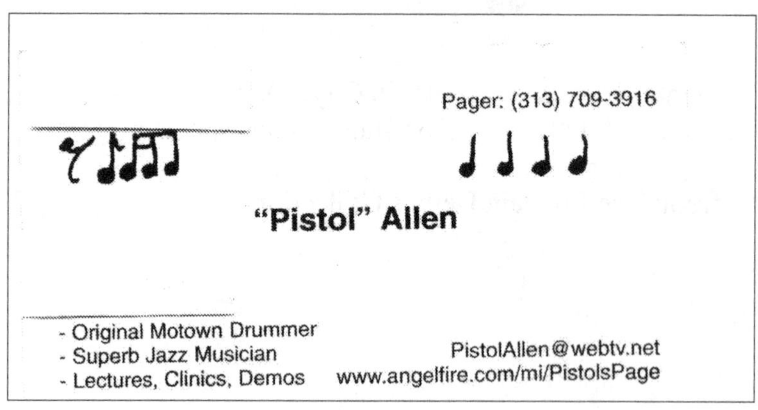

Photo credit: Louvain Demps Collection

July 15, 1925 April 20, 1969

IN MEMORIAM

— Of The Late —

William (Benny) Benjamin, Jr.

SATURDAY, APRIL 26, 1969
AT 11:00 A. M.

Peoples Community Church
8601 WOODWARD AVE.
Detroit, Michigan

REV. D. V. STEWART, Officiating

Photo credit: Louvain Demps Collection

Motown Artist Drowns

A man identified as a Motown Record Corp. star and a male companion drowned in the Detroit River Sunday when their small craft capsized off Sandwich Island.

The recording star was identified as Frederick (Shorty) Long. His body was recovered. The identity of his companion was not immediately learned. Dragging operations to recover his body are to be resumed Monday.

First reports said the wash from a passing freighter swamped the boat but the Coast Guard said later no passing ship was involved. They could offer no reason for the sinking.

The island is off Sandwich, Ontario.

Long wrote and recorded "Here Come da Judge" and "Function at the Junction," two of his top hits.

Long, born in Birmingham, Ala., was both a singer and a pianist.

Obituary

Frederick (Shorty) Long was born to Mr. and Mrs. Richard Long, May 20, 1940, in Birmingham, Alabama. He was their only child.

He attended Washington Elementary and Parker High Schools in Birmingham, where throughout his school years he left no doubt that his heart's interest was music.

It was during these formative school years that Frederick discovered that his given name had almost been totally substituted by "Shorty," a name less formal, more endearing, and more adaptable to his infectious personality.

Shorty's total dedication to his art was indelibly marked by his early commitment to Christianity. He was literally raised in the church.

To be exact he joined the Broadstreet Baptist Church in Birmingham pastored by the Reverend J. H. Holmes and later transferred his membership to the South Elyton Baptist Church pastored by the Reverend Morelan Lanier.

Shorty's professional tutoring was done by Musician Greats Alvin Robinson and the Great W. C. Handy. He expanded the soulful dimensions of his voice by listening for hours to recordings of Little Willie John and Johnny Ace.

Shorty's musical genius was boundless and limitless. With equal finesse he played piano, organ, drums, trumpet and the harmonica.

It was a natural for a young entertainer with such genuine soul, character and ability to gravitate toward Berry Gordy Jr.'s Motown Record Corporation in Detroit.

Shorty became a member of the Motown family.

At Motown he polished his style, became an accomplished writer and a record producer. He penned such tunes as "Devil With The Blue Dress On", "Function At The Junction", and "Here Comes The Judge".

Beyond a doubt however, Shorty cared more for one of his most recent tunes: "I Had A Dream".

Indeed, Shorty had a dream, and perhaps his dream shall become his legacy.

Shorty died last Sunday at the age of 29, leaving the fulfillment of his dream to relatives and friends who survive him.

Left to mourn the loss of a true and vibrant spirit are his widow, Mrs. Pamela Lisa Long, his stepfather and mother, Mr. & Mrs. Coleman Sanders and his father, Mr. Richard Long.

Order of Service

Organ Prelude
Hymn
Invocation
Scripture
Selection. . . . . .Bobby Taylor
Acknowledgment of Condolence
Selection. . . . . .Stevie Wonder
Eulogy. . . . . .Junius Griffin
Recessional

Pallbearers

Clarence Stamps	Edward Cooper
Henry Barrow	Johnny Dawson
Roger Fletcher	Toki Wade

Louvain Demps Collection

The lovely Syreeta.

Photo credit: The Louvain Demps Collection

I Heard It Through The Grapevine

The Andantes literally were grapes on the grapevine. The rest of the grapevine had a lot to say about them too. Now it's time to turn the tables as we hear more testimony and stories from some of their closest friends and family, people who were in Detroit with them during the time they were working at Motown and have firsthand insight to the era, music, and The Andantes.

One of Jackie's beloved cousins is William Brooks. William passed away shortly after being interviewed for this book. As you read, we hope you can capture William's wit and sense of humor. He spoke with an Atlanta, Georgia drawl and accent. He had this to share: "We didn't grow up together, but our relationship was close because I was always in Detroit growing up. My grandfather actually lived in Detroit part of the year, so we would be back and forth with him also. Our mothers were sisters. My mother's name is Inez.

"I grew up in Atlanta, Georgia and I went to Detroit often because my dad worked for Delta Airlines. I grew up having flying privileges, so I was always back and forth to Detroit. Jackie was always bossy, but a good bossy. Her family spoiled her rotten because she was the baby. She is a caring and giving person, full of love and life. She loves her nieces and nephews and she just loves kids in general. She makes them kids mind. If they are around Jackie, they will behave. Jackie and I never had kids. We never married either. We had that in common; we took after our aunt Ethel who never married or had children.

"I would get tickled when I went to the studio with Jackie. It was exciting to have a cousin in that line of work, knowing she was working with the legends. My friends would be so envious when I would go to Detroit and have such a good time with Jackie and everybody. My friends in Atlanta couldn't believe I had a cousin who worked at Motown. They loved hearing the stories I would tell them about my cousin's famous colleagues and the people that we knew. The Spinners were the ones I got to know the best, but I met everyone, from Diana Ross to The Vandellas. The first time I met Stevie Wonder, he was wonderfully friendly. He was sitting at the piano and they introduced me to him. He sat there and composed a song about Atlanta right on the spot. Those are memories and times I will never forget. They're very special to me.

"Whenever I was in Detroit and Jackie was working at Motown, she took me with her. I was there all the time. I recall being in the studio when they were recording parts of Marvin Gaye's 'What's Going On'. It was unbelievable being in the studio and watching them work. They would learn so fast what the producers were asking them to do and get it done so quickly, and sound so good the first time. They'd take what they said and make it brilliant. They had that musical church background and that helped them work so well, nothing seemed hard for them, and it was effortless for them to sing like that.

"They would deny when they were moonlighting and when people said they sounded great on a certain song, Jackie would tell them, 'I don't know what you're talking about.' They had to keep a lower profile to earn a living outside of Motown because Motown did not want them out there singing on other records. They had a gift and when you think about it, they shouldn't have had to hide that they were working other places. I was so proud of everything they did and it was a shame that they had to keep it quiet. It was about business for them and working. They didn't want any trouble. If you heard the records, you knew it was them singing, but they kept it quiet at the time.

"I think The Andantes have voices like angels. They were just phenomenal. To know my cousin had that kind of talent! The whole family was talented like that: Emory, Aaron, and her mother and father. They gave concerts at Hartford Church. The whole family was musical. It was a joy being with them and being part of that. I think we are a very friendly family. You'd hear them everyday and their jobs gave everyone something special later in life; they gave us many musical memories. They didn't think what they were doing was going to last and still be around and be so popular. Jackie told me to come to the Motown picnic in Canada. I flew in and went with her to the picnic. That was the first time I really got to meet Diana Ross. She was a star and I was the country cousin from Atlanta. She was so nice. I was amazed how little and tiny she was. I met Tammi Terrell. She was such a pretty and nice girl.

"Jackie and I were inseparable when I was in Detroit. We did a lot of ripping and running back in the day. She loved to shop and was obsessed with shopping. She'd have a ball shopping. I liked to shop too, but I couldn't keep up with Jackie. When I was going to Motown with Jackie I bought a lot of records. Jackie got a discount on records. I have all of the albums that she sings on. I like everything and I was truly a child of the Motown era. I listened to it then and I still enjoy it today.

"Jackie didn't flaunt or brag about what she was doing, but I sure did. I told people all the time 'My cousin sang on those records.' Several times I was in Detroit, and when we were in the car a Motown song would come on, I'd look at Jackie and she'd say 'What are you looking at me for?' I'd say, that's you all singing on that', and she'd just say 'Yeah, I know', and back to business as usual. They want to be respectful too because it's them singing on a lot of the songs. They were lucky to have been in that era and make that history. Marlene keeps quiet too; they are similar. Their personalities are very humble.

"The impression I got from being around them and spending time with them was that they loved what they did. This was a job that they loved and they had fun going to work. They loved to sing. I went to the Motown Museum with Jackie and I had to tell them who she was. She keeps a low profile. I made them open up a case at The Museum so she could sign the memorabilia that was inside this case. I told her, you're signing that like everyone else has. They did open it up for her to sign it.

"I feel so proud when I hear the music and know that it's Jackie singing on those great classics. Our cousin Miriam came into Detroit with me one time. Jackie's sister Annette would act as our chaperone so we could go to the Motown Revues at The 20 Grand. We were too young to get in; Miriam would end up somewhere in a chair asleep. She was younger than me. Annette was a life-saver when it came to getting us into those shows. That was a real treat to be able to get to see The Motown acts on stage. I think about her now and how nice she was to take us to those shows. It was a lot of fun. No matter what time the show was, Annette would get us in because she knew people. We would have just died if we couldn't go to those shows. My cousin Miriam was about twelve and Annette was so sweet to make sure her young cousins from Atlanta got in to see those groups. They would not have let us in without Annette.

"I feel Marlene is my cousin too. She and Jackie have been in each other's lives for so long, so Marlene is family for me. I didn't get to know Louvain as well, but she was always so nice and friendly to me and I always liked her. Oh and that beautiful voice she had-Whoa!! They really sounded like angels. One time I went to California with Jackie and Marlene. They flew in from Detroit and I met up with them there. They were working the whole time we were out there. Louvain wasn't with them for this trip. They were singing the background vocals for a T.V. show for The Supremes. They weren't on camera, but they did the backing track for the special.

"While we were in Los Angeles, we went to some parties with The Temptations and we went up to Mary Wilson's place in the hills. Everyone was going further up the hill to Diana's place. Jackie and Marlene didn't want to go up the hill because we had rented a little Volkswagen and I was the only one who could drive a stick. They said we were far enough up the hill. Mary and Diana had houses on the hill above Sunset Boulevard. Jackie and Marlene were too hesitant to take the car up further because it was so steep.

I remember when the special aired. I recall the elaborate gowns The Supremes wore on that special. We were in L.A. for about two weeks. It was a great trip and a lot of fun. I had never been to L.A. before. Norman Whitfield's wife was hanging out with us the whole time too; they were looking for a house out there. His wife would treat all of us to dinner and was a wonderful host. She was in L.A. first and she was showing us all of her shopping she had done while she had been there. She was a truly nice woman and an all around great lady. The Andantes had a good life during those years. It was fun times and good friends and great times. I want everyone to know they're good people. They never let what they did go to their heads or have an ego about it. I know they don't talk about it and still today, they keep it to themselves most of the time. The Andantes just weren't cherished for what they did. It's coming to them now though. They deserve it."

Ronald Rice is Marlene and Jackie's childhood friend. "I became close friends with them and there were about ten of us who ran around together. I was about sixteen when we really began to spend more time and hang out in a group. We had picnics and went out together. When we could go out without chaperones we would go to The 20 Grand and The Gray Stone Ballroom. After they started singing at Motown, I would go with them to the Motown Revues and watch the various acts perform. I attended the Motown Christmas parties with them and I went to the big picnic in the summer. It was family-oriented at the gatherings and everyone loved everyone.

"We grew up in the same neighborhood. It was a relatively self-contained, working, middle-class, black neighborhood. It was well-established in the city of Detroit. There was every church denomination within two square miles. St. Stephens AME Church, Hartford, and New Light were the three churches that all of the youngsters would attend for Sunday School and Church. We would hop from one service to the other and sometimes we would go to Tabernacle where a lot of the Motowners went to youth group. St. Stephen's is where a lot of the record-hops took place. I would go to all of the parties and dance with ladies such as Martha Reeves, Mary Wilson, and Gladys Horton. It was a great time. I had fun during those years with my friends and with the music as the backdrop, it was special memories.

"I remember seeing Marlene, Jackie, and Louvain sing at a Hartford Baptist Church concert; they were guests at the concert at the time and they came as The Andantes to sing. I will never forget what they sang: 'Give Me Your Tired, Your Poor'. That's the inscription on The Statue of Liberty. That's how I learned it. I heard them sing that song and it was beautiful. They were so talented beyond what people knew. I am still a member of Hartford Baptist Church.

"I went to many of the studio sessions with them, not only for Motown, but when they did other sessions in town as well. The sessions sometimes wouldn't start until late in the evening and it would be a long night for them. Other sessions would be out in the suburbs where a producer had a studio in their basement. Sometimes it would be white artists. They sang with black and white artists. They weren't under contract, so they freelanced.

They felt they had more freedom if they freelanced.

"Marlene has a perfect ear for music. She could get a piece of music or listen to a group of musicians play and if there was something wrong or off, she could re-write it and fix it. They come from church and musical backgrounds. They were great at the old standards and their training gave them great insight when they recorded. They blended so beautifully. I was in sessions with The Four Tops, Stevie Wonder, and The Supremes. I'd sit off to the side and watch them work and listen to the musicians play. I was right there in the studio watching everything. At one point they had me clapping on one of the records. I believe it was a Four Tops session. Marlene loved hamburgers from Woolworth's. I would pick up a burger and bring it to her in the studio when she was in session.

"Marlene was loyal to The Andantes. She went to fill in with the Supremes but wanted to remain true to Jackie and Louvain. She wanted them to be able to sing as a trio and be able to work. Motown used The Andantes to get that full sound. They had that quality and sound that made it the Motown sound. I was with them riding in the car many times and we always had the radio on. Their songs came on and they would sing along. They were joyful when they sang. They were more joyful just singing along to the radio than they were excited about being on the radio. I like their work with Stevie Wonder and I like the Mary Wells sessions. I love 'My Guy' and Marvin's 'How Sweet It Is To Be Loved By You'.

"They sang with Liz Lands, who had a beautiful voice, and their work with her was amazing. They sounded great with her. I like their work with Brenda Holloway. In those days lyrics had much more meaning. Smokey Robinson had a way of writing, just as did many of them. It was a time that has yet to be captured again. Etolia White is another friend of ours. Her brother Frank White was a piano player and church musician, who was very well known in the city. Etolia sang with The Andantes for a little while.

"I would be in the studio watching the ladies work and sing. I witnessed them to be inventive and creative; they would improvise and make things better. I saw them take ideas that were given to them by producers and make them better. They came up with better solutions for sounds and blending the vocals. They loved what they did and they enjoyed working there with the other artists. It was joyful when one of the Motowners had a hit record. The Motown artists loved The Andantes. It was a time in our lives when we were feeling hopeful. Doors were opening up for blacks and we were encouraged by the movements at the time. Our groups of friends weren't into drugs. We hung out and had house parties, but no one was into the drug scene that I saw. Our group was a group within a group within the Motowners, so we saw a lot happen.

"What I would want the world to know about The Andantes is they're everyday people with big, warm hearts. Their hearts were in the right place. They were joyful, optimistic, and they enjoyed seeing their peers become successful. They got along with everyone and are very much respected by their colleagues. It took them a long time to realize how important they were to the history. They have remained young at heart even through their hardships. We've remained friends all of these years. They're always surprised and very grateful when people recognize their work and know who they are. I can hear them on the records. I know their sound and voices. I love them very much and I am very proud of them."

Give Me Your Tired, Your Poor

Give me your tired, your poor
Your huddled masses yearning to breathe free
The wretched refuse of your teeming shore
Send these the homeless tempest-tost to me
I lift my lamp beside the golden door

Emma Lazarus wrote 'The New Colossus' poem in 1883. It was affixed to the pedestal of the Statue of Liberty in 1903.

Coleman Castro is Louvain's cousin. He spent a lot of time with Louvain in Detroit and offers great insight. "I grew up outside of Ann Arbor. I spent the summer of 1967 with her family. Her mother and my father's mom were sisters. I called Vainy's mom and told her I wanted to spend the summer with them, they were a big warm family. I stayed there with her mother, Ruth, and Ella.

Louvain's mother was a very strong woman and a very nice person. She was beautiful with long beautiful hair, a Creole woman. Her father was a quiet man and kept to himself. Vainy was married and that's when we really got to know each other. This is when I found out she was a singer at Motown. I later moved to Detroit and worked at Wayne State University.

"Vainy is a sweet, warm, and affectionate person. She was quiet and mild back then. The best way to describe her is the mom I wished I would have had or the sister I never had. She was a good friend. She was the type of person you wished you could marry. She was everyone to me, all wrapped up in one, and I'm happy that we're family. She's about ten years older than me. We bonded in a good friendship and talked a lot about life and what was going on. We are cousins, but we talked like old friends and we were there for each other and were encouragement for each other. We would catch the bus together because she didn't have a car. I have a lot of good memories of us and her sons just being together and doing things together. I worked at night and she worked at night so we would hop the bus and go downtown and go to the movies and go shopping.

"She's always a mother to everyone. She was the kind of person that you could just talk with. She told me one of The Holland Brothers and she were talking and he wrote a song on her kitchen table as they were talking. I don't remember what song it was. They were just talking and having coffee after a session and he wrote it. She would talk to Marvin Gaye and counsel him. She is so easy to talk to and she is truly there for people. Her favorite place was the kitchen table and we would just sit there and talk about life. That stands out the most for me because it happened regularly with her. Louvain sees me as someone special. The way she treats me, it's like I am special. We always listened to each other and showed respect for each other. Sometimes you don't realize that you're giving someone something they really need when you're just listening to them and connecting with them. That's what we did for each other. She is a generous person.

"I went to several recording sessions with Louvain. The Andantes were always the number one choice for the producers. I met The Originals there in the studio with Louvain. Everyone at Motown was very friendly and I knew that they thought of her as a dear friend. I recall her voice being so strong that she would stand back a little from the microphone and Marlene and Jackie. She could really belt out a song. She's so tiny to have such a powerful voice. You can hear her on 'Love Child'. She's so powerful on that song. I was young and I'm sure my mouth and eyes were wide open. They literally sang on every record, they really did. So many years they were part of Motown. They were a significant part of Motown. They're just as important as everyone else.

"I also went to several sessions that she did at other studios. It would be late into the night. It was a lot of work. I was in a session with Martha Reeves and The Andantes. I think it was without her group members. I think they had already disbanded. I was so in awe and I cannot recall what song they were recording. I was in sessions where Ashford and Simpson were producing. I asked Louvain why they never sang their own records. She told me they wouldn't really allow them to be a solo group, that they wanted them to remain the backing voices. If they complained then they gave them a raise to keep them from wanting that. They were just so perfect-sounding that they could've done more as a group. They should have been recognized more back then. Everyone gets credit now on CD's but back then you didn't know who was doing what on those records.

"You have to tell different aspects of a story. They have their history and story to tell. Motown has its own story. The Andantes have their story apart from that. I've told my children all about Louvain. I am very proud of her. I was the black sheep in my immediate family and kind of different than my brothers. I was more artistic and out there, so Louvain and I bonded. I've read jazz musician biographies and autobiographies and I'm a great lover of music. I'm always looking for those types of books to read. Creativity runs in the family. My favorite songs that she sings on are The Four Tops tunes. I love 'Baby I Need Your Loving'. They sound so great on that.

"When you listen to just their vocals, without the lead, it's pretty amazing. I was able to hear that when they did the playback in the studio. Vainy loved to sing, but she didn't love the political part of it. There's so much that goes into fame. If she could sing forever she would be very happy. Louvain is still beautiful and was a gorgeous woman in her youth. She was confident in her singing. I know that she was a great mother and didn't want to be away from her children, so being on the road and fame would not have been easy for her.

"It was an amazing time in the 60's for black people. During that time, rapid change was happening. I started college in 1964 and I marched with The Black Panthers on campus in college. Dr. King was killed and amazing change was happening for everyone. The Civil Rights and Voting Rights were passed. There were so many fabulous clubs in Detroit. It was a social time and a musical time. It was a beautiful city with gorgeous homes. I will never forget seeing The Temptations. I saw Marvin Gaye in the Motown Revue. I recall how he stood out onstage.

"You can see that when Vainy started singing, black people had very few places that they could go for a career. You didn't have very many rights and there weren't a lot of people that could help you, such as lawyers and executives. It was a different time and you made the best with what you had. My dad made me proud to be black. I read a lot about our history. We grew up in a period where, being black, you had to know your place.

"The sixties and seventies were the best times. What makes America what it is today isn't so much what's in the history books. What helped to make Motown were the political and social issues of the time. The point of view of the people who lived it and what they think is Motown. I would love to know how The Andantes interpreted what was going on around them. How could those three girls, who were just out of high school in the inner city of Detroit, be able to work with everyone and make music history?

"It was a dogfight at Motown to make hit records and everyone wanted to make money. They were the central core along with The Funk Brothers that everyone was working around. Everyone wanted them on their records. With all of the different forces around them, they were able to stay consistent and loyal to each other. Some of the girl groups didn't like them singing on those records. They stayed connected to each other for the fourteen years they sang together, even with all of the turmoil of the times and what was going on around them. They persevered and remained respectful to the music and to their colleagues. They were right in the middle of history and a major part of making history. Yet somehow The Funk Brothers and The Andantes were ignored until recently.

"Louvain is bursting now. Back then there were forces holding her back and I think she bloomed late in life. Her confidence had to grow. She isn't afraid to tell this history now. They were the worker bees making those hit records. At the same time they were held back because they should have been a girl group of their own. When you look at the times of the fifties and sixties and what it was like for black people then it says a lot about how things worked out for them. They are in the age group that spans periods of time where, as a young person, you had to keep a lower profile because you were black and keep quiet. You referred to your elders as 'Mr.' and 'Mrs.' and children had manners. There was a breakout for blacks and women and when it happened later, they missed it because Motown was over.

"The main reason why people like The Andantes were ripped off was that the oppressors of the time were oppressed themselves. If you read a little about Paulo Friere, think in terms of Black Americans then and the traits of the oppressed people. They took on the traits of the oppressor. You would think that a person would do more for their people if they came from an oppressed background, but instead they take on the traits of the oppressors and the cycle continues."

Joe Castro is Coleman's brother. "I remember when she started singing at Motown, my brother would visit her. I was proud of her. That was the music of my childhood and all of my friends loved Motown. The Motown sound was our music. I cannot pick a favorite song that she sings on. When I was a teenager, I had all of the Motown records. I loved the music but I never could dance. I loved all of the artists who sang at Motown. What I think about when I think of Vainy, she is one of the sweetest people I know. She is a very sweet, kind, and loving person and she always has something positive and good to say. I would like to be around her more than I am."

Louvain's son Michael Demps has these memories: "I would visit Hitsville and I didn't realize who my mother was or what she was doing. I understood that she modeled and sang. When I was about seven years old, I understood it more. I would see a Bentley in our driveway and when I went inside, Edwin Starr would be over visiting in the living room. He was always dressed so sharp. I never saw him in a pair of jeans. It was funny to me because I would play his records over and over, and to have him sitting in the living room was a little surreal. I remember she dressed us cute in little matching caps and corduroy pants and suits. I was in the studio with her when she recorded 'For Once In My Life'. I remember Stevie playing the piano. I began to recognize my mother's voice on the records because The Andantes have a special sound. I knew when I heard mom. One of my favorite songs is 'Mickey's Monkey'. I remember being at the studio one time, seeing Smokey in the booth, and he called out, 'Is everybody ready?' just like he did on 'Mickey's Monkey' and I thought that was really cool. That's just what he did at the start of a session.

"One of my favorite songs is 'For Once In My Life' and my ultimate favorite is 'Love Child' because I can hear my mother so well on that one. I absolutely love 'Bernadette' and the part where the music goes silent and I can hear her stand out on that high note. It sends chills up my spine—that is *my mother*. It's a good feeling to know my mother's voice is going to be in history, long after we're all gone. They'll still play those songs generations from now.

"I have a memory of her learning to drive. We were in the car with the instructor and I was in the back seat. I remember getting tossed around a lot. I think I was the original bobble-head at age five. It was funny to see her learning how to drive."

Etolia White has more to share about Marlene and Jackie. "In 1962, we made a car trip to Chicago. There were six of us. We called ourselves The B6 (I named us that). It means The Boss Six. Everyone was trying to be the boss and we all had strong personalities. Jackie was the oldest, then Marlene, then me. I gave us each a number according to our ages, so Jackie was B1 and Marlene was B2. There were six of us: Louise Walls, Yvonne Harbin, Yvonne Washington, me, Jackie, and Marlene. We've been friends for more than forty years. Each one of us has a different dynamic relationship with the other. When my daddy was sick and I had to go to work a 'real job' because singing was only part time, Marlene and Jackie would stop in and feed him lunch. They made certain that my daddy got his lunch and they paid for it. They made sure they took care of that before they went to work.

We are a close group. We are real friends and share a true friendship."

Yvonne Rashida Harbin adds, "There aren't a lot of people who can say that they have had great girlfriends for fifty years, but I can say that. Jackie would keep us entertained all the time. She missed her calling as a comedian. She has the absolute funniest one-liners of anyone I have ever known. She would get a wrong-number phone call in the middle of the night with some woman asking if her husband was there. Jackie would give her the line, 'Well what's his name?' She keeps us in stitches all of the time. No one is on their feet like that late at night when the phone rings. She is always funny with something comical to say. Jackie is the mother-hen of all of us. She'll tell you what's up, where we're going, and that the car is leaving. She keeps us in check and keeps us in balance by addressing the silly stuff. Oh lord, do we have some history together. We were in each others' lives all the time and in each others' face everyday. We are all like family. Jackie has been quite a character all of our lives. Marlene and Jackie love what they did for Motown and are very proud of what they did. I'm always so proud of them and I tell them all the time. My very best girlfriends are The Andantes and they're people who will go down in history. I feel blessed to have them in my life and have shared my life with them. They get embarrassed when I tell people who they are. I want them to have their place in history and not ever be forgotten.

"Etolia's memory is phenomenal. I used to date a guy who had a lisp, and he couldn't say 'Etolia', so he muttered 'Toby'. I have been calling her Toby for over forty years. We have been such good friends for fifty years and I feel so blessed to have that friendship with these women. We are such characters together and have so much fun together. Etolia is afraid of heights but she became an air traffic controller. I tell you, we are a funny bunch of women. Another one of our friends is Barbara Bolden-Dillard, she lives in Texas now, she was a hairdresser. Diana Ross and I had the same hair appointment with her at 6:00am on Saturday mornings back in the day."

Mickey Stevenson had more to share about Motown. "Motown wasn't a lucky situation. It was a lot of hard work that made that happen and a lot of stuff that happened behind the scenes. Motown could've happened anywhere. Berry took a city that only manufactured cars and turned it into a music capital. I went through this in my mind's eye. I just thought *man, that really was incredible*. It was a moment in time for a purpose. You have to have a spiritual mind to understand what he did and what happened. When you look at it in other ways, it comes out as something different altogether. When you tell these stories, you can do them without the negatives and the smut. You cannot look at a person's life as a whole and pretend that they didn't have any problems. You have to make it a reality and tell the human side of the story. You have to protect the families of those who are gone. It isn't right to tell another's history that can possibly hurt their children or families."

Marilyn Stewart met Louvain in 1959. "Our friendship is one of those friendships you just have and it lasts because of a common love bond. We have maintained it over the years. We stay in touch and we still laugh, clown, and cry together. My husband and I met Louvain in 1959 in Detroit. We moved into her neighborhood and lived on the same street on Arlington, about four houses apart. I went to the studio with her many times. I would drive her and help her get to work and back home. The studio was on the west side and we lived on the east side. Some days I'd drop her off and some days I'd go in and hang out. One day I was there and they wanted clappers. I clapped my hands on a record and they paid me for it. I don't remember what song it was. I had no idea she had that kind of voice until I went to the studio and heard her sing. I was older than Louvain. I met Marlene and Jackie and I thought they were all very nice young ladies. I felt like a big sister making sure they were all okay and I watched over them. I don't think they realized I would keep an eye on them when they were out at the nightclubs. I wanted to make sure Louvain had a ride at night when she was coming home late. I would tell my husband that I didn't want to see her taking the bus that late at night.

"She and I would go to The 20 Grand. I would drive her down there. That was when she, Marlene, and Jackie would sing behind whatever acts were performing on stage. I would sip a Coke and watch the show until she was done with work. The Motown music really helped seal our friendship because I loved music so much. I was a lover of Motown music, but that was not the direction I was going in with music. I played the organ and directed choirs. One day Vainy and I were hanging out and playing with my new organ and Joe Hinton came over. We started writing a song together. We all put words in and he put the melody in. Joe took it to the studio. The song was called 'One Step Away' and Gladys Knight recorded it. That was a very exciting thing for me. It was on Gladys' album *If I Were Your Woman.* I loved Gladys Knight. I love her voice and the way she sings.

"If I had to sum up Louvain for her fans, I'd have to say that she's just a happy, upbeat person who is full of life. Even when you know she's going through hard and bad times herself, she will lift your spirits up. She's that type of person. She'll turn the focus back on the good and positive and lift others higher, rather than have whatever she is going through bring another down. I loved all of the music that they did at Motown and I love all the songs that The Andantes sing on. Hearing her high voice, it was such a wonder to me how she could sing like that; such a clear and great voice. I like Motown music more because Vainy sings on it. I love The Supremes' 'I Hear A Symphony'. I can hear her on that. Her voice was always so clear."

We hear again from Jackie Harper, Louvain's godsister. "I had a brief encounter at Motown. I'd be there for some rehearsals. I sang with a group called The Vocalettes and I don't know if they used us on any records or not. I would see Louvain there because we both had business there. She continued on at Motown and I went more into gospel music and singing for the church. When Motown was here it was normal to be in the company of any one of the artists: Tammi Terrell, Marv Johnson, Marvin Gaye, or The Spinners. They were out and about, were approachable, and were just normal folks who we interacted with.

"I would go to clubs and everyone would be there. It was a fantastic time for entertainment and music and it was all through the city. It was a magical time and I am happy I was a part of that era and witnessed it up close and personal. There was a place called Idlewild where performers would go on the weekend. We would see Della Reese and other performers there. This was a tourist city where blacks could go. I lived across the street from Ron Banks and The Dramatics. His mother would play the piano, his father would play the horn, and my sister and I would be over there singing with them. Our family knew The Four Tops. My brother and Duke were friends and sang on the corners doo-wopping together. I loved all of the Motown acts. I can't say I had a favorite, I loved them all. It was so magical to grow up with this type of energy and creativity. I thank God I experienced that.

"I grew up singing with music and Motown in my life. I went to the Motown Revues at The Fox and The 20 Grand. They were always filled with excitement and electricity. The stars were open and mingled in the crowds. They met their fans and gave autographs. What was so different about this time is you would go to the show to see them onstage, and then you would end up at a party with them after because everyone knew everyone. You would end up at after-hour clubs and back then it was good, clean fun. Everyone would be there: David Ruffin, Tammi Terrell, The Four Tops, The Supremes, all of them.

"My sister and I backed up Dinah Washington when we were very, very young. It was at the Gray Stone Ballroom. It was I, Virginia Hines, Joyce Holmes, Charlene Tyus, and Gloria Jean Holmes. We called ourselves 'The Vocalettes'. We were young and didn't get paid. We had a manager named Daniel Newsome. I don't know where he is now. He got us some gigs. Daniel was getting ready to sign us and my father said 'No.' We were going to go out on the road. My father worked for Ford and he said he would have to quit his job to be out on the road with us. That's when it came to a halt. He didn't want us out on the road because there was too much drugs and drinking out on the road; he was strict. He said we could sing locally but that was it.

"When The Supremes and everyone took off and began to have success, I wondered if that could have happened for us with Mr. Newsome. We would go to the State Fair and see The Midnighters, Billy Ward, and The Dominoes. We loved singing back then. I had music in my bones. We would go to that fair, get home late, get a whipping, and go back the next night just to be near the music. We couldn't make our curfew because we stayed until the last shows.

"What I remember most about Louvain is that she cared about people. Her love and kindness has always been there for people. She remembers you and she takes the time to stay in touch with you and shows she cares. She keeps you alive in her life. I am grateful to stay in touch with a dear friend. Some people go on in life and lose touch with their roots and closest friends and Louvain is just not like that. She doesn't let the connections she has in life fall away. She is family-oriented, so even if you aren't a blood relative, she treats you like family and she makes her family with those she knows and is close to and keeps a close circle of friends.

"We have meaningful, precious memories because we were girls together and we're family. I'm grateful to hold her friendship so close and still have her in my life. She's a praying woman and we prayed together many times and that kept us together as friends. The glue that kept us close was our spirituality. Whenever we talk, we pray for one another. As a mother, she held on to her children and she raised them and brought them through with her during hardships. She is seriously a great mother. She did what it took to be a good mother and she's a survivor and a provider. I have never known her to be without employment of some kind. She's a diligent worker, a hard worker. She worked hard to make a life for herself and her sons even though things didn't come easy for her. She pulled through and was like the Energizer Bunny-she took a licking and kept on ticking. My hat goes off to her."

Emory Hicks remembers, "One occasion we were all hanging out at my house and The Temptations were playing at The Copa and somebody said, 'Lets go.' Next thing you know we were all in New York with reservations and tickets watching The Temptations. That was the kind of stuff we got into, having parties and fun times. It was fun times and not like it is today. A party would be dancing and playing cards and just hanging out. We would dance all night until we couldn't dance anymore."

Childhood friend Ed McQueen adds, "Louvain was Catholic and I was Protestant. We went to the same high school. I was her first date in high school. We went to a sock-hop together. My older brother drove us to the sock-hop. I was the one who couldn't dance but Louvain could dance very well. We sang together in glee club. She sang with the girl ensemble and I sang with the boys. Abdul from The Four Tops was in our glee club. Little Willie John and Sylvia Moy were in our glee club also. This was at Pershing High School. She was an outstanding first soprano singer. She was always a serious person and she took singing and music very serious. I appreciate the music of Motown. It will always be here, it is part of American History. It came along during a time of change in our country. No matter whom you were-black, white, or whoever, Motown was appreciated by the music fans. That's what was going on at the time. Anytime there was a Motown Revue, people would be in line to get there and see it. Then and now, Motown has maintained its popularity. I rubbed elbows with the stars of Motown. They were good, pleasant people.

"I knew Louvain from the ninth grade on. She was a great kid. She was a live-wire and kept you laughing. She was a very personable person, sweet and sincere. She is very open and sometimes too much; she makes herself vulnerable. We had a close friendship like a brother and sister relationship. She is a true friend and I would do anything for her then and now. I think the world of her and always have. I think she is a wonderful person. I think highly of her. Her children are like my own. She has the drive to keep the legacy she helped create out there in the public eye."

Harold Stone says, "I went to quite a few of the Motown shows and saw the Motown acts. I knew The Four Tops and a few others. The 20 Grand and The Fox Theatre were *the* places to go. I guess my favorite act would have to be The Four Tops. Berry Gordy could have done what he did in another town, but it was in Detroit that it happened. He had many talented people in this town. Everyone was into music at the time or had a group—I even had a group, and wanted to sing. There were so many groups at that time singing on the street corners. We all did it. My group wasn't as dedicated. We had jobs and we liked to sing, but we didn't press on with it. That's why I admire The Four Tops and people like Louvain who stuck with it and hung in there trying to make it. They had the drive to succeed with singing and they followed their dreams. Success takes a lot of hard work, and you have to pay your dues. Everywhere you go, you hear Motown music. If you were from Detroit, you knew that music came from your city and you were very proud of it."

Some Things You Never Get Used To

It may come as a surprise to some people, but others have heard throughout the years that Marlene Barrow was a Supreme for a short period of time. Jackie and Louvain were very supportive of the venture. Louvain says, "Marlene had a great opportunity. It was a fair chance for her to get out there and finally sing and perform. I was all for it and supported her one hundred percent." Mildred Dobey adds, "I was so proud when Marlene was a Supreme for a brief moment." Yvonne Rashida Harbin says, "Another thing that we lived through was that Marlene was one of The Supremes for a little while, and that was very exciting. Marlene was always so beautiful. I can tell you it bothers me, as their friend, that they didn't get their credit over the years. I wanted to see them get their due. Marlene sings on some very big Supremes hits and doesn't get the props for it."

Marlene was respectful and modest about the times when she filled in for Florence Ballard onstage. Prior to the experience, she was singing in sessions with Mary Wilson. There are a block of Supremes songs that are just Mary and Marlene backing up Diana Ross. Marlene recalls, "Holland-Dozier-Holland took me aside quietly and asked me to come into the studio and sing, so I did. That is me and Mary on 'You Can't Hurry Love'. There are a few others on which I sing. It was Harvey Fuqua who approached me and asked me to fill in for Florence onstage. I informed Louvain and Jackie so that they heard from me what I was going to do. I never felt it was going to interfere with The Andantes because I knew it was a temporary situation. For a brief period, while they were negotiating to get Cindy Birdsong, I stepped in and sang with The Supremes. I didn't see Florence during this time and it was kept very quiet that Cindy was in Detroit. I wasn't told any of the details. Cindy was singing with Patti LaBelle and The Blue Belles. I filled in on the engagements that The Supremes had booked until Cindy was free from her contract with The Blue Belles.

"It was fun while it lasted. I didn't have any dreams of it going any further because I knew I was just filling in while they were negotiating with Cindy. It was a great experience and one that was truly a lot of fun for me. I'm glad I had the opportunity to say I was a Supreme for a little while onstage. The first thing I did as a Supreme was a private performance for the Fisher family, here in Detroit. It was at Gross Pointe Country Club. A daughter of the Fishers wanted The Supremes to perform at her coming-out party and the crème de la crème of Detroit was there. The Fishers were General Motors. I was able to fit the gowns and of course I knew the songs very well. I just had to learn the routines.

"I performed with Mary and Diana in Philadelphia, Cleveland, and a few other places. I had no problems with either of them. Mary and I were close and she helped me with the routines and the dance steps. I was fortunate because I already knew The Supremes' music from all of the sessions I had done. Mary and I had rehearsed with Harvey, Cholly Atkins, and Gwen Gordy. Diana kept to herself on the road and was more private, plus her mother was with her. There was a venue called 'Basin Street East' in Boston. This was the dress-rehearsal location for The Copacabana. The Copa was the biggest place you could play at the time. The Supremes were booked and they were getting the new show ready for The Copa. They were trying out new show tunes, new routines, and of course, the classic Supremes songs too. Berry flew out to see how the new tunes were fitting into the show.

"When The Temptations and The Supremes performed at The Copa, and other big venues, they did a lot of the old standards and show tunes. We had a break one day from the show in Boston and there were Motown affiliates who wanted to host us on a picnic and a boat ride. Diana didn't come with us but her mother did. Mary, Diana's mother Ernestine, and I had a very nice day out on the boat with the affiliates. I wouldn't have gone on to be with The Supremes had they asked me. I felt loyalty to The Andantes and my young son. I knew I was just filling in and it was a wonderful thing to have happen." Before the end of the decade, things were changing at Motown. Not only was Florence gone from The Supremes, but The Temptations would see a change in their lineup as well. Mary Wells and Kim Weston were gone from the company too.

Louvain was seeing changes in her own life and would soon go through a divorce. "Somewhere along the way my marriage went sour. I had stayed so busy working I didn't notice it until it had gotten so bad. I didn't see it fall apart until it was ugly and I couldn't deny it. He was with me from the beginning and we had two children. He was supportive and encouraging in those early years of my singing at Motown. As I worked more and more, our marriage went downhill. We married so young and maybe that was part of it. He was the breadwinner and I was working, so that also put a strain.

"Home was a hard place for me to be, so I worked more. Agnes Bowles was Beans' wife and she drove me to work and was a very good friend of mine. While I was going through the divorce and moving out, she helped us move. I had a statue of praying hands and I was running around in circles with them. She was conducting the movers, ordering the people, and organizing the move. She was a real card, a great lady. I met her when Beans was in that horrible car accident where he almost died. I took things over to the house for her and her sons and we became friends. She was a good friend to me after I left Mr. Demps. We lived with them for a little while until we got our own place. She checked on us and made sure me and the boys were okay. For a while, it was quite emotional and traumatic for my sons and me. She would later divorce and I would be there for her through it.

"Work was my escape from the heartache. Everything that was inside of me, that I was unable to express, came out in me through the music. I was able to feel the emotions and they came out when I sang. Sometimes the lyrics could be turned around to fit my own life. When I sang those songs they were an outlet for me. They gave me an emotional and verbal release because I didn't' share with people or talk about how unhappy my marriage was. I was miserable and I let it all out when I sang. I said things I wished I was able to say to people out loud and I sang it loud. I know music is healing. It was a tool for me, then and now. The lyrics were inspired sometimes by what was going on around us directly. You have to be kind enough to let sleeping dogs lay, and not tell who or what some of those lyrics are really about.

"Marvin Gaye and I became kindred souls for one another at this time. Tammi Terrell had fallen ill and Marvin was in a different space in his life. His life had taken a turn and it was showing in him and his work. You could feel the depth when you were with him, at least I did. Great artists have difficulties with communicating. They are able to communicate in spirit form easier than in human form. He had a lot of suffering inside of him, not just because of Tammi but his personal life. It seemed he was working through his life and it was showing and moving through him. I witnessed his spirit moving and I saw a change was coming. Marvin and I talked a lot during this time. We both had things going on in our lives. He would give me a ride home after the sessions.

"One day Charles and Anita Russ's daughter Tonya was watching my boys. Marvin came by and she was overjoyed with excitement when she opened the door and saw Marvin Gaye standing there. I definitely liked working with Marvin as an artist and as a producer. He was exceptional in the studio. I recall a difficult session was 'What's Going On'. There were many people singing on that record with us. I think this was a hard session for me because Marvin was in another realm and he would try to tell us what he heard in his head. It was hard for me to hear what he was hearing. I knew that he was creating a great piece of work. He really was a mastermind over the session and it was hard to grasp the full essence of what he was conveying to us as an artist. He would stop the tapes and after a while, it would get frustrating. This was different from a session where it was a producer/ songwriter. He was producer/artist and he was fretting over the work. Him being the artist that he was, it was a different experience working with him and this was a deep session for him. It moves you when a person is coming from and creating from a spiritual place within them. It was an amazing experience for all of us. It was the first time we saw our name on the album credits."

By late 1971, the writing was on the wall that the end was near and times were changing. Just a few signs were: Holland-Dozier-Holland were long gone from Motown, Tammi Terrell had died, Diana Ross had left The Supremes and Marvin Gaye was isolated in grief.

Marvin Gaye would be honored in his home town of Washington DC.The Funk Brothers and The Andantes would accompany Marvin during the first performance he would give after Tammi's death. Funk Brother Uriel Jones recalls, "Marvin Gaye Day in D.C. was the last time I worked with all three Andantes. Marvin Gaye was given the key to the city in D.C. and he wanted the best on his show. That's why he had them come in to sing with him.

"I would have to say that I love everything that The Andantes sang on. They did extensive work behind the male groups and the girl groups. They're just amazing. I don't have a favorite song because I love everything that they did. No matter where you go, you are going to hear Motown, in stores and everywhere. The Andantes really stand out, so the public should really finally know who they are. They sang on the records for the female groups and didn't get their names on the record. It was The Andantes doing the singing for many of those groups. It's hard to explain how great these girls were. They taught the other singers a whole lot about singing. Their personalities were so dynamic too, which made them even more so pleasurable to be around. They were so humble and they were my girls. As far as The Funk Brothers were concerned, The Andantes were the best in the world vocally. I believe if they had put records out on these ladies, they would have been the top singing group around because there was no comparison. They were great singers and talented. I am glad that the public will learn about them; they deserve this finally.

"They went through the same situation we did. The Funk Brothers and The Andantes did not get the recognition. They were kept in the background. They should be remembered for what they did, like everyone else. Their contribution to the Motown sound was significant. The fact we weren't recognized made it hard to prove to people what we did. We have bragging rights for what we did, but nothing showed up for it. Since our documentary came out, we have bragging rights, but now we have something to show for it and proof to tell it. People put a face with the music and when people love a record, they only know who sang the lead on it. The rest of the record had The Funk Brothers and The Andantes on it. The music helped make those records hits and the background vocals helped that too."

Louvain remembers Marvin Gaye Day. "Marvin begged The Andantes to perform with him at this event. It was the three of us and The Funks beside him. Marvin and I talked a lot the night before. He told me he was so scared. I asked him to please not smoke anything. I knew he smoked and I knew he was scared. I told him 'I will be by the piano, so when you feel scared just look over at me and it will be okay.' It was the first time he performed since Tammi's death. He had stage-fright so bad and he told me he would look at me if he got scared.

"I was always worried that something awful was going to happen to him. Marvin and I talked on a spiritual level when we discussed things and I think that's why I worried about him so much. I would tell him that he already had a deep connection with God and that drugs weren't giving him the meaning in his soul that he thought they were. He would sink deep and not be able to lift himself back up when he was high. He could get into the deepest, darkest places of the mind. At other times, he was Marvin Gaye the priest because he was deep in soul and spirit. He told me I was a deep and funny person and we had that in common. I went to his house after Marvin Gaye Day because he had me come over to pick up my check. He hugged me and kissed me and said, 'Thank you baby for being there for me and helping me.' "

Jackie adds these memories of Marvin, "Sessions with Marvin were memorable and fun too. As an artist, and when he produced, I never saw a dark side of him. Marvin was a certain way and he really just respected women. You witnessed it with the people around him such as Kim, Tammi, and us. When you're singing with someone and you click in personality, and on top of that you sound great, that's just magic. Marvin made magic with his duet partners. He respected them and that made the music special. Knowing Marvin as I did, he would've been devastated had any of his girls passed so young the way Tammi had. He cared about us: Mary Wells, Kim Weston, Diana, and all of us. Even when it came to working, he didn't want to wear anyone out or make you so tired that you had to rest. He was a gracious, respectful person.

"He would make you drink water and rest and not work us too hard. Tammi Terrell was a really nice person and a lot of fun in the studio. I wished I had known her better after having spent all that time with her. Then she was gone. She was a great singer and such a friendly person. It really wiped Marvin out when she died. You never know how many people you touch until something like that happens. If I had to pick a song that was my favorite, I would have to say 'I Heard It Through The Grapevine'. I love all of our work though. I think we have a great sound. When I hear it, I feel good because I remember feeling good when we were doing the work and making it happen. 'Grapevine' is the ring tone on my cell phone. I figured if I was going to have a ring tone, I wanted to hear myself singing and I wanted it to be something I liked."

Marlene's memories of Marvin: "He was just a musical genius. Paul Riser would write out music charts for the musicians and Marvin would tell them to forget those charts and follow him. He would sit down at the piano and play and the musicians would follow what he was doing. It was fabulous. That was his way and how he did it. You could not box him in. He had to have his way and be able to free flow with his creativity. They may have rehearsed it one way yesterday and were recording it today, but when Marvin got there he would do it his way and say to forget the sheet music. I never saw a dark or disturbed side of Marvin."

"We've got to find a way, to bring some loving here today."

Marvin Gaye

What Is So Good About Goodbye?

With the end of Motown nearing, The Andantes had no clue they would soon be out of work. Louvain, Marlene, and Jackie all suffered personal losses around the same time. Jackie lost her father due to complications from a stroke in 1970. Louvain lost her mother April 1, 1971. Marlene lost her mother in October of 1972. These were trying times for the three ladies who had worked the last fourteen years together. Now in their early thirties, times were changing and it would never be the same for the musical trio.

Rita Lumpkin-Daily remembers when they heard the news. "When they found out that Motown was going to close, we went out to Belle Isle Park. The Andantes made an announcement to everyone that Motown was closing and leaving. We had a huge crowd of cars following us to the park. The whole neighborhood came down. We told everyone to follow us because we had something to tell them. Everyone was so mad because no one from Motown told Marlene, Jackie, or Louvain, or even warned them. We had everyone come down to the park and we made an announcement ourselves about what Berry had done and what was happening. We were spreading the word to everyone and rebelling because they were left high and dry. People didn't believe us at first that Motown was leaving. We were telling everyone that Hitsville was gone and over. There was such disbelief that this could ever happen."

Marlene says, "Those last days were sad. We were not told anything. I believe the last sessions we were doing were the 70s Supremes and some of the Diana Ross solo sessions. It was a crazy time and we noticed that work was slowing down more and more, they were calling us in less and less. It seemed a change was coming. We had heard it in the air that they were leaving Detroit and we would ask them repeatedly if it were true. They would deny it and tell us everything was okay, and not to worry. They were not being honest with us about their plans. As much work as we had done for them—for the nearly fourteen years we were there, it seems they could have told us the truth. The date is embedded in my head: January 16, 1973. Those people who were going to Los Angeles knew they were going and the ones that weren't simply were not told. This was our livelihood and it would have been nice to know our jobs were ending. We had one hell of a time getting unemployment too. It took several attempts at getting the paperwork through because Motown didn't label this a lay-off. In our minds it was. The work ended and they left—after we worked fourteen years for them. I felt they showed us how little our hard work meant to them. I felt taken for granted and unappreciated. Had they given us some notice that they were leaving I would have a different opinion of that today. It was disrespectful how they left."

Jackie shares, "We weren't asked to go with the company. I for one wouldn't have gone because I wouldn't have left my family. I have always been close to family and I wouldn't want to move away from them. It was also too much of a risk to go. In Detroit, we had a guarantee that we would work and have a paycheck because Motown was here. There was no guarantee that would be the case in California. It is better to be close to family if you're having troubles and looking for work. It's another thing to be across the country and not have a job. Some of our colleagues and The Funk Brothers went out there on a limb with very little and they just didn't make it. They got out there and Motown didn't give them the same amount of work, plus everything was more expensive in California. When Motown left here, it was gone for me emotionally. I just didn't go on and on about it. I didn't bring it up or tell people about it. If I'm doing something that I really like and it ends, I have to be through with it emotionally and let it go. I just could not pine over it. People become run down trying to chase a lost dream or a dream that has ended.

"Motown wasn't coming back to Detroit and I had to accept that quick. It would have been nice if it could have continued. I would have continued to do that for many years because I loved it. I truly loved it. I'm not one to pine over things. The music business was beginning to change at that time and work for background vocalists just dried up. It wasn't just Motown. My brother Aaron owned a recording studio called Gloreca Records Inc. and Gloreca Publishing, named after his wife Gloria. He didn't have a lot of artists going there but Aretha's father used his studio. Aretha's family lived within walking distance of Motown but she never recorded there. The music scene in Detroit seemed to end. The whole city changed."

Cousin William Brooks adds, "Jackie is a full on Detroiter. She loves her city and she was never going to leave it when Motown left there. She loves her sports teams and she supports her city. She was always a family person and just too close to her family. I knew Jackie wouldn't want to go to L.A., and Marlene was probably not going to leave either. They weren't about to leave their families and friends. They worked a little after Motown left but not much. It dried up."

Emory says, "When Motown left here it was time for them to get jobs, think about the future, and have a retirement and benefits."

Paul Riser adds, "Motown moving to L.A. was the breakdown; the Detroit era of music is what survived in the long run. The reason it fell apart was he didn't take to L.A. what had made the company strong. He took the boat out but he didn't take the people. The people were what made the boat float. Those people were The Funk Brothers, The Andantes, the writers, and arrangers. The people that ran the boat were left behind, so it sank. It should not have happened like that."

R. Dean Taylor says, "I made the move to Los Angeles when Motown left Detroit. It was so depressing. They didn't have the sound anymore the way they did in Detroit."

"The ladies had to pack up the sidewalk and everything to start over again" says Sylvia Moy.

Coleman Castro shares, "When Motown left, the girls felt let down. They worked there for so many years, longer than most. All of the sudden Motown left and Louvain thought they would be going too at some point. Come to find out they left and didn't even tell them about it. And they never came back. Louvain and the girls were hearing rumors that Motown was leaving. They never thought that the music would end or that they wouldn't take their house-singers with them or at least keep them working in Detroit in some capacity on the recordings. They up and left and everything ended."

Harold Stone says, "Entertainment was not the same here after they were gone. The nightclubs didn't draw the crowds they used to. Things were on the way out after Motown left here."

Yvonne Rashida's insights: "When you ride the high wave for a minute and all of the sudden the bottom falls out of it, that's a hard adjustment for anyone. It doesn't matter who you are when your bottom drops out or what level of success you are at, it is an emotional thing for anyone and that is what many of the Motowners went through. So to cope with it they end up with the drugs and drinking. They try to find that high again and it's a difficult adjustment when your level of fame and fortune changes.

"For what The Andantes went through versus what their colleagues went through, they got the better deal. They may not have gotten their credit and acknowledgment, but they didn't crash as hard as some of their peers did. They know this. They have remained silent in the background all of these years and been very respectful to everyone. They sucked up the pain and went on with their lives and that was a good thing and their silence shows how much they respect the work they did. They have a lot of class. They need to express their truth about what they did now. Too much time has passed by. If people knew the extent of how their voices were used at the time, it would not have been acceptable."

Louvain has a lot to say about this moment in time. "I got Jackie and Marlene's last paycheck for them. I had to raise hell to get it. Marlene and Jackie called me in the middle of the night and told me that we didn't have any money. When they went to get their paycheck there was no money for us. I asked, 'What do you mean we don't have any money?' I told them I was going to look into it in the morning and call them. That was a hard day, a cold winter. I called Jackie and Marlene and told them to go get their money. The way it happened for The Funk Brothers was very different. They just had a note on the door when they came to work. Motown could have left town without ever paying us our last check. We had plenty to be hurt over, trust me, the way the whole thing happened. What hurt was the heartlessness of it.

"I went down to Motown and asked to see Berry. I said 'Someone in this place knows where he is.' They said Billie Jean was in a meeting. They kept telling me she was coming, she was almost done, she would be out soon. I went in and tore up a meeting that Billie Jean was having and I raised hell and disrupted her meeting. I wanted to see her. I demanded our money and I got it. They gave me mine. Jackie and Marlene's checks were ready when they went down there. I was so angry that they did this to us. I felt bad about what happened with Billie Jean, that she was the one who felt my wrath because I asked to see Berry. I rode to the bank with her to get the money. It makes me angry when I think about what they did and how they did us wrong. I don't know about anyone else's life or the details. It seemed that so many people crumbled after this happened and you have to ask why.

"Every word of this is true and there is much more that is true, but I will never say it. I have grown enough to know that you have to express your truth and be true to yourself. At the same time there are things that have to die. You cannot grow and flourish if you attack or harm others. I do not want to harm or hear that anyone is hurting from what I've done. I want people to be happy and I want to be happy.

"We knew something was wrong, but they kept saying everything was fine and to not worry about anything. We heard the rumors and they lied to us and denied it when we asked them if they were leaving. Everyone denied they were moving the company to California. As far as we were concerned, we didn't have a job anymore. They left town and there was never anything to go back to. We wondered why we couldn't do sessions from Detroit.

"Maybe everyone meant their intentions at the time they said it—in their heart it was true for them. People change and grow cold or heartless. In the confusion, you begin to blame. Eventually you know you have to clear it all out, forget what a person's intentions were, and depend on God.

"I was living at a location where I was told I either had to buy the place or vacate it. This is what hurt so bad, that I didn't have enough money to buy it. I had no notice whatsoever, that work was coming to an end. Since work ended for me, I was truly struggling with no way to raise even enough money to get a new place and start over. During this time, I was very angry and hurt with everyone. I felt as a group, and as individuals, we helped so many people make so much money. At that time I thought someone could have helped us out. All of the studios and people we had worked for and all the favors we did over the years…I was willing to do anything. There were no options. I called many people and just about begged for jobs.

"During this time, it was known by those close to me that the man in my life was Joe Hinton. He isn't the Joe who sang 'Funny How Time Slips Away'. My Joe also went by the name Jay Lewis. Joe was from Atlanta Georgia and we had been dating for a couple of years. I knew I had to move from where I was. The situation was either someone had to hire me quick so I could have money coming in to get an apartment, or I had to leave with Joe. Singer and songwriter Andre Williams went to bat for me. He sought out Mother Waddles who was building a ministry. I went to meet with her and I could have had a job with her. Joe Hinton told me he didn't think I qualified for the job and, looking back, I think he said that so he could get me to Atlanta.

"I called Mr. Wingate and told him I was in trouble and asked if he could please help me. Ed Wingate told me he'd get me an application for the factories, but I needed a job, not an application. I was so desperate and I knew nothing about a job like that. I never worked like that and I had already made up my mind to go by now. I couldn't wait to see if an application would go through. I needed a job and money fast.

"At the very last hour, and I mean the end of it, after I had already decided I was going to leave, Jackie and Marlene said that Barrett Strong would give us some work. But it was too late, I had to go. I was nervous and scared but I had to go. Agnes Bowles was so sad when I left. I felt incredibly guilty and bad about that. I also felt awful because I did not tell Jackie and Marlene the whole story of what was going on with me, and the fact that I was going to lose my duplex. I was just so hurt. I can't even really explain it now, so I know I didn't know how to explain it to them then. I just had to get out of Detroit. I had no options to stay there after Motown left. My situation included a lack of choices, you could say, after mistakenly believing in another's promises and words. I went to Georgia July 4th, 1973.

"I was angry with the ones who did not do right by us. There were certain people at the top of my list. I have since forgiven them and I can tell this now with a healed heart and spirit. My time at Motown was a little longer than Jackie and Marlene's. I worked there and it was all I knew as an income, and that was the same situation for them. We had no warning and it all changed. All of the work dried up for singers."

Marlene had to make some changes in her life also. "I had to get out in the world and find another job. This job ended. Many days I was mad and I was putting in applications everywhere. I won't deny I was hurt. I had to sit a minute and collect myself. It was a financial, emotional, and mental hurt. I had to keep moving and I couldn't sit and wallow because the singing had ended. I had to get going and raise my child and pay my bills. An interesting parallel for me was when I had a basement flood. Jackie and I both had floods and lost everything relevant to Motown. I lost all of the pictures and record albums. We had pictures that would make you cry. I really had nothing to wallow over once that part of my life ended. All of the memorabilia went too. There was really nothing for me to cry, look, or pine over. Our careers as singers completely dried up. We could no longer earn a living singing. I could've done that on and on because I loved it, but it ended. Jackie and I may have gotten an occasional call to sing, but they were few—few and far in between, and nothing that you could earn a living from. Eventually it was just time to call it quits to the whole idea of singing for a living.

"I'm glad that I had this attitude of 'on to the next thing' and that my feeling wasn't to pine over it or cry over what had ended and what was lost. That will truly eat you up inside if you carry that with you. I was hurt, very much so. I had hoped for more recognition as years passed on, more than what we were given. I had to put it behind me. I would still be hurting and crying if I hadn't. If we stood around and cried, we could have cried the hardest, loudest, and the longest. We sang on more of it than anyone and have no royalties or credit for that work. Some just couldn't heal or get past this and move on. You run into friends over the years, mainly at funerals and sadly and you see that some didn't move through the years very easily.

"These were trying times. My mother had died and I was a single mother trying to make ends meet and survive. I would work until I found something better. I did several different jobs. I made it through with a lot of prayer and letting go everyday. This was a work in progress to speak the dialogue I am speaking today. There were hard times and sorting to do, but you heal that over time. It was hard to move on but we had to have jobs, raise children, and have health insurance. From 1973 onward, I had very little contact with my fellow Motowners, except for Jackie.

"My life changed drastically. I had to get myself in bed at a decent hour because now I was getting up at 8:00am for work. I worked at a photography studio and I took classes at Jedco Business School; that's where I learned clerical skills. I worked at the University of Detroit in the Human Resources Department until 1978. I took the Civil Service Test and finally someone from the State of Michigan called and I said, 'Thank you, Jesus!' The date I started with the State is the same date as my last paycheck at Motown, January 16th.

"What got me through the transition of singing to having a normal life was a lot of prayer and that I had a son to raise. I couldn't start crying. During these times, my father was a major role model for my son and they did many sport activities together. My son was a lovely child and was a great artist; he could draw very well. My son and I have come through some very hard times together. I received so much love and support from my former in-laws, Mr. and Mrs. Thomas Barrow Sr. My son and I could not have made it through without them. My son has the background of prayer not just from me, but from his grandparents. He had a solid Christian background and spent a lot of time with my ex-husband's parents. In my life I have learned that you can't force spirituality or God on another. They have to learn from seeing and witnessing what works in your life. Everyone has to make the decision in life how they wish to walk with God."

Jackie was ready for a rainy day. "I didn't work for a year after they left Detroit and then I had to get a job. I was taught to save money for a rainy day that may come, and when the rainy day came, it was clear to me that the singing was over and I had to get a real job now. They weren't going to record here again, like they had. I never really understood why it had to happen that way. Even though some artists had left the label, new artists would have come from near and far to record for Motown. I started working at the Detroit Historical Museum for a little while.

"Some of our colleagues hit much harder times than we did. Anything other than singing was beneath them, so when they needed to work a nine-to-five job, they didn't want to do that. For us, when the work ended, we had to keep on going. We loved singing, but it was time to work and pay the bills. Marlene and Louvain, they had young children. There was no time to cry over the fact the singing had ended, we all had responsibilities and families. The downfall of many was the move to California by Motown. You can't give yourself a label and say 'This is what I am and this is what I do.' So many ended up bitter and they still are. You're not accomplishing anything by being upset and bitter about something that happened forty plus years ago. As for us, it was more of a hurt that we didn't get the credit we deserved or the acknowledgment. So many people were chasing fame and fortune. Many became bitter when others got it instead of them or when they didn't get it at all.

"Fame didn't earn some people respect. They may have had the money and achieved the fame, but they didn't win friends or respect. The days of Motown may be forgotten, but not for those who lived at that time and worked for that company. You can't change how things happened and some people have not forgotten the way things happened to them or to their friends. When you carry animosity over the years, it hurts only you. The people you stay mad at don't care and don't even know you're mad at them half the time. They've gone on with their lives and don't even know you're angry. I'm not one to put on or pretend I like someone if and when I don't. I have always spoken my mind. If someone who wasn't nice is having hard times, that wouldn't make me happier.

"In 1974, I landed a good job with the City of Detroit. It was alright for me and it was an interesting adjustment. I actually liked it very much. I worked for the Water Department. There were no more egos. Entertainers are very ego-driven and when you're in it you don't really notice it until you're not in it anymore. You can see a huge difference. I loved the singing, music, and my friends; but the egos I did not miss. I enjoyed my job and got along well with my co-workers. Marlene and I got lucky; she worked for the State and I for the City. At one point, she and her son came to live with me and it was like having a sister live here.

"I lost all of my photographs in a basement flood. Then I had a break-in where they stole the photo albums. I had pictures from all of the picnics, parties, sessions, and sometimes when we were just down at Hitsville taking pictures and welcoming back our friends after they came off the road. I had pictures of them getting off the bus. I never saw any of those pictures turn up anywhere so whoever stole them didn't circulate them. It's sad because they were sentimental to us and they probably ended up in the trash somewhere."

With Marlene and Jackie settling into regular jobs there were many life lessons along the way. Both of them were at Florence Ballards' funeral in 1976. Marlene recalls, "Flo was such a nice person. It was overwhelming to be at her funeral. She was just so young and it didn't seem possible for her to be gone. People were overwhelmed and the lines to get in to see her were up the street. People were waiting for Mary and Diana to get there. Everyone was caught up in it. This was so sad to me because she was so young. It was unreal. The night before at the viewing you couldn't even get near the place. For me it started and ended with Florence's death. The people were falling out of the sky to be at her funeral. It really was the circus people have described over the years. That's what I witnessed. It was at Rev. Franklin's church and it wasn't big enough to fit everyone who wanted to see her.

"The crowds spent the night in the streets. The police had to get the people back so the funeral procession could come through and the family could get into the church. The night before was just as bad as the day of the funeral. The people just kept coming for Flo. The people, of course, wanted to see Mary and Diana. It was unreal that a Supreme was gone now. They were begging the people to get back so people could get in. Her husband Tommy and the girls finally were seated, and then Mary and Diana came in.

"My God, such a commotion trying to get the people calm so they could start the service. I had never seen anything like it. Jackie and I were sitting in the choir stands. Stevie Wonder slipped in quietly and no one even noticed him. You realize the phenomenon that The Supremes were as you witness something like this. By 1976, The Supremes had been long over. The emotions that they evoked then still remain today.

"The same experience happened at David Ruffin's funeral. This tells you that what happened altogether was a once in a lifetime connection. When it was lost, chaos occurred. The fans feel very connected to this music and to the voices that created it.

When you have a voice that is connected to a great talent like a Ruffin or a Marvin, they feel that loss deeply. Florence was lost too young and we never saw her full potential and what could have been. It was a very special time and very special people came from that time. Mary Wells didn't have any hits after she left Motown and Flo had a hard time getting work and singing again. I believe her heart broke when she could no longer sing. It affected her."

Jackie adds, "I went to her funeral. I was waiting to go into the church and Carolyn Franklin said, 'Why are you standing out here? Come on in and go with me.' She and I sat in the choir stands along with Marlene. It was a very sad, sad funeral. That's a sad story anyway. Florence didn't live that far from me so I would see her from time to time. A niece of Flo's is married to one of my second cousins."

Marlene continues, "In 1979, I lost the man who I called 'daddy'. My son graduated from school in 1979 as well. In 1980, I married Harold Tate from Inkster, Michigan. We dated for two years. We had a very nice wedding in the chapel at our church. Our reception was in Aaron Hicks' backyard. Mildred Dobey played the music at my wedding. I lost a sibling in 1988 and my birth-father in 1989. We began losing our brothers and sisters in song. It's very sad when the ones closest to you in song have passed on. Obie and Lawrence were very hard to lose. Marvin was hard to shake and that was just devastating to all of us. You have to realize that we spent so much time with these people. It was just shock and hurt when they left so young. Marvin was so talented and it was sad that his life had such turmoil at the end. He had such a good, good heart. What I witnessed with Tammi was she was so young and a really sweet person. Seemed to grow up fast, she too died young.

"If someone came to me for advice about this business, I would tell them to make sure to read everything and know everything. Know the fine print. It was too late for us. We were naïve and we thought our agreement was one thing and it was another thing. We trusted blindly. You should always know what you're in. So many artists became consumed by drugs and drinking because of the pitfalls and the cutthroat things that happened to them. Drugs are everywhere in the entertainment industry. It's a common thread in this business, especially the music industry. You have to be balanced in some way before you get in this business and have some grounding or you can get caught up in that and eaten up by it. The temptations are constantly there with fame and fortune.

"There are people who will hang with you and say they love you, but they only love you for what you can do for them. They do not truly love you. Most artists are vulnerable people. They are also people who need reinforcement and oftentimes they do not see or realize that their environment of support is coming from people who don't love or support them or even really care about them. To maintain a music group and have success as singers in a partnership, you have to have a foundation of friendship and trust and must love one another. To sustain, you have to like each other. You are together all the time, on the road, in rehearsal, in the studio, onstage. That bond has to be strong. It has to be closer than family at times. The Andantes had a foundation of love and friendship. We enjoyed each other and would be there for one another through hard times. I feel we are friends first, The Andantes second, and that is the bond that we share.

"I would tell any singer now to make certain they knew how their voice is being used when it comes to sampling and what have you. People get paid for that now. I know I was naive about this back then, so there's no need for me to say I knew exactly what was happening when it came to how these things were credited every single time. We would sing on things where we didn't know who the song was for. We would go in and do a track and then it would become a Diana lead or maybe a song for Martha, or Marvin. We should have been writing down our sessions and dates. We also had the non-Motown sessions. I remember names of people I worked with, but not really songs. I wish one of us, if not all of us, had written things down.

"We didn't have the foresight to write it down. For the times we recorded in Chicago, it would be so helpful in compiling our discography now and the history. We just went, did the work with the producers, and came back home. We never thought about it again. We did so many favors for people and friends back then where we sang when someone needed girls on a record. The whole reason we went to Motown was because we were helping Popcorn as a favor. Everyone was helping each other make records and music back then. Who would have thought all of these years later what we did would still be here? Life went on and I wish I had written it down. You don't think about that part of your life again until it comes up or you hear the songs and then realize there's so much you just don't have written down.

"We simply didn't know we were making history at the time. There should be some way for us to flip back and find out why we weren't compensated since we were in the union. I would tell a person starting out in this business now to write down every session they did, with whom, and what song, so that forty years later when your voice is on TV and in movies you can say that is you singing and you can prove it. Over the years you see how many people from our era of music took legal action over one thing or another. I wish someone could have stood in my shoes and seen what it feels like when those thoughts crossed my mind. The next minute those thoughts would be gone and life would go on. I couldn't let that get on my mind for too long. Above all, life is to enjoy what you do, even though it is a job and it is work sometimes. Enjoy and live in that moment, because that moment will sure enough end. And keep a diary of it.

"I know we all have our trials and tribulations. I know that Louvain being in Atlanta alone was hard for her and it bothered me that she suffered so much alone down there. We really didn't know all of the facts when she was down there and doing this book brought us together in a sense because we're learning about her life at that time. No doubt about it, we all love each other very much, but at the time it was hard to understand why she felt she had to go there by herself with her sons and go through so much heartache alone down there. Everyone has their ups and downs through life. We were hit by the same experience. Jackie and I had each other. Louvain was alone and that bothered both of us so much.

"I wish she stayed here where she had people who could be there for her. I thought I had it bad until I talk to Louvain about it and learned how bad it really was for her down there. She was private and held it in. She didn't want to burden anyone with what was happening with her. She kept it to herself and rode through it. Singing was her whole life. It was her outlet for her trials and heartache. When the singing ended, her trials really had begun because now she had no outlet. I look back and think about it. She didn't have a close girlfriend like Jackie and I had. She was alone down there and her life was wrapped up in keeping her family together. The outlet for her stress and heartache was the singing. That was no longer in her life everyday as a job. Everyone had a scar and processed it in a different way.

"Perhaps it was not intentional, but the scar is there and most of us had to heal it. We were witness to so much and what happened to us, The Funk Brothers and many others; I don't think it can ever be documented properly. A once-in-a-lifetime moment. You're a major piece of the puzzle and left out. I feel it has been a matter of doing what is right by us, and we have to do that for ourselves, our history, and our families. God has his way of working in our lives. The only way this can be told accurately is if we enlighten people. The only thing Berry said in his book about it was one sentence, that we were the backup singers.

"I had questions during this time. Why was everyone so unsettled by their experiences and their contributions? Why was there no compensation for what they did? I'm not saying that I, Louvain, and Jackie should be living in a castle on the mountain top, but we've struggled very hard and should have a house to show for the work that we did. There was certainly enough money made from the Motown sound to compensate the contributors. I wouldn't want to trade places with some of the people who had the fame and fortune. Being compensated and acknowledged is what I am talking about. We had to get used to the fact that this was never going to happen for us. We would read in the paper that Motown had sold for so much or how a Jobete catalog is worth a certain amount. It just makes you mad if you let it get a hold of you. You cannot let it get on you. I don't understand it, but I also don't worry over it because life goes on."

Life did move on. Marlene and Jackie would join Louvain and many other Motown alumni for recording sessions produced by Ian Levine. Jackie recalls, "When Ian Levine came over here from England, Marlene and I had our full-time jobs. Some of the others had been singing or trying to get their music off the ground again. We sang on those sessions. For us it wasn't a great thing because we couldn't leave our jobs here in Detroit. We were unable to go to England and promote those recordings. It was nice that we were able to see everyone again here in Detroit. What happened financially afterwards was not a good experience for most everyone who was involved with him. He didn't compensate many people. What baffles me about the music business is that there is so much money and enough money to make sure people get compensated, but instead you encounter these people who want the whole pie for themselves and try to beat you out of your share of the pie. They couldn't have that pie if you hadn't put your voice on that record in the first place. This was like round two of what we had gone through once already in our music careers. This was the last time The Andantes sang together.

"We had several deaths in our family. Two of my sisters' children passed away young. I lost my mother in 1986, my aunt in 1990. My brother Aaron and my sister Annette are both gone. Most of my immediate family is gone. Many of our colleagues passed away so young. I cannot believe all but one of The Temptations is gone. It's difficult to ponder at times what some of our colleagues were going through. I never really understood the attraction to drugs in our business. I wasn't caught up in drugs even though I was around it. As a group, we saw a lot of it, but none of us ever had any problems with alcohol or drugs.

"Before my mother died, she encouraged me to lose weight. I lost about 85 pounds after I turned forty. My mother wanted me to get in better shape because I was getting older and she didn't want me to have any health problems later in life. I went to the diet program ERASE. I never felt bad when I was a larger person, so I didn't do it to feel better. My mother had a good point in that once you get to a certain age it gets harder to get the weight off. You do feel better when you eat properly. I think food addiction and losing weight is a much harder addiction than some other things because you have to eat to survive. You don't have to smoke or drink to stay alive. Keeping a healthy diet and staying balanced, now that is work. For me, I just like food. I like a good meal and I enjoy eating. I always had someone to cook for me up until my mother and auntie passed away.

"My mother had a heart attack and left here very quickly. I called her on the phone that day. She was staying with my brother. I told my mom that I bought a new car but to not tell anyone. We talked a few minutes and then we hung up. I called her back and I said, 'Did you tell anybody yet?' She started laughing and said, 'Girl, no. We just hung up the phone. If I was going tell it, I haven't had time.' I asked her if she had talked to my auntie today and she said, 'No.' I then said, 'Don't be a motor-mouth and tell her momma, I want to tell her I got a new car and surprise her too.' So she said, 'Ok, I'm not going tell her.' Then we hung up. About ten minutes went by and I called back. I said, 'You haven't told anyone about the car have you?' She just fell out laughing and said, 'Look girl, I have to go to the bathroom. Don't call here for twenty minutes.' She went to the bathroom and called out to my brother and told him she couldn't breathe. He took her to the couch and put a pillow behind her head, sat her up, and my mother died. She didn't suffer at all and she went quickly. She had a good laugh at the end with me and I had a good memory of talking with her.

"Our family always had a great sense of humor. I told my aunt and sister that my momma sure could keep a secret. She didn't tell anyone that I got a new car. When something dies with you, that is really keeping a secret. I have such fond memories of my mother. Every time I think of my mother it's something funny. She was warm and sweet. She was a comical person who made us laugh all through our lives. I've never had a bad day since she died, where I felt bad or guilty. My life and memories are so wonderful and positive. My mother enjoyed her life and remembering her makes me feel good.

"My mother loved Red Lobster restaurant, we would go out to dinner there. She lived a good life and went everywhere. She loved to travel. One time she was in Acapulco, Mexico with her traveling buddies. They went to the casinos and she won some money. The day she was supposed to be coming home she called to tell me she was going to Hawaii with some other ladies she had met. I said 'Momma, they could be axe-murderers.' She said to me, 'Well, if they are you can come to Hawaii to claim my body because I am going to Hawaii with these ladies to have fun.'

"Everybody says I am just like her. My mother just had a great fun about her. We'd be out shopping and I'd say, 'Momma, can we eat something?' and she would say, 'Didn't you eat yesterday?' I'm a lot like my mother. She was just a funny, happy person."

Emory adds, "Jackie was very close to our mother and spent enormous amounts of time with her. She tended to her every need and after all of us kids left home Jackie was still there. After our mother moved to a senior citizen home, Jackie was with her everyday. That was her right-hand lady."

I'll Walk With God

This is Jackie's mother's favorite hymn

I'll Walk with God from this day on.
His helping hand I'll lean upon.
This is my prayer, my humble plea,
May the Lord be ever with me.

There is no death, tho' eyes grow dim.
There is no fear when I'm near to Him.
I'll lean on Him forever
And He'll forsake me never.

He will not fail me
As long as my faith is strong,
Whatever road I may walk along.

I'll Walk with God, I'll take His hand.
I'll talk with God, He'll understand.
I'll pray to Him, each day to Him
And He'll hear the words that I say.

His hand will guide my throne and rod
And I'll never walk alone
While I walk with God.

Words by Paul Francis Webster
Music by Nicholas Brodszky
Singer is Mario Lanza

Louvain's Cousin Ruthie Satterfield.

Photo credit: The Louvain Demps Collection

A pensive Louvain (left)

Ella and Ruthie Satterfield with Martha Reeves and Louvain (below)

Louvain Demps Collection

Max Jr. and Michael Demps. Louvain's handsome sons, all grown up.

Photo credit: Louvain Demps Collection

Jackie's mother Clara with aunt Ethel

Photo credit: Jackie Hicks Collection

Lawrence and mother Marlene

Photo credit: Marlene Barrow-Tate Collection

Jackie (in black shirt) with sister Annette and her children...Brett is behind and Bridgett and Kevin are on the right.

Photo Credit: Jackie Hicks Collection

The Hicks Family; Annette, Aaron, Emory, Jackie, and mother

Jackie, Marian, Emily and Edith.

Photo credits: Jackie HIcks Collection

Marlene and Harold Tate

Photo credit: Marlene Barrow-Tate Collection

Jackie with sister Annette

Photo credit: Jackie Hicks Collection

Jackie's cousin, William Brooks

Photo credit: Jackie Hicks Collection

Midnight Train To Georgia

With Detroit and Motown behind The Andantes now, they each had to move on in their lives. Louvain says, "Although it's not a Motown song and we don't sing on it, that 'Midnight Train to Georgia' got me in a lot of trouble, not to mention brought me quite a lot of heartache."

Cousin Ruthie's daughter is Ella Satterfield and she recalls saying goodbye to Louvain. "I was about seven years old and she decided to make the move to Atlanta, Georgia. Oh, my God, that was the saddest day. Louvain came in and she sat me down. She always called me 'Ella Wella'. She told me, 'You know I love and you have always been my Ella Wella.' Louvain always wanted a little girl but didn't have one. She would always pamper me and tell me I was her little girl. She said, 'You're still going to be my little girl, but I'm moving to Georgia and that's really far away.' I was just so devastated because I was still a little girl and I was still grieving from Louvain's mother dying. Her mom had raised me along with my mother. She assured me we would remain close. It just felt like the end of the world. It was just horrible. I hated it. We saw her one last time and then the day she moved she called me. It just was awful."

The flight to Atlanta was a memorable one and Louvain remembers the heartbreak all too well, "We flew to Atlanta and the boys brought our St. Bernard on the plane with us. Joe was supposed to have everything ready when we got there. Our apartment was not ready when we arrived. It was a holiday weekend. Lady Darwin was our dog but we called her Pony. She had nowhere to go when we arrived and when the apartment was ready in a few days they told us no pets allowed. Joe ended up paying some teens to take care of her and eventually we lost her and that broke our hearts. She was our family.

He made promises to me that it'd be us together if I moved to Atlanta; this was the kind of stuff you see in movies. It took me some time to realize this wasn't going to happen the way it was promised. Joe ultimately left Atlanta with another woman. I was down here alone with my sons and really had to begin again all alone. I asked God to get me out of this relationship mess, so I was done with him before he left here. God got me out of the mess, thank goodness.

"A couple of years had passed and I was going to the post-office one day. I was driving down the road and I saw this man with a gas can walking down the road, so I stopped to help him. When he got into the car, he was nice and I was nice to him too. It was Joe Hinton. I had a real strong desire to light up and smoke. I thought to myself like the cartoon characters do with that little grin, 'I can just light up one cigarette.' Then I realized it was my car and I would have burned down my own car. At first, Joe was really good for my boys but our relationship ran its course and I would found myself alone again. I was too embarrassed to let my friends know I had made a mistake and I was too prideful to ask for help. I was determined to make it here on my own, so I stuck it out and I raised my sons in Atlanta, alone. I didn't even tell my family how bad it got. I was ashamed it had gotten so bad.

"A little bit of bitterness creeps out when I remember these stories. I just wanted to sing, raise my boys, and have a good man in my life and things went against me for too long to have that. Now I sing, I have raised my boys, and I don't need a man in my life. The first line of duty now was to get a job. I put in an application to the Georgia Retardation Center. I got a job there teaching retarded children for five years—five of the longest years of my life. You think you have problems until you see what problems other people have. I saw real problems at the center.

"With these children, it was hard for me. The people there weren't very nice and I had to make that up to the kids. My job was late at night and I was to make sure everything was okay. In the morning, I was to get everyone dressed and ready for the day. This was a real learning lesson for me in having compassion. At the time I needed to have some compassion for others, I was mad and angry. God puts you where you can work through some things. The children helped me through that. My state of mind was not great at this time. I was terribly depressed about life and my situation and what had happened back in Detroit. Working there was really hard and a challenge because I was a singer at heart. I was borderline suicidal a couple of times and then I would get a jolt back to reality. What would happen to my boys if I wasn't here?"

Michael Demps adds, "We had some very hard times when we first came to Atlanta and it was tough for her as a single parent. When I look back on it now, when she worked steadily at Motown she had the means to provide for us. Then to come here, she had a much harder time. The best way I can describe my mother is very giving. There were times where we didn't have much, including food. She worked two jobs to support us and we didn't get to see her much."

Louvain continues, "I had to get through this. Working at the center took some of my harsh feelings away. I had to have a heart to deal with these children because they needed love and caring. Some of the adults were mean to me and mean to the kids. I had no experience in this field and I only went there because I really needed a job. Once I saw the injustices to these children, I think that's what made me stay as long as I did. I saw them give unnecessary medicines and surgeries. They knew I liked to read there late at night and they would turn all of the lights out on me. This was a life-changing experience for me and I worked through a lot while I was there.

"Late at night, I would hear us on the radio singing with The Supremes or The Four Tops and here I was in this retardation center. All I wanted to do was sing again. I sang along but there was a pain deep inside of me. The joy I felt from singing had left my life. The people at the center really didn't believe me when I told them what I had done and I was too mad to tell anyone all of the details about it. I had to put on my application I was a singer. They had the 'whatever' attitude if one of our songs came on.

"I found out that you could be at your lowest state of mind and still sink lower if you allow that to happen. When I told people I sang at Motown, they just didn't want to believe it. During this time, I stopped telling people and I suppressed it. That clogs you up more when you can't express yourself. I owed it to my sons to overcome things like this. These other little hurts in the aftermath of it all made me stronger. I just had to keep going.

"They assigned me to a little six-year old boy named Jody. He was very small but very strong. He had to be restrained and he was retarded, spastic, and a self-mutilator. I came to love this little guy so much. He would beat himself. He had no nose from his mutilating himself. He was real strong and real mean and I was just so fond of him because he was a fighter. He was the person they assigned to me, thinking I couldn't handle the place or him and leave. I tell you, Jody and I worked through some things together. I was to get him dressed and ready by 7AM.

To put one shoe on him was a fight, and frustrating. He would squint his eyes because he didn't talk, and when he squinted you knew he was going to give it to you some kind of way. When you tried to dress him, he would stiffen up like a board. You couldn't move him for nothin'. He wouldn't let you dress him. Jody didn't sleep well. He laid awake a lot and one night I was with him beside his bed and I told him, 'Look here, you are smaller than me and in the morning I am going to dress you and I don't care what you do to stop me.' He understood me. We got through that morning. I started clapping and I guess he thought I was a crazy one. The other people who worked there didn't want to deal with him because he didn't have a nose. It was upsetting to look at him. It was my golden opportunity to work with him. As time went by I began to talk with him late at night and I would tell him that I loved him. He didn't talk but he started to call me by the name of 'Juice' so I was Juice to him. It was the only thing he could say. I knew that was my name. I taught him to say 'yes', so when I asked him if he felt good he would say 'yeah'. He had feelings and he knew I loved him and protected him. Some people were cruel and would say things in front of him and he understood what they were saying. I wouldn't let them hurt his little feelings anymore. Jody's brother was also in the center and he was spastic too, but he wasn't a mutilator.

"These boys were the products of incest. Their grandfather was their father. I came to love him and I'd watch his eyes and could tell he loved me too. At one point he developed kidney stones and had to go to an outside hospital. The center called me and told me not to come to work that day but to report to the hospital and give him his medicine. He wouldn't take it for the doctors and nurse at the hospital. As soon as I got there, his eyes lit up and I said, 'Jody, why aren't you taking your medicine? You need to take your medicine, now open your mouth and take it.' He took it that simple. He was my friend and I treated him as my friend the whole five years I was there.

"There was another little boy named Leonard and he was breakable. I got to the point where I could pick him up. He wasn't retarded but he could break a bone just by turning over. Then there was Loretta, who wasn't retarded. She just had a speech impediment, a 'lazy tongue' I called it. I went to a meeting and told them that she needed testing. I went to them and told them she wasn't supposed to be in here, so with the help of one woman she got out.

"One day everyone was talking that a Supreme had died, I could not believe it. That hurt me so deeply. I thought there was no way a Supreme could be dead this soon, she was too young. It broke my heart and it took me a long time to shake Florence's death. That got on me and in my spirit for a long time. I could relate in a sense to what I believe she felt back then, her broken heart. She just wanted to sing.

"The Retardation Center was a hard place to be and when I left it felt like someone had lifted a manhole cover finally and I was able to come out. It was hard because of the adults who worked there. It was a dark place and there was a rumor that it was built over an old cemetery. I'm sensitive to energies of that nature so I would see things and hear things, or feel things. By the end of the five years, I had to get out of there. I had been placed there for a reason and the reason was over. I never found out if the cemetery rumor was true, but the place had strange happenings and it was a dark place with dark energies around it. They have since torn it down. I felt bad that I left Jody and his brother. I had a talk with him and I felt his spirit understood. The last time I saw him he had a sparkle in his eye and laughter because I made him laugh.

"My sons needed me and I had to keep going. I put them in schools that were close to our apartment. I was also lucky enough to connect with Richard Law and sing some jingles for TV and radio. The jingles weren't consistent enough to pay the bills and take care of the apartment. It made me happy to sing because if I didn't have that, I don't know how I would have made it. I had to keep going because I was still hurting at this time and mad and if I had stopped moving I know I would have surely died. I met Richard through Joe Hinton. We sang at GRC Records and when the pay was not consistent, I took a part time job at Northside

Hospital. I worked three jobs to pay the bills and I had good benefits. GRC was founded by Mike Thevis. Many people were coming into town and at the time people were recording here. They thought it could be a hot spot for recording such as Detroit was or Chicago. We worked with so many people like Bohannon and others. It was a busy place for recording. I would even see my old friend Eddie Kendricks. They told me that he was here and he wanted to see me. He always made my heart light up. I came down with my friend Francine Owens to the studio where he was recording and when I got there, he had everyone in the room give me a standing ovation. I could not believe it. R. Dean Taylor had come down to Atlanta to record at GRC.

"Mike, the owner, was good to us and we had the opportunity to record many sessions. Mike did a little bit of everything at his studio. Richard and I recorded backgrounds along with a woman named Kim, a friend of his from Nashville. Mary Fielder was another who did background work with us. We worked at several studios. GRC Records and then RKM Records is where we did the commercial jingles. We also went to Nashville to record."

Richard Law helps fill in the Atlanta years. "I had the opportunity to join a jingle company, plus I knew a guy with GRC Records. Louvain was beginning to sing at GRC as well. GRC is General Recording Corporation. It was started in Atlanta by a business man named Michael Thevis. I didn't know any singers in Atlanta. I was hanging out and writing jingles. Then Louvain and I started singing jingles together.

We did a lot of work in Atlanta. We did TJ Swan Wine, Coca-Cola, Schlitz Malt Liquor Beer. There were different levels for jingles and commercials. There were local, regional, and nationals. We got a lot of airplay with the jingles. We did the Coca-Cola commercials when they switched from 'It's The Real Thing', to 'Have A Coke and A Smile.' We sang on those. We did a jingle with BJ Thomas for Muscular Dystrophy along with the Atlanta Symphony. It was a sixty-piece orchestra. The thing that was happening at the GRC Label is they were bringing artists from Philly and Chicago to record in Atlanta. We did an album with Clarence Carter and we did sessions with Loleatta Holloway. I think that was some of the first records Louvain and I sang on together.

"We did a tribute show for Bill Lowery. It was his 25th anniversary in the music business. We backed up all the acts from Joe South, Tommy Roe, Billy Joe Royal, and The Classics IV. Bill had bought an old school and turned it into a studio. Tons of hits came out of that studio. Louvain and I worked there recording for a long time. We called ourselves 'The Richard Law Singers'. The mainstay was Louvain and there was a woman named Barbara South who sang with us. She was Joe South's sister in-law.

"We did records with Meadow Lark Lemon and Major Lance. We did sessions with John Edwards who went on to be with The Spinners. We recorded with Peabo Bryson and Paul Davis was the one producing those records. Paul went on to have hits in the 70s. 'I Go Crazy' was one of his big hits. We worked with Lobo and sang on some of their records. We did a lot of everything together. We did a record with The Funk Brothers in Atlanta. They came in for Joe Hinton. He produced it and sang. It was a song I wrote. Paul Riser did the arrangement. It was called, 'We've Got Each Other'. I was just thrilled that these guys played on it and Paul Riser worked on it. Louvain and I did the background vocals.

"I grew up fascinated with music and actually watched the Nashville scene grow. I was familiar with Motown as well. Being a singer, I knew when I heard the records of Motown that the voices were the same people singing. I knew there was a collective sound they were going for. I figured there was an in-house vocal group that they were using. I didn't know it was The Andantes until much later. I knew when I heard those records; they had the same voices on all of them.

"My life and career has been an assortment and a variety of music. When you are a studio singer, you don't know what to expect until you get there. Sometimes you don't know the song or the artists, just the producer who hired you. We did the music for the film *Black Starlet.* It was thrilling to hear your music and singing in a movie theatre. It was like the poor man version of *Mahogany* and the only person I recognized from it was Al Lewis from *The Munsters."*

Louvain continues, "There was a man name Randy Roman who knew Richard Law and he helped me get a job at The Record

Shack. This was a big record warehouse. In between sessions, I had to find regular jobs. The Pips had come in and I was embarrassed that I was working there, even though I was feeling better about myself and life was a little better. That was my foolish pride again. I was too prideful for people to know I was working there and not singing. I worked there for a while and put the gospel catalog together.

"They told me I could get someone to help me so they let me hire my son Michael and he worked there with me. He was a teenager. We organized the whole place. There was a lady who worked there and she wanted the job I had. She would go around to the sections of music and scramble them up so it would look like I wasn't doing a good job. I was always going behind fixing it again. I didn't get to it fast enough one time and I was fired. I cried over that so much. Randy and his wife were so good to me. I loved the record shop because it put me close to music again. I was also happy because I was learning new things.

"There was a moment when there was enough money to go back home to Detroit. I asked the boys and I left it up to them. They told me they wanted to stay because it was green all year in Atlanta and the winters were not as bad. They liked it here so we stayed. So many things happened during those years in Atlanta. I promised the boys I would get us out of the apartment and into a house. I was able to do that in the late 70s. I saved and saved and I bought us an inexpensive house. One time Richard and I were working for Bohannon and we met his beautiful wife and children. He was getting his car serviced in Detroit and he had his driver Robert take me and the boys back on a free car trip home. We didn't have any money at this time. We were talking about Detroit and he said his driver was going to take care of his car and that we should go along. We were able to go into Detroit for a weekend to see Ruthie and Ella. It was one of the kindest things to happen for us while we were in Atlanta. I just loved him for doing that for us. I would work for him anytime he called us. He was producing an album and I came in and put all of the harmonies and the background on it.

"Richard and I worked with a Caucasian woman named Sammy Johns and she looked exactly like Diana Ross, it was amazing. We were doing a five-night gig with Sammy and we rehearsed with her. She didn't sound like Diana, but she looked just like her. We sang so well with her. I had a solo on stage where I did a Louie Armstrong impression. During the intermission, she went to her room. Her manager came to us and said that Sammy wasn't used to singing with other people onstage. They paid us for the rest of the night and the rest of the week and we never saw her again.

"I was the voice of Magnolia on recordings for Pinnacle Records. Magnolia was a group with no lead vocal yet. They were trying to launch it and couldn't find a lead person. It was a good record and they were hoping for a smash with it. They called me and asked me to come be the front person for this press conference and photo shoot and they would pay me. I was behind very badly on my house payment so I told them that I needed five house payments, so they did it. They paid it and flew me down to Nashville. It was a huge party and press event. I was the person they were announcing as Magnolia. This was a miracle for me and the boys. What kind of miracle could have happened where someone came and paid my house note for five months? The whole thing just fell away. The whole Magnolia thing never happened. I never even saw the pictures from the press event. I look back at this and I think I was given this because I treated the kids at the Retardation Center right. I had done something to receive God's miracles, because he saved us. He sent me angels. They made sure they paid me and took good care of me and they even paid the house payment directly to the lender. Pinnacle Records folded and I never heard from them again. To me that was a true miracle.

"There was a Toyota national commercial I was up for. It was going to pay very good money. When I went to the audition, they knew I was from Motown so they would ask me to sing like Diana Ross. I would do my best Diana voice and I ended up getting the gig. This was going to pay $16,000. Sadly, this was a missed opportunity because I got the job, and all of the sudden Toyota went on strike and so it never happened.

"During the years when I was distant with everyone and everything relating to Motown, I thought about Jackie and Marlene a lot. I thought about them the most actually. I would think about them all of the time and what we did together. There are so many memories inside of me. The memories are a big part of my life and so are Marlene and Jackie. It just hurt me so much that our lives had to change like that.

"I joined the music union and I hadn't worked in a while. Tom Evans from the union called and told me he had a job for me. He was always very nice to me. He told me it was for Six Flags. He told me the pay amount and where to go. I was so relieved and grateful and then he said, 'I don't know how many times you'll have to ride it.' I said, 'What?' I couldn't take the job because I was unable to ride the Scream Machine over and over and over for this commercial they were filming. I just started crying and the kids came home and said, 'Momma, what's wrong?' I told them I got a job riding the Scream Machine and I couldn't do it. The boys were so sweet. They offered to ride it for me.

"By the 1980s things were looking up. I became an ordained minister and I was working things out in my life. I had found my niche working with children. I began to build credentials. Every job I had, there was a child who was uncontrollable and needed more supervision. I could tune in on the one who needed it the most. I always had this thing for the underdog.

"I was riding home on the bus one day and I saw a place called, Academy of Early Learning. I noticed it was a big building, where kids were playing and I was always job hunting. The next day I got off the bus and went inside. As I was in there I talked myself into a Teacher's Assistant job. It was remarkable. I started out with the after-school kids who were a little older. They grew to like me. I was a tough and short lady to them, but I loved them. I worked there about three years. The bosses there couldn't figure out how I was stern and how the children still loved me. I had really wonderful kids. It escalated to me having a class of my own because I helped all of the kids so much after school. My class was called Sharing & Caring. My methods of teaching were unorthodox but they worked very well with the kids.

"I was always looking in the papers for jobs, so I answered an ad for a woman who was running childcare from her home. She was looking for someone to help and teach and I was hired right away. Then I was fired and I went to jail. It was coming up on Halloween. I was doing very well with the kids since they were preschoolers. She was putting up decorations of spiders, bugs, skeletons, and other things. I don't like things like that and I told her that some of the kids may be a little scared too. She said she was going to put a coffin out as a decoration. I told her that I wouldn't let her do that and scare the children. We ended up in a big fight and she tried to beat me up and threw all my stuff in the street. I grabbed her by the throat and threw her through the window and I went to jail. I was only in jail overnight. When they were booking me, they asked what I had done to get in jail. The judge threw the case out and he asked me if I wanted her to go to jail for a night. I told him no because it was not a pleasant place for anyone to be.

"I would become the nanny for a beautiful family, The Boltzs. Bob and Christine Boltz had two children, Adam and Sarah. I began working for them when Adam was six months old. I stayed with them for seven years and I was at both Adam and Sarah's High School Graduation. They surprised Adam by having me come to his graduation.

I was the nanny for Bob Fierer's children for several years, the boys were John Michael, Mark, and his daughter was Gillian. I started working for The Attorney Meg Campbell and Dr. Richard Gitomer in 1990, Richard and Meg. I have been with them since their children were born. Austin is a very pretty girl, she is seventeen. She used to play with me and hide things from me in boxes and bags. I had so many jobs in Atlanta but this one is the very best one. They are good to me and I love them as my family. They love Motown too. David is their son, we call him Campbell. Both children have the middle name of Campbell. When David was a little boy, I would put him on my lap and sing to him, a little song he liked."

Campbell Cake
Campbell Cake
You sure got what it takes – uh huh
You're mom and daddy's bouncing baby boy
You're mame and grandad's pride and joy – uh huh
Campbell Cake
Campbell Cake
You sure got what it takes – uh huh

Meg Campbell & Richard Gitomer share this, "Before our daughter Austin was born we advertised for a nanny and had very little luck finding someone who was acceptable. One day we answered the doorbell and Louvain was on the doorstep. She came very highly recommended. She shares the music history with our children. Our children absolutely love and adored her and she loves them. They have bonded and they are fiercely loyal to her and protective of her. She has been a wonderful part of their lives and an essential part of their growing up. She reinforces all of the values we have taught our children. They have perspectives on the world that they may not have had. We found out she was a singer from Motown because Mary Wilson was in town promoting a book. Louvain's car wasn't working so we drove her down to see Mary. When we got there Mary introduced Louvain to the whole crowd at the book signing."

Louvain continues, "The 80s and early 90s were some difficult times as far as Motown. For starters, Marvin Gaye's father shot and killed him. This shook me up and still does. My own father died one Thanksgiving morning. We would lose other legendary singers from our past life: David Ruffin, Eddie Kendricks, and Mary Wells. It was sad to see our colleagues die so young. The last time I saw Mary she came to me and asked me to pray for her. It wasn't long after that we found out she had cancer. I called her and she was unable to talk. I was able to talk with the woman who was caring for her. I was able to tell Mary that I loved her.

Hattie Littles was another who I befriended over the years. She would tell me how her end with Motown really happened. In the early days she was to open for Marvin Gaye and a gun battle broke out where she was staying. She was afraid to come out of her hotel. She called Mrs. Esther Gordy and Berry and told them she was afraid to leave her hotel to perform. She told me that they fired her after that. Hattie developed some problems and never really got back on her feet until later. This knocked her off her foundation and she drank a lot from the depression of it. She had a great gospel voice and was very involved in her church and senior work. She has children and grandchildren. I told her she had to forgive and move on and I do believe that she did heal those wounds before she died. After Hattie died, Mr. Steve Holsey, a dear friend and journalist in Detroit wrote a wonderful article about Hattie. Steve is a great friend to the Motowners."

Michael Demps adds, "About a year before Marvin Gaye died my mother and I went to see him. When he arrived in a limo he recognized my mother right away, and he shouted out 'Louvain, aw baby!' and they hugged and kissed. She used to tell me how they talked a lot back in the day."

Louvain's dear friend Mary Andrews was with her and her sons early on in Atlanta. "I met Louvain in Atlanta when she first moved here. We lived in the same neighborhood and have been friends for over thirty years. We became acquainted through prayer and church. I'm a fan of the Motown music. I'd like for her fans to know she is a courageous woman. She's a hardworking person and when she has obstacles in front of her she takes them as a challenge, puts her best foot forward, and moves on. I had taken ill and she invited me to be in her home during this stressful time. I was able to recuperate from my heart attack in her home. She took me in and I lived with her and her sons.

"I was able to see in my spirit vision that great things were going to happen for her. We would pray a lot together and we are both ministers. I would tell her that she had to move on from her past. I encouraged her. The Lord was going to open a door for her and that she needed to stay steadfast, unmovable, and believe in Him to receive His blessings. I saw in my spirit that she was going to travel and sing again. Louvain will never hit bottom because when she is low she becomes inspired and she knows she can do whatever God is bringing her through. She knows that God is on her side. She has had hard times and in her hardest times she has been there for other people. We have had a long journey and she has come through some hard trials and struggles. God was always there for her to bring her through. Her time has come to get her just due.

"I prayed that she and her friends healed and forgave the hurts from the past so they can enjoy their blessings that are flowing to them now. She came to me and told me thank you for believing in her. She is a very loving, caring, and concerned mother.

"She was very protective of her children and now they are protective of her. She is a minister and she ministers very well and is a great teacher. I learned that when she's not saying much, to leave her be alone with her thoughts. I learned not to say anything because that is when she's talking with God. After a while, she will talk and open up. She had some very hard and trying times when she worked with children at first here in Atlanta. I would tell her to stay strong and we prayed that God would open a door for her and that is when she became the nanny for those children Sarah and Adam. She had a good job in their home and she went on to do it again for the Gitomer Family. She has come a long way and I thank God that she came through the suffering. She ended up with a church tribute that knocked her off her feet.

"They honored her with a beautiful tribute and gave her an award. I told her this is her time now. I am thankful that Jackie, Marlene and Louvain are able to see and know about the recognition they are receiving. You cannot hold in anger and jealousies or resentment. The Father will bless you and you will block those blessings if you do not forgive."

Louvain continues, "My sons are wonderful young men. Michael and Max are wonderful fathers."

Janece is Michael's daughter. "I'm inspired by my grandmother's singing career and I haven't really told her. I am just beginning to pursue that path for myself. I'm very proud of her. I know all of her songs. I spent most of my days with my grandmother when I was little. I remember she prayed with me a lot when I was little. She would pray over the phone with her friends and I would listen to her. I tell everyone, 'That is my grandmother singing on Motown records.' I feel proud when I hear her on the radio. I know her voice now. My dad and grandmother have performed together. I want my own children and grandchildren to know about her. I'm a fan of Motown and can listen to The Temptations until my legs fall off."

Ella adds this about her cousins Michael and Max: "Max is the happiest person you will ever meet. He is very adventurous. You never know what he's going do and where he's going to show up. He is a great father and grandfather. Michael is spiritual. He attends church and is following the word and is very much into family. He has been working really hard to raise Janece and has done a beautiful job. He loves to sing and he loves to perform. Max was involved not in one but two fires. In each he almost died;

it was very serious and was televised."

Louvain continues, "My family is truly blessed and the years in Atlanta were blessings. I worked through so much hurt. I was placed in situations that were essentially for my own good. It was trying times to say the least. I got a call one night a few years ago and it was Joe Hinton. He asked me if I would ever consider working with him again. I said sure, business is business. I knew I would never be involved with him again on a personal level, but I could work with him. He apologized to the boys and me for what he did. I told him to let me know the details of work and we could figure out something, but nothing ever happened. I don't know where he is now. I will say for a little while he filled a space in my sons' lives when they needed a male figure.

"When I do see others from Motown now, we all have children, and our children have children. We were kids when we started out. When we see each other at events such as the Esther Gordy Edwards Tribute, it's really something that boggles your mind. It really is a family, so to speak, because in a real family, you don't see your cousins and distant relatives. You go to the reunions and family functions together. There is an underlying love for one another even if you don't see eye to eye with a few of your relatives.

"Everyone had their own journey but what happened was people lost their homes, their health suffered, and their children didn't eat. They needed rehab or their children needed rehab and help because their parents didn't get their royalties. There is a right and a wrong and it could have been better for people. I think when you do wrong to people you suffer with that. You have to forgive yourself and ask God to forgive you when you do injustices to people. Some things make you hard and some things make you soft. For the people who walk around in shame and don't correct it, you must pray for them. If the best was done, it was not done very well because many people were hurt.

"Hurting people begin to hurt other people and what happens is you become immune to hurting others. You don't see the ramifications of your actions. If you are the leader and you have been leading people, and all of the sudden you go away with no warning, well you are not a very good leader. When great leaders mess up many can suffer from that. I made amends with my own past and those I had hurt. There is a closure that comes when a person apologizes. It was a magical time in our past and those were the magical days. Everyone started out so innocently I feel. When I met Berry Gordy, he was someone I thought would be transforming our lives into our dreams. You end up spending so much time with people. We were young and some of us goofed up and didn't mean to. There was a very gracious woman who I loved dearly and after all of these years I ended up going to her and apologizing for the wrong I had done to her. Forgiveness is a gift that you give to yourself. It is part of the human psyche to want forgiveness from others as well.

"I had to find forgiveness all over again for Ian Levine. People have asked about the sessions with Ian Levine. I had some solo work and so did Pat Lewis. Some of the fans wrote to me and wanted to know how Marlene and Jackie feel about those sessions and why they aren't singing lead. I don't know why they didn't sing any leads. When Ian Levine approached me to come to Detroit, I was working and had to leave my job in Atlanta to come to Detroit. The agreement he made with me was he would let me sing lead on something. I thought everybody was singing lead on the songs anyway. I just assumed and it is not good to assume. I didn't question when he offered to let me sing lead. I figured he was letting others sing lead as well. Some people refer to these sessions as The Raping of The Andantes, among other things. This turned out to be a negative experience for us and caused more hurt. It was salt in the wound for us. This was the last time that Marlene and Jackie sang and it was the last time the three of us sang together. The hurt from this experience was another deep one.

"Although it was nice to see everyone again, the experience was the same. I became closer friends with Frances Nero at this time."

Frances recalls, "We became friends when we were at Sylvia Moy's studio on Webb. I really got to meet The Andantes and know them during the Ian Levine sessions. Louvain and I developed a friendship and I wanted her to have something from me as a token of the friendship we had started. We spent a lot of time together and did a lot of recording for Ian Levine. When we recorded it was like being at a manufacturing plant; that was the way we were recording. Turning out record after record and it was so busy for those sessions. Everyone did so much on those sessions and worked so hard, it was a shame how it turned out.

"I was making erotic chocolates at the time and I had a thing for dainty little tea cups. I liked Louvain so much as my friend. I surprised her with a teacup and a little chocolate penis. We all had a big laugh about the chocolate and she was showing it to everyone; she loved the teacup too. We stayed in touch all of these years and it developed into a great friendship. Our friendship has been maintained over the years because we have many spiritual talks and we are there for each other."

Louvain adds, "Marlene had to tell me what that little chocolate thing was. We had a good laugh over that. I can look back at some really fun and good times even though they're attached to some negative experiences throughout. I'd try not to feel resentment or bitterness when I would read in the paper about Motown being sold and then I would see how well some people were doing.

"I have to say that Diana Ross, for me, represented some issues that brought up heartache for me after Motown left Detroit and the years that followed in Atlanta. She was the face that reminded me of it all. I had to forgive myself for having negative feeling towards her. When I hear things about her now being hurt or negative news in the press or derogatory statements, it hurts me because she is hurting. I don't dislike her. If I could get to her now I would pray with her. Diana comes on my heart often and I think of her often. I wish to tell her that I am sorry I was angry and envious. I wanted to keep singing too and I was mad at anyone who was able to do that and she was everywhere on the radio and TV in the 70s and 80s to remind me. Looking back at myself before I ever knew Jackie and Marlene…I had a dream to sing. Looking at what Diana had, it represented the dream for me. In the dream I lived I had it better because I had Jackie and Marlene as my partners, our sound went down in history, and the hand I was dealt wasn't as bad as I thought. When I was the lowest, it seemed I wanted what she had but I know now I had the better hand because she had just as much, if not more heartache and pain than I had, and she suffers it publicly. I do pray for her happiness. I now appreciate her courage, strength, and endurance. God has a plan. I have the opportunities to sing now and I am very blessed and happy with my own life.

"What I would say to Diana Ross now is that I want to see her continue to ride out the rest of her life in happiness and peace. I honestly know the woman has suffered, publicly and privately. You can't tell me she hasn't known pain. She doesn't know me well enough to know my heartfelt wish for her and her family is sincere. I would sing for her again in a heartbeat and I would really try to get Mary Wilson too. You have to understand, although some of us were not the very best of friends, we are tied together in song and on those records. We are sisters and if Mary and Diana could sing together again, that would be something special for everyone."

Ain't No Mountain High Enough.

What's Going On?

The Andantes have come a long way. It has been nearly 50 years since they stepped foot into Hitsville and made musical history together. They've watched people come and go in the music business and witnessed firsthand some of the pitfalls of show business. They've said goodbye to many of their friends and colleagues who were part of the history we know as Motown and 'The Sound of Young America'.

Andante is a musical term that means "moving along". They have lived up to that term and then some. They have maintained their friendship and bonds with one another. They've remained loyal not only to each other, but to the music they created and to those who stood beside them for all of those years. They have respected the Motown legacy.

What's going on with them now and what have they been up to in recent years? Jackie is retired and has been very busy traveling. Marlene is enjoying retirement with her family and Louvain has been working and keeping up with her singing.

Jackie retired in 2002 and shares a little about some of her hobbies. "I love to go shopping and I love clothes. I enjoy watching basketball. If there is a good game on I like to stay in eat, relax, and watch the game. The Super Bowl was in Detroit in 2006. I watched Stevie Wonder and Aretha Franklin open the Super Bowl Show. I went to some of the concerts and outdoor events. I had to get out and support my city and wear my Super Bowl hat and T-shirt. I love The Pistons, they are my favorite team. I had season tickets for them at one time but now I hold tickets for the women's team, The Detroit Shock.

My favorite Piston is Tayshawn Prince. My Jersey is Ben Wallace, but I like them all. Back in the day Dennis Edwards had tickets too. Many times he would give his tickets away and I would be fortunate enough to get them. I usually sat up high, but Dennis' seats were in the 4th row. I do some volunteer work for The Detroit Lions at Ford Field. We have a group who sell merchandise at the games and the proceeds go to cancer for children and their families. I also enjoy track and field. I went to

The 1996 Olympics in Atlanta.

My niece Bridgett is my sister's daughter and we spend a lot of time together. I had plans to spend more moments with my sister but she died in recent years. Our plans were to enjoy our retirement together."

Bridgett says, "Downtown Detroit used to have a vibrant shopping district. We would park at Paul's cut-rate garage and walk over to Woodward Avenue. Hudson's, B. Siegel's, and Winkelman's were a few of the stores I remember visiting. We always ended up at Otto's for caramel and cheese popcorn. Jackie would take us out to eat also. We would go to the restaurant that was inside Hudson's but my grandma and grandaunt loved to eat at Red Lobster, so we would go there. As early as I can remember my aunt has always been a caring and giving person. As I have gotten older, our relationship has evolved into a great friendship. She is like a second mother. Jackie, my mom, and I would spend a lot of time together and do many things. We took bus and train trips to places like Toronto, Minnesota, Chicago, and Philadelphia. We would also see plays, shop at the malls, visit family, or go out to eat. Ten years ago I began working for the Fire Department and I was suddenly unable to do a lot of things with Jackie and my mom. They continued to be together to the point where if one went somewhere without the other, the question would be 'Where's your sister?' That's how rare it was to see them apart. My mom passed away on September 1, 2003. What a terrible and sad time it had been for all of us. I would have loved for my mother to be a part of this book. She would be so proud. My memories of Jackie consist mainly of her just being Aunt Jackie and when I was younger, my grandma and my grandma's sister lived in the same building. We spent a lot of time there. Jackie took excellent care of them. One of the things she, my cousin Carryl, and I would do was their grocery shopping once a month. I hated grocery shopping. I used to tell my mother that when I grew up, I was going to hire someone to do mine. Jackie would make us go. We would always get one basket for grandma, one basket for Aunt Ethel. Jackie and I continue to be close. We still travel together and do things together. I'm very glad that The Andantes are finally getting their 'just desserts' because as everyone has been saying, and I am now seeing for myself, it's about time."

Jackie adds more, "I really enjoy concerts. In recent years, I have seen Stevie Wonder and I saw Luther Vandross about ten times. It makes me so sad that he's not with us. Luther was amazing in person, he made you want more and he put on a fabulous show. I love Patti LaBelle, she puts on a great show too. One of my favorite female singers is Gladys Knight. I still love her after all of these years. I really love Aretha Franklin too, as well as Dinah Washington and Sarah Vaughn.

"I love that some of our colleagues are still out there working, like The Velvelettes and The Funk Brothers. It amazes me how many of us are gone. It's hard to believe there is only one original Temptation left. I'm telling you, I was happy to see The 50th Anniversary Special that they did for The Four Tops at The Opera House; those guys really stuck it out and maintained their group.

"I thoroughly enjoyed the film *Standing In The Shadows of Motown* even though it was a little painful to relive that and they didn't mention us being there with The Funks. I went with a friend and when the movie ended she looked at me and said, 'Jackie weren't you there too?' The film was a perfect example of what happened to people. My family has mostly passed away and they wanted to see Marlene, Louvain, and me get our credit one day. It didn't bother me that we didn't go to Los Angeles or make a fortune singing. The fact we weren't mentioned in history was more bothersome than anything else. We have to mention ourselves and say it for us now. Every once in a while someone will call and want to include us in a book and talk to us. It came out slowly about The Andantes. It even took us a long time to do this.

"I do hear myself on the radio everyday. When I go out shopping and go from store to store, they're always playing Motown music in those shops. I'll stay in there longer just to hear us singing. That's something that I never get tired of. I hear us singing on the radio everyday, it's refreshing. I just feel terrible that I don't sing anymore. There is really no reason why I don't do it now. When you don't practice something on a regular basis, you lose it. My singing voice is not the same as it once was. I like to think it is still in there. It's amazing to me that people still enjoy what we did over forty years ago.

"What I would like to see happen for us now after all of these years is The Andantes' name in history. I would like to solidify what we contributed to music. In recent years we have begun to see some honors for our work, but our story is not anywhere in print, until now. I am very proud of our history and our work together. I know that preserving our legacy is up to us. We do have a story to tell here and telling it should come from us and only us.

"I have my daily life now with family and friends. They make my life more fun. I still attend Hartford Baptist Church and I judge the bake sales and contests. I can't hold a grudge over what happened to us in our youthful years at Motown. It wasn't right but I cannot change it. There are enough good and fun times about it that I look back with fondness and good memories.

"Friendships are very important. When you are friends with people you can trust and they have your back that is wonderful. Always keep loyal friends close. Marlene, Louvain, and I want to be here for each other. When I see Louvain it is like no time has passed. As time does pass, we intend to spend more time communicating over the phone.

"Marlene and I have lots of fun over the phone. Often it takes us at least four phone calls plus the call-backs to get all of our talking done. We finally remember everything that we want to say to each other in the conversation. There is always a joke in there that throws us off. We just love it and cannot wait for the call-backs. We laugh a lot together.

"I stay busy. Marlene and I have switched roles. She was the one who was social and went out when we were younger, now she's home and I'm running and ripping with my friends and family. I really love going to plays. We attended the play about The Marvelettes, *Now That I Can Dance*. It was at The Mosaic Theatre. It was really wonderful and put together very well. I enjoyed it. They had us there as special guests and introduced us to the audience. I went to New York with some friends to see *The Color Purple*. I also went to Toronto a couple of times to see *The Wiz* and I saw it here as well. I saw *Les Miserables*. That was excellent. I saw *Lion King* three times. *Phantom of the Opera* and *Rent* were great too. I also frequent the ballet and modern dance. I remember the first time I saw Judith Jamison. That was a fantastic night at the theatre.

"I go to a lot of art fairs and museums in the summer months. I don't paint but I love the arts and support the arts. I have quite a lot of art in my home and I collect and enjoy it. It doesn't matter who painted it. I love colorful paintings and I appreciate and admire them. The abstract art is over my head sometimes but there is enough art at my level for me to enjoy. In the summer months I attend an ethnic festival on the river front. I like seeing the different themes, one week is African, Spanish, and so on. I like the different foods and the clothing and seeing the cultures come together in one place together. I get bored easy and I like to stay active. I joined a bowling team and was bored after about six months. I like to try different things and move on to the next new thing. I started walking with my brother. He stayed with it but I got bored. Traveling and shopping is my exercise and that never bores me. Put me in a mall and I will walk it. I usually get out every weekend and go to dinner and a movie.

"Being single has allowed me the freedom to do pretty much what I want. It has provided me a lifestyle that has allowed me to afford some things that would have otherwise been impossible. I travel with friends and family and this single life leaves me with no regrets. I love and like myself and have no problem enjoying my own company. Some people pick the wrong person and find themselves alone and unhappy in a marriage. I prefer to say I am by myself but not alone. I enjoy reading and staying on top of current events.

"I enjoy a good night of television. My favorites are all of the *CSI's* and *Law and Order.* I watch the nightly news. Soap operas are not for me. They all have the same plot; one man, one town, and every woman in town has to have him. It's kind of sad and very funny. Give me a good murder mystery instead. I also like a good comedy that is clean, refreshing, and funny that does not offend anyone to get the laughs. My favorite women of comedy are Lily Tomlin and Carol Burnett."

Marlene lives a very quiet life with Harold. Marlene says, "Our life is very family-oriented because our children are older now and we have grandchildren. I have two grandchildren from Lawrence; their names are Marlene and Racing. If my grandchildren wanted to pursue singing, I would support what they chose. They already sing in their church and their mother directs the children's choir.

"Our family takes trips to Atlanta and Vegas and we get out of Detroit every other year on vacations. Oftentimes a nice weekend is to have Yvonne and Fred come over for a game of cards. I'm enjoying doing nothing really. We're just relaxing with family and enjoying the days. It's nice not to have a daily obligation of work and just spend that time with loved ones. I have ten siblings and I'm much closer to them now than when we were growing up and when I was a young adult.

"I had a few health scares in recent years and that's the main reason why I don't sing anymore. If I happen to be in the car, turn on a particular station, and something of ours is playing, I will hum along. But because I had a heart attack in 2002, I can't hold my air and breathe the same as I used to. It was frightening because anytime doctors tell you something about your heart it scares you. It was a life-changing event for me. It was a mild heart attack but it scared me enough to make some changes in my life. God is watching out for me. I had never been sick or in the hospital except to have a baby. I take better care of myself and get plenty of sleep and a B12 shot each month. I have definitely had some emotional times in my life and I credit getting through them by being able to move on, let go, and through the power of God and prayers. I do a whole lot of praying.

"My church foundation has stayed with me. I may not be in church now every time the door opens and I know I should go more often. I was raised in that environment and have never forgotten the principles that I learned. The teachings remain inside of me. I use them in my life. They are a part of my foundation. The music is still in me. You never forget it. It helps get you through the rough times in life and helps you get through the week. No matter what you end up doing as your life's work, you can draw from that foundation. You have to stay in that fellowship with others and you need that connection when you have a strong belief in God. I went to a funeral recently and the music took me back. The old songs made me feel connected to my faith and I do not want to be distant from it. I was humming those songs and was thinking of my childhood when I sang them. Songs like 'Oh How I Love Jesus', 'Oh Pass Me Not Our Gentle Savior', and 'His Eye Is

On The Sparrow'. God needs time just like anything else in your life. I can see in my life now where God helped me and where He made me wait and He had me be still so I could hear Him. So many occasions in life, we are in a hurry to heal and God has a plan. You have to hold on and be still so you can hear God speaking to you. Healing doesn't happen overnight. God has to bring you through it in divine timing. I also learned in life that sometimes you are praying the wrong prayer, sometimes without realizing it. You think you want something you don't need. We're selfish in our prayers and we don't realize it. That's when you don't get the answers you want the way you want it, because it isn't what you need. You want to often say 'Lord let *my* will be done' when it's, 'Lord, let *thy* will be done.' We want what we want and He has to bring us through things to realize we don't want them or need them. You have to be careful what you wish for and what you pray for. There's a law of attraction and you can bring the wrong things into your life and it takes time to get that corrected. What God has planned for you will come to you.

"I hear us everyday on the radio and I never get tired of it. Harold is very proud of what The Andantes have done. You do not have to look for Motown on the radio. It's just there constantly everyday. It reminds me of a beautiful time when I hear it now. Jackie had a cousin in London and he heard us all day long over there. In the clubs they still play Motown like it just came out, it's so current over there. Vickie played Karaoke for me over the phone and I couldn't believe how great we sounded. I hadn't heard it like that since the days when we recorded it and heard the playback in the studio. She would ask me who sang these songs and I couldn't deny it was us. I finally had to say I got her point. We sang those songs. We are prevalent on that music and I will be forever proud of what we did. My son loves listening to Motown and Stevie Wonder is still his favorite.

"I have peace now about my Motown years and what happened. It was something that had to evolve in me. When you love something and it's taken from you, there will be emotions over it. I came from a stable two-parent home where we talked about things and worked them out. Over time, I talked about this with my friends and family. I felt I had to make a decision about how this would affect my future life. Life happened to all of us and some things were placed on the back burner. For me to explain my Motown years to my grandchildren who are eight and ten, I would first have to explain who Marvin Gaye is and sit them down so they understood it.

"Marvin was before his time and what he wrote and sang about eventually came to pass. I know that the reason things fall away is because people don't address them and that is why we're doing this book now. Our friends and families have wanted us to do this for a long time, so we owe it to them as well to do this. I recently saw on television the demolition of The Donovan Building. I know my feelings have evolved because it was a bittersweet moment for me to see history come down. The papers in the building were flying everywhere and it seemed the building was abandoned and full of memories just as many of us were. We actually worked there too and recorded there. Berry's office was there for a while. You can't be crazy and live in the past, for it is unhealthy. Bittersweet is the best way I can describe it: bitter because we felt left out of the history and sweet because it was the best times of our young lives. Our parents are gone. Many of our family members are gone. For us to finally have some of the awards we've received and to get recognition is something that those people wanted to see happen for us. The unraveling of the story has taken so long because by the time people began to write books in the eighties and nineties, some of the key people were already dead and gone.

"Emotionally we were unable to tackle this then. The time is now. It's a joy now when I see our fellow Motowners and when I see the ones who are still out there performing and making it through. There are lots of hugs and love when we see each other. Sadly, we see each other often at funerals. I look at many of the entertainers, past and present, and it pains me that some were caught up in drugs and drinking. The lifestyle is hard out on the road and the schedule is grueling. Life in general is hard enough, but life and the entertainment business take its toll. It makes me feel lucky and sad at the same time. If everyone could be together once more, the sound would be the same. You couldn't touch it.

"Movies and television are something I do enjoy now. I love to watch The Pistons on television with my husband. I like old television shows like *Laugh In* and *Sonny and Cher.* I have always loved Michael Douglas and *The Streets of San Francisco*. Jay Leno tickles me and I never miss Oprah's show, I love her. I like *CSI* and I am hooked on *Law & Order*. I like *Commander in Chief* and I hope I live long enough to see a woman become president of The United States. I like *West Wing* too. Washington D.C. is a lot like the music business where everyone is smiling in your face, but you don't know what's going on behind the scenes. I know it's just television and the entertainment business, but if you really put a lot of thought into this it would truly frighten you how things go down in our world. Power in the wrong hands is just dangerous, whether it's politics or the music business. You have to pay attention to what is going on around you. When you get too comfortable, that's when you get blindsided. We're all sitting at a round table and karma will soon come to you. That's life and how it happens. I believe what goes around comes around."

Louvain has maintained communication with the public. She has a presence on the internet and we have seen her recently doing TJ Labinsky's *PBS Specials*. TJ recalls, "A very special moment was getting Louvain on the show we did with Edwin Starr. Reunited were Louvain and The Originals and they sang '25 Miles' together just as they did on the original record with Edwin. Sadly, Edwin passed away right after we taped that special. Another time, Louvain and Pat Lewis were on a PBS show in 2005 and they were reunited with The Four Tops. Sadly, right after that taping Obie Benson passed away."

Louvain is a sentimental person and when she watched the *PBS Motown Special*, it hit her hard. "I've been throwing a pity party and it has lasted too long. No one came but me. I ended up becoming very depressed after I saw the PBS show on television and it took me some time to shake those feelings and get over it. Obie died right after we did that show. It's so hard to describe how I feel when I sing this music and hear this music. It puts me in the clouds. For the ones who are no longer here, I can feel them in my spirit as if it were yesterday. When I close my eyes and listen, I remember like it was yesterday when we were all together, then reality sets in and I wake up. They're mostly gone and I sink low sometimes when I realize most of our friends and colleagues died young. It just gets to me. Obie was so happy when we taped that show. He blew me a kiss when we were singing 'Bernadette'. I love that song still to this day. It makes me feel good. Obie always had a smile on his face when he sang. If you watch the clips from the old days he has that huge smile when he was onstage.

"When I saw him backstage the night we taped the special I mentioned to Pat that he didn't look right to me and she agreed. His coloring was off. It wasn't too long after that he passed away. I was glad to see him so happy that last time singing onstage. Some of our colleagues died when they were making a comeback, so to speak, or were out there on the road enjoying their careers. Edwin Starr had moved to England and life was good. He was in a good space and he was working more and more and enjoying his life when he passed. I wish he could have continued doing what he loved. When I did the PBS special in Pittsburg I had the opportunity to sing with Lou Rawls. That was a real treat. We had a memorable talk and we cut up and laughed together. He died since that taping also. Marv Johnson was making a comeback when he died and he had learned so many great lessons and he was coming into more wisdom and experience. I know he had to be happy out there performing again. When I've seen people in the past get all puffed up over their fame it bothers me. I don't think they realize it can be taken from them so quickly. You have to be grateful to have those opportunities to perform and be in the public's eye. It is the public demand that makes you the star you become. Marv Johnson was a loving man and when I see him in my mind's eye, I remember him as a kind man.

"There are a handful of us still out there and we're trying to work and keep the music alive and the legacy alive. I was so happy to see The Funk Brothers get their recognition finally. I saw Jack Ashford at *The Men of Motown* event in Detroit and we connected again. It was after that he called me and I went out on the road to do some shows with him. It made me feel good that I was wanted in that way to sing. I love to sing and knowing that people enjoy it makes me feel very good.

After doing those shows with Jack I went in for a physical and mammogram. The results were that I had cancer. I talked it over with my children and my boss. I told Vickie, Marlene, and Jackie. I wanted it to remain quiet and it wasn't known except by those closest to me. I took treatments for several months beginning in early 2006 and now today I am cancer-free. I've changed my diet and I'm taking much better care of myself. I'm trying to make organic choices and trying to enjoy them. I've been using my George Foreman Grill to grill fish and vegetables. If I can find organic 'Green Eggs and Ham', I would be in great shape. Some of my favorite foods aren't organic. I like pizza and frog legs and I love Chinese egg-drop soup.

"I, Marlene, and Jackie have spent the last two years keeping in touch more because we're working on the book and we've received some long overdue honors. Paul Barker, who is our dear friend in Detroit, really pioneered for us to receive awards in Detroit-two, in fact. He was responsible for our Women of Motown Award and also The Distinguished Achievement Award that we received at The Detroit Music Awards in May of 2006. Janie Bradford honored us at her Heroes and Legends Awards in September of 2006."

Paul Barker wrote the following speech for The Detroit Music Awards. The Andantes' dear friend Paul Riser along with Robin Terry from The Motown Museum presented their award:

"The success of the Motown Record Corporation has been greatly celebrated and vastly documented in the annals of history. Over the company's forty-seven year history, we've heard countless stories of how the music bridged racial barriers, bringing people together and stories of countless musical success. We know about the great artists like Marvin Gaye, Stevie Wonder, Smokey Robinson and The Miracles, Diana Ross and The Supremes, The Temptations, The Four Tops, Martha Reeves and The Vandellas, just to name a few. We know about the incredible house-band The Funk Brothers who helped craft what became known as the Motown sound or 'The Sound of Young America'.

"Yet, in over forty-seven years of history, one story seems to have eluded all the history books, all the television shows and all the documentaries made about Motown and the Detroit music scene. It's the story of tonight's Distinguished Achievement honorees: The Andantes. Do you know who The Andantes are? If not, you're not alone, but pay close attention to the story I'm about to tell you.

"Marlene Barrow, Louvain Demps, and Jackie Hicks comprise the vocal group, The Andantes. Although known by diehard Motown enthusiasts and Motown circles in Europe, The

Andantes have remained Detroit's best kept secret…a producer's secret weapon and a writer's silver bullet…and an intimidation to most vocalists. The average person would never know Marlene, Louvain, and Jackie were instrumental in contributing to some of the greatest recordings in popular culture. The Andantes were with Motown from the inception of the company and for over a decade, they exuded a quiet sense of class, professionalism, elegance and talent which is still unrivaled today. It's now time we all know and celebrate their contributions.

"Louvain Demps came to the newly formed Motown company in 1959 with the desire to record a song written by her friend. She became the company's first recording client, paying for studio time to put the recording on tape. Although the record was never released, Motown heard amazing potential in Louvain's soprano vocals and hired her as an in-house background singer. A short time later, Marlene Barrow, Jackie Hicks, and Emily Philips entered the Motown story as backing vocalists for newly recorded Motown singer Richard 'Popcorn' Wylie.

"They called themselves The Andantes. Motown founder Berry Gordy was often impressed with how quickly The Andantes learned their parts and continuously called on the ladies to add vocals and handclaps to songs being recorded in the now legendary Studio A. A short time later, Emily Philips would leave The Andantes and would be permanently replaced by Louvain Demps, creating a perfect, irresistible blend of harmony that would become a main gear in the Motown machine.

"One of the sessions recorded using the newly formed Andantes was for Eddie Holland's hit 'Jamie'. This was just the beginning of what would turn into over an estimated 20,000 recording sessions in just over twelve years-an amazing and almost unparalleled accomplishment for any artist, band, or musician. The Andantes became Motown's number one studio vocalists with their smooth, chorale sound as valuable to the record label as The Funk Brothers' rhythm section. The group recorded and released one record as The Andantes called 'Like A Nightmare', but it was decided the company could not afford to lose The Andantes' vocals in the studio in exchange for extended traveling needed to promote the single. (Their single remains the most sought after 45 record in the world) The Andantes were now recognized as a pivotal part of the Motown sound and to change the 'assembly line of success' now would affect all the artists. So, The Andantes remained in Detroit contributing their voices to songs by legends such as Marvin Gaye, Stevie Wonder, Martha Reeves and The Vandellas, The Temptations, Diana Ross & The Supremes, Jimmy Ruffin, Edwin Starr, Kim Weston, and countless others.

"The Andantes were most prominently used on all of The Four Tops' Holland-Dozier-Holland-produced hits including 'Baby I Need Your Loving', 'I Can't Help Myself (Sugar Pie Honey Bunch)', 'Reach Out I'll Be There', as well as Stevie Wonder's 'For Once In My Life', Mary Wells' 'My Guy' and the Marvin Gaye classics 'Ain't That Peculiar' and 'I Heard It Through The Grapevine'. In fact, Marvin Gaye was adamant about using The Andantes on his now historic album *What's Going On*, on which the group received their first album credit. The ladies' moving and emotional vocals brought life and emotion to such socially-conscious songs as 'Mercy, Mercy Me' and the title track 'What's Going On'.

"Other artists began to hear stories of Motown's secret weapon and quietly hired The Andantes on the side in an attempt to cash in on Motown's famed formula. The Andantes worked with music legends such as The Dells, John Lee Hooker, Bobby 'Blue' Bland, and Jerry Butler. Jackie Wilson brought in Marlene and Jackie to lay down some of their most recognizable lyrics on his international #1 hit 'Higher and Higher'.

"The Andantes continued their incredible run until Motown's move to California in 1972. The ladies continued to contribute to Detroit recording sessions until the early 70's when life's path took them in different directions.

"Over the years, the music industry has changed…the city has changed…but The Andantes have always remained exactly who they are. Three INCREDIBLY important women who helped usher in an amazing era of popular music. They were pioneers in the Detroit music scene and have no parallels to be compared to. The Andantes have an amazing story to be told, yet maintain a gentle and yet seldom seen sense of class and decorum. Marlene, Louvain, and Jackie…tonight is your night to take a bow and receive acknowledgements for your outstanding accomplishments. They will NEVER be forgotten. Ladies and gentlemen: please stand up and welcome The Andantes!"

Louvain continues, "Steve Holsey made sure we had coverage in the Detroit paper and he has been a great supporter of ours. He has helped to maintain our legacy in Detroit. We are very blessed to have such support from Janie, Steve, and Paul. I'm so glad they're in our circle of love and family. We love you very much.

"I have spent a lot of time in recent years writing letters to organizations seeking to get our name recognized in more places. I began that campaign several years ago. I felt we should have something to show for being on all of those records. I wrote to everyone I could think of who may be able to help us. I got two responses back from that letter writing campaign.

"One was from Berry Gordy and the other was from Jerry Butler. Berry had his assistant call and she told me he didn't know we felt this way and that if I was ever in California I could come sit down and talk to him about this. That was as far as I got with my letter writing campaign. In 2004, my church honored The Andantes and myself here in Atlanta. The woman who organized the tribute was Charlotte Dudley and she sought out Berry to add his insight to the tribute. He sent a letter back and I want to share it in this book.

"It was the first time we ever had the personal acknowledgement from him that The Andantes were part of that history. We weren't invited to Motown 25 or Motown 45. The letter read, 'Louvain, Congratulations on a much deserved tribute. The Andantes were true unsung heroes who made such wonderful background music for so many years, on so many Motown hits, Berry Gordy.'"

"Pastor Ruth Smith of Atlanta had this to share about the tribute: "Ms. Louvain and I met at Georgiann's House of Styles Beauty Shop located at the West End Mall in Atlanta, Georgia. We were both getting services but as a Christian woman, I try to be aware of my surroundings to see if anyone needs to meet the Lord Jesus Christ, according to Romans chapter 10, verses 9 and 10. I also try to notice if there's some weary soldier of the cross who needs to be encouraged.

"Ms. Demps struck me as a person who had given much and could use some encouragement. So, I opened a conversation with her. She shared with me that she was a singer and named some of the places and people she had worked with. I invited her to sing at Light of the World Christian Church which was headquartered in Decatur, Georgia at the time. We're now in Stockbridge, Georgia. Ms. Demps came to the Decatur location and sang to the Glory of God. It was an awesome ministry!

"We encouraged her and she encouraged us. This is the way God always does it, when we give to others it comes back to us. My goal was to encourage her but she really has been encouraging me every since. Her fans should know that she is a gift from God to minister in song. She loves her music and it shows in her ministry. When I think of Ms. Demps, I think of someone who is determined. She has faced much that perhaps would have caused others to quit, but not her.

"Once I realized that she was an unsung hero I decided to do what I could to give her some of the honor due her for the contribution she has made to the music industry. I assigned one of my daughters, Charlotte Dudley, who has a gift of research and organization, to find every one she could and invite them. We developed a group of background singers from the church and we re-worded some of the songs to be 'God-focused'. She did her own concert! It was awesome! For example, when we sang, 'Someday We'll Be Together', we said, 'Someday we will be with our Lord'. Many of her old friends came and we had a service dedicated to her and presented her with gifts and her crown. It was a very touching moment. We were all blessed!

"I am not familiar with her Motown years but we spoke with Berry Gordy and many others from that era and they did confirm that she was who she said she was in Motown. This was a little before my time and I am not really into the secular music. However, I know that every good gift comes from God.

"One of my favorite secular songs that she sang on is 'Someday We'll Be Together' by The Supremes. This song was popular when I was leaving my parents home and starting my adult life and I missed them so much! My favorite song now that she sings is 'Great Is Thou Faithfulness'. God is being faithful to her even in what Vickie is doing for her. She still shares at our church when she is in the city and we always enjoy her ministry. One of my favorite moments together as friends was when I had a tea party at my home with 100 of my favorite women. Ms. Demps was one of my special guests. She was also kind enough to sing at that event and she was wonderful! I would like to say to Louvain, 'Ms. Demps my friend, It does not really matter how you began. What really matters is how you finish.' "

Louvain continues, "This past year I've been to England and Wales to help put our name out there. Jeanne Sorensen has been a great friend to many Motowners. She books these shows so that England can see the legends. My dear friend Mike Critchley offered this review of the show I did with Karen Cherokee Pree and her sister Lolita."

Mike says, "The show was a huge success. They were sharing the bill with J.J. Barnes and The Contours. J.J. Barnes opened the show, and was good, good, and very good-a hard act to follow. When Louvain and the ladies hit the stage, the crowd, just over three thousand people, went quite wild. They looked good and sounded great. Opening straight into 'Like A Nightmare', at that moment they became a new group. After the first song, Karen introduced Louvain and she got a three-minute standing ovation. The happiness, both onstage and with the fans—you could feel it like something of serious substance. Each song got the ladies more comfortable and the crowd became quite frantic. They were great on all their songs. It was fabulous the way the sound was mixed, so that whichever two were on backing vocals, their microphones were put at almost equal volume to the lead singer. It was amazing. The showstopper was when they did 'I Got A Feeling'. They had the audience in the palms of their hands and they made that song their own. There was no doubt that Louvain, Karen, & Lolita had stolen the show. As an encore, all of the acts returned to the stage. Mind-blowing stuff, we have these weekenders every year, and this one is already being hailed as the best balanced show to date."

Jeanne adds, "Pontin's Holiday Center is where they performed. About six or seven years ago they began to bring over the Legendary Musical Acts, Northern Soul acts, and the Motown Stars. In March the Northern Soul Legends perform and in October the Motown Legends. The venues are huge and the crowds know all of the songs and they know who The Andantes are. They have a wonderful understanding of who The Andantes are. The audience loved them and went crazy. The fans in England are the die-hard fans who know the actual catalog number of the songs. They treat Motown as if it were alive today. I feel that the people now who help do right by the legends, and for anyone of us to do a really good job, you have to be a fan. There are people in the business who make it about the money. They don't want to help. The Motowners were my heroes. I had a rough childhood and the music helped me through really hard times. I could escape into the music. I've had multiple jobs over my life but music is my heart. I spend time now paying them back for that and helping them. They mean so much to everyone. I have to say to Louvain, 'Do you know who you are?' If The Andantes went over to England for a book signing, it would be insane. They wouldn't even have to sing. People would go nuts to be in the same room with them, they are so loved. People lined up for hours to get autographs at this last show we did."

Louvain continues, "For me, dealing with our legacy and writing a book was a healing process. To get from one thought to the next was a challenge. The way I deal with things now is much different and is a much healthier outlet for me to heal. I've been able to express my feelings and write them out to Vickie and the healing that has come is what gives me peace now. Some things were for the book and some things were just so the hurt could come out and come to the surface. The wounds had to heal and the hurt had to escape because it was in there, and I know it was in there for other people as well. I have been grateful for this opportunity because some things were so pushed back in my mind and emotions, that I thought they were gone. The poking and prodding got the feelings up and out and that was a good thing. This was about the inner-feelings and I hate to think I carried that hurt around with me. It was apparent that I did because I would write to Vickie and the feelings would come out.

"If you put me in a room with everyone again, at this stage in my life, I can say I honestly love and want the best for all of them. I have to forget the times where I would open the paper and see how great someone was doing when I was living on one can of soup. I know that I survived and that can of soup saved me and my family. I'm still alive and my children are healthy. I made mistakes in my life and I corrected my own wrongdoings to people. I cannot change the past. I know now is a better day and I depend on God because people change their minds too much.

"I pray for Berry often and I pray that he has peace. I want him to know that I have peace now and that I have forgiven him. I feel it is important that he know that his choices in the past sorely affected my family and me. This is why overtime when I see him now I say, Berry I am praying for you.

"Everyone wants to see the good in people and everyone knows there are things that can happen to a person from their childhood and that they've suffered hurts in their past. Everyone, no matter who you are, will be accountable for what you have done in your life, accountable to God.

"Through Berry and his company, I was introduced to many amazing and wonderful people, sometimes by him. I am thankful for that. He may not remember but he introduced me to Sammy Davis Jr. in the lobby. He told Sammy I was one of his singers. In the end, he did not do right by us after all of the work we did on those records. I was loyal to him always. I think about the people in my life and how they've touched me and I can't deny the bittersweet part of it. I thought with my silly self that Motown would go to L.A., get settled, and we would record again. People would have done anything, including me, to help Berry and his company. I believed him when he said we were family and his talk of helping everyone and not letting people down. From the time I met him, he always talked about helping the ones who helped him. I believed he cared about us, so it hurt when the company left. I believe he had good intentions, but my mother used to tell me, 'The road to hell is paved with good intentions.' Maybe in his heart of hearts he will make things right one day. One good gesture that Berry did was he created The Gwen Gordy Foundation and that made monies available to help the artists when they'd been sick or needed medications and surgeries. We saw his heart when he began to make funds available to the legendary people who pioneered this music.

"I think he can soften if he looks at the past and really looks at what people went through and what he himself has gone through in his personal life. I know it hasn't been easy just because he's wealthy. I know he has suffered in ways that people do not know. He may not know how to change something now but there is a way to make peace with it and make it right when you have done wrong. It is almost like a Humpty Dumpty situation and once you have that, you may not be able to put it back together. You can acknowledge that you let Humpty fall off that wall and get cracked and hurt. It is about being accountable. Say you are sorry. That was the hard part, trying to remain loyal to a person you're mad at, someone you appreciate and at the same time, you don't respect them for what they did. If they just apologized or admitted that what they did was not in the best interest of the people who worked for them, you could at least have closure easier perhaps.

"The initial incident that hurt the three of us was never dealt with on an emotional level. It was dealt with over a period of years because life happened. We had to heal this in spurts. I would have to sort and rationalize the whys and hows in between my life unfolding and raising my children. The anger was with me for a while and you inflict that again on yourself by the anger and resentment that you carry with you. God is bringing me through this healing process. In spite of everything that went down, the additional healing came in recent years when we were finally acknowledged and honored as a trio. I can see how far I've come by how I feel about the past now. I have no more hate but I do have questions. I'm not sure they'll ever be answered. I am okay with that now. Each time I see my friends from back then I have noticed significant changes in them and in myself. We're all getting older and we know how much we mean to each other. We've grown up and matured.

"Now we deserve respect, and I don't mean from the public, but that we are respecting each other and ourselves now. Everything has a season and you cannot hold back the things that are hidden under the surface. They will come out. You cannot hold back truth. It finds its way, sometimes generations later, but it finds its way. People come into your life and you love them. Sometimes they don't know how you feel. As time goes by you are brought a new kind of life when the seeds you plant in goodness grow and people see where your heart is coming from.

"Marvin Gaye said in his biography *Divided Soul* that we were the best vocal group at Motown and that no one pushed us. There was no peep from anyone for many years about us. It went unspoken where the credit was due. It's important to me that people know. Mary Wilson has since been outspoken about our singing on The Supremes' records and Martha had been open about it as well. The Marvelettes also have come out with telling it.

"I was so happy to learn how Cal Street felt about us singing on The Velvelettes' records. This was needed for us. I am so proud of our history and sound. We share rich history with so many wonderful legendary artists and people. You can bury your hurt for many years and you can convince yourself that you have moved on, but when you talk about those times and memories, it resurfaces. The self-dialogue doesn't reflect healing even though on the outside you appear healed. Inwardly you want answers and you have questions. I'm willing to bet that my questions are the same as many of my colleagues, especially Jackie and Marlene.

"I feel very good these days. I think we are all feeling good. Even though we live separate lives, we are together in spirit because of the music. We came from the same place and had the same hurts and yet our lives took different roads. We are bonded in a way that people may not understand. The dreams I have now tell me I have healed. Here I am and I have survived. If left over hurt comes up in me now I ask God to show me where I need to forgive someone. Through prayer and meditation God continues to lead me through and shows me in my spirit where I need to do the work and maintenance to stay in thankfulness and gratitude. God deals with everyone and you have to listen to Him when He is talking to you. He may use other people to deal with you or He may use images. I don't ignore these promptings now. They are meant to lead me to healing and I follow them. People often miss God speaking to them and I do not want to miss Him. When He shows me something now I pray for me and the other person he is showing me.

"The saying 'forgive and forget' is not an easy task. One can never really forget when it is in your subconscious mind. Your mind can get a hold of that hurt so easy and you can stay stuck in it. The key is to forgive. God shows me where I need to forgive and I listen now. I saw where The Donovan Building had come down and the documents were still inside of it. To me, that is just disrespectful for the entire history as if someone died and they weren't given the proper burial. It was abandoned and full of archives and memories and no one cared enough to retrieve that information and preserve it. Motown was a great place and many great people and things came from it. How can you let any parts of it fall away? The memories have to be preserved. I did not understand that, but I could relate. I had to forgive what I saw happen with that building. The Detroit music scene didn't thrive after Motown left the city. The city and the music went hand in hand and the place was booming in the 1960s. The history of that building should have been saved.

"God is a healer, but if you are holding on to any kind of jealousy or resentment or even a malicious thought He can not deliver you from that pain. I had to surrender all of that to Him. I intend to live the best life I can and I ask Him everyday to show me how to do that. Since I had cancer I ask Him daily to be a better person with each new day He gives to me. My thought process is different now and I can accept that a person's behavior is their own responsibility and that I can't turn that behavior inward towards myself. I see now that it is a reflection on them and not me. It only is on me if I allow that to manifest in anger and hurt. Now more than ever I am released by the past and I don't want to be a victim of the past again. I want to rise above it and forgive.

"I felt bad for so long just as many of us did. I just no longer can internalize another's actions. I know that they must have felt bad and I forgive this for my sake and for theirs. I pray for them and I let them go in love and peace. I am beginning to find all of the 45 records and albums I had buried away when I put that life behind me. I was mad at everything and I hated everyone. I have recently moved and when I was unpacking, I found those little treasures. I see how they mean the world to me now. I am on a path of love and forgiveness now and I grow with it more and more. Now I want to celebrate because I know we deserve that. Had I stopped and thought too much on the past I would have surely died.

"I had to keep moving so I could survive and take care of my boys, I had to shovel the shit around. I had gotten myself into in Atlanta and I made a life for us here, a decent life. Sorrow kicked in for me at one point and sorrow for my colleagues as well. My heart was heavy and I felt bad for everyone else. I know at times the people who seemed to be doing good were in just as bad shape as I was. I realized some of my hatred was misguided towards them and that they were in the same boat as me. It was a living hell on the inside of me and I was trying to make a living on the outside and tuck that pain away so people could not see it. Then add not talking about it to anyone or dealing with it. It's insane that so many of us have the same story of heartache and struggle and you can't help but ask 'why?'

"When Universal Motown released *Motown Karaoke*, my sweet friend Harry Weinger made sure I had a set. It took me a while to listen to it because I knew it would sound like it did during the playback and that was something I hadn't heard in forty years. When I heard it, I wished that those times were still here. The fans got a real taste of what it was like back then before the lead vocal was put on the record. The Andantes have our individual lives now but maintaining our legacy and what we did has always been important to me. It has only been recently that the resources became available to pursue this. It has been so many years since I have spent a significant amount of time with Marlene and Jackie. Doing this book has brought us together.

"I hadn't been in their company for a long period of time. I am learning who they have become since I've been in Atlanta. I've learned from their homes who they are now. They have grown and matured. Marlene asked for what she wanted in life and now she has it—a good man and a nice home. Marlene has a nice quiet life and a good retirement.

"Jackie's home shows her talents and interests. Her wisdom and her travels come through in her home. She is a world traveler and is enjoying life. I am very happy for her that she has that opportunity now. She always wanted to travel. She's such a fun-loving person and she'll keep you laughing. She goes on shopping trips often and has the absolute best wardrobe. Jackie and Marlene are my friends and they are simply elegant women in their ways. They are connected to me and I want them to come to Atlanta to see my new home. They are happy with God and God has provided them good lives.

"Every little girl has a dream. Dreams come true. To have them, you have to let go of pride and let God put you where you can flourish and grow. I feel God has brought each of us to a healing place and I am blessed and honored to have shared my life with these women. Doing a book was a dream of mine and now it has happened. I hope there's a chance we can sing together again. For as long as I live, these ladies are a part of me. You find out in life there are only a few people who are really for you and that God is always with you."

Reflections
Memories, Accolades, and Favorites

This chapter is dedicated to The Andantes from their colleagues, friends, and family. Many people had so much to share. We wanted everyone to have a place in the book. Some people sent letters while others talked on the phone or sent emails. Some correspondence came in when they received awards in Detroit and Los Angeles.

Claudette Robinson
The Miracles and First Woman of Motown

"Congratulations Jackie, Louvain, and Marlene on being honored as The Distinguished Achievement Awardees at The Detroit Music Awards. The three of you have contributed much to the 'world of music'. It's exciting to know that you're being honored for your extraordinary musical sounds that helped to shape 'The Sound of Young America'. This is just the beginning of many more awards to come. May God continue to bless you with health, peace, and prosperity, and God's daily miracles. Your Sister of Song, Claudette Robinson"

Jeanne Whitlow-Mosley
Childhood Friend

"I was in the choir with Louvain and her sister at Holy Ghost in Detroit.

We met up by chance again several years later in Atlanta working for the same company. She was always a lovely young lady. From the early years of singing in the choir with her, she was always interested in music and singing. She was a wonderful singer. I knew one day she would go on to great heights in her life because she was determined and focused to get there."

Mildred Dobey
Choir teacher and the woman who named The Andantes

"I know they're legends now and I am so proud of them.

What they did back then was real singing and it made the Motown sound famous. They didn't get the credit they truly deserved. I knew their voices and I can hear them clearly on so many records."

Keith Summers
Fan and Friend in Baltimore

"The Andantes are long overdue for recognition and respect! They have been at the top of my list for many years. I've loved Tammi Terrell and The Andantes for most of my life. Some of my favorite songs are Martha's 'My Baby Loves Me', Kim's 'A Thrill A Moment', and Tammi's 'Come On and See Me'. I send much love to all. God Bless."

Rita Lumpkin-Daily
Childhood Friend

"My favorite song of theirs is 'My Guy'. They sound so great on that and it is their signature sound and song. I want to see the world give them a standing ovation everywhere they go. They deserve it. To sing on thousands of songs that people have loved for years, they deserve the credit finally. Everything happens in its own time and perhaps there's a reason why they weren't given credit then, but they need to be acknowledged here and now in the present. Many things happened in the record business and maybe they weren't meant to get the credit then. The Creator is giving them their due now, because the time has come."

Louis and Jean Burton
Friends

"My family and Louvain's family are like extended family. We have been in each others' lives for a long time. My wife and I remained friends with Louvain and Max Demps even after their divorce. She was a very nice lady. I find her to be a very congenial person and her children are very kind people as well. I'm an old jazz man and I had that in common with Mr. Demps. I came through the jazz era. A lot of the Motown musicians were jazz musicians and they played excellent music. What I witnessed with Lovuain was her determination and focus with music. She was diligent to pursue music."

Jackie Harper

Louvain's Godsister

"Over the years I hated that her talent was hidden behind a curtain. I feel she deserves recognition. I'm proud of her pursuit and determination to continue with the gift that God gave to her. She blesses many with her gift of song. She not only carries the gift of song in her heart, she carries it in her spirit. I am so glad she didn't put her gift in a drawer and leave it there, and that she continues to share the gift that God gave to her. She means so much to so many people. She has a lot of fans and I am proud to know her and proud of her success in life. I know people really appreciate Louvain's contribution to music. Tourists who come to Detroit want to see Hitsville. I'm so proud that my friend is a major part of that historical place. Ester Gordy did a great job for her brother, keeping that memorabilia alive for the public to see. I take it for granted sometimes because I live here, but it is pretty amazing to know Marvin Gaye, The Supremes, and The Temptations all got their start there at that small little house on Grand Blvd. I have fond memories of Motown."

Pat Cosby

Friend

"Thank you for your beautiful voices, the ultimate Motown sound.

"I love you so much."

Carl Lyons

Jackie's Cousin

"I can remember when she was a little girl and they had a piano. They were always around the piano singing and dancing."

Pat Washington

Fan, Friend, and Author in New York

"This award has been long overdue. I have always admired The Andantes for being great songstresses. A lot of backup singers can learn from them. I love them on 'Whisper You Love Me Boy' by Mary Wells because the harmony is so tight and crisp and I love that! I am grateful to The Andantes."

Michelle Murphy
Fan and Friend
"Congratulations on your honor! You deserve it! May God continue to bless you!"

Candace Wolfe
Jackie's Friend
"Jackie is a straightforward and honest person. She is a lot of fun and is an avid shopper. I feel very proud when I hear The Andantes on the radio. 'Baby I Need Your Loving' is my favorite. They're heard everyday on the radio and I'm happy and proud that they are getting their recognition."

Dan Verona
Fan and Friend in Long Beach
"The Andantes are the one consistent connection between nearly every single Motown song. I think they are wonderful and I'm glad they are getting this attention."

Sharon Davis
Author
"Like The Funk Brothers, The Andantes were the backbone and musical lifeblood of Motown Records when it mattered most. Fans have always acknowledged this. Now, with The Distinguished Achievement Award, the world can pay tribute to these wonderfully talented and grossly underrated ladies of soul."

Garnett Carter
Fan
"I would like to add my congratulations to The Andantes for them being honored."

Darlene Gist
Friend and Fan in New York
"We were playing records of all the songs that The Andantes were on. Their blend was so powerful with The Four Tops. They are the strong undercurrent. Without their voices on so many popular favorites, there would be a noticeable void. We didn't know their names until later in life, but we sure knew their

sound. These singers are like part of your family, because you had the same archetypes in your home with family and church and all over the community. They were our role models. I didn't know Tammi, Martha, Wanda, or The Andantes personally, but I knew them because we all came from the same root of homegrown southern families. Having the world know about The Andantes, changes a lot of stuff; such powerful icons as Tammi Terrell and The Andantes release more truth into the air. Clearing out the old stale air of misconceptions and hidden facts and giving the world a fresh new supply of clean oxygenated air for us to breathe! This is a good thing and the planet is happy about it!"

Michael Demps
Louvain's Son

"I want the world to know that there were people behind the scenes that made things happen. The Andantes helped put Motown on a higher plateau and you cannot deny that there is a sound. It's about time they're getting their recognition now. They need to tell their story in history. If you don't tell your story, whether you are sixteen or sixty-five, it won't be accurate and documented in history correctly. This is history that should be known throughout the ages. In the 60's the look was more important. Now everyone is realizing the music is important. You can look like anything now and become a superstar. It was always the music that mattered. I imagine that they felt used. They were needed and used in a way where they weren't fully compensated for their contribution. Unfortunately, nice people get pushed aside because they don't make a lot of noise."

Phillip Howell
Fan

"I'm a big fan of Motown 60's music. I liked all of your backup vocals with The Supremes, Martha and The Vandellas, The Marvelettes and The Four Tops. You had us fans fooled. Thank you for everything."

Bob Bosco
Fan

"Best of luck to The Andantes. They've never gotten the

credit they so richly deserve."

Joe Rivera

Of Earl Lewis and The Channels

"I met Louvain at the PBS Doo-Wop Special. When Louvain walked into the room I knew immediately who she was. I hold artists such as Louvain in high esteem and I want her to know how wonderful a role The Andantes played in the Motown sound. We have a common factor in Jesus and I thank Jesus for bringing us together for that brief moment. We have been friends ever since."

David Bell

Fan from Melbourne, England

"Like most fans I had never heard of The Andantes, as you were Motown's best kept secret for the longest while. Now your history is slowly unraveling and I realize how important you were in the story of Berry Gordy's legendary record company. For me, the defining moment for The Andantes is Mary Wells' 'My Guy'. The background vocals are awesome and make a great record sound more awesome. Thanks for all of the wonderful work that you did with my favorite artists."

Gert Pereboom

Fan in The Netherlands

"The girls worked so hard in the glory days of Motown. They are equal and an integrated part of the family. I guess you could call them The Soul Sisters. Wow, what a family. I was and still am amazed about their voices and how hard they worked. The amazing blend of voices from Marvin's 'I Heard It Through The Grapevine', to David Ruffin's 'Dinah'. It was always my dream to sing with The Funk Brothers. The tour that followed the film *Standing In The Shadows of Motown* allowed me to do that. I was up on stage to sing 'My Girl'. I was the last one to leave the stage and met the guys later. Despite the respect The Funk Brothers now receive I always thought The Andantes deserved a place in the spotlight as well."

Scott Taylor

Fan

"I wouldn't be honest if I didn't tell you that I was disappointed when I found out that many of my favorite songs had The Andantes singing on them. Later I really grew to appreciate what the group brought to the table. They added sweetening to the infectious Motown sound. Their sound became synonymous with the Motown sound. The first time I heard of The Andantes was within the credits of Marvin Gaye's LP, 'What's Going On'. A few years later Martha would reveal in *Right On Magazine* that The Andantes sang on 'My Baby Loves Me' and 'I'm Ready For Love'. I now know The Andantes sing on too many releases to count. It saddens me that they aren't in The Rock and Roll Hall of Fame. Their angelic singing is what helped to create the Motown sound. The Andantes are truly an American treasure."

Tony Willis

Fan in Wales, United Kingdom

"I too was somewhat disappointed to realize there were so many cuts by the 'stars' that were in fact backed totally by The Andantes. Don't get me wrong—it just seems a bit wrong now that the girls who were used so much and were so prominent on the recordings and someone else got the credit for them. This leads me to think about the Motown sound and I have to admit, there is a sound which was unique to Motown. It wasn't the lead singers or the groups that made the sound, it was the whole package. I am one of those people who buys discs and I want to know who is singing the backing vocals—is it The Raelettes, The Ikettes, The Sweet Inspirations, The Waters, The Jones Girls, Darlene Love, or The Emotions? It's now more obvious to me that The Andantes were the Motown sound for me. If you girls weren't on there, it wouldn't have sounded like Motown. You didn't get any label credit, liner notes, or sleeve credit. I think it is long past time for you to get major credit for the truly big part you have played in the production on all of those songs. Thank you for the pleasure that you have given me personally over the years with your recordings."

Julian Kent

Friend, Gritty North Recordings

"We all know how great The Andantes were, and what fine, kind ladies they are. Motown Records was blessed to have had them as an essential ingredient of the Motown sound. The number of recordings that they contributed to is incredible (over ten thousand!), and you won't find a less than excellent job done by them on each and every one. As a Hip Hop/R&B producer I hope that I may be gifted one day to work with a group that can even come close to emulating the talent and accomplishments of The Andantes."

Mary Andrews
Friend in Atlanta

"I actually love the song 'Money' and 'I Heard It Through The Grapevine'. There is a song called 'Lightening Never Strikes Twice'. I just love that song. It got airplay in Atlanta all the time."

Bridgett Jackson
Jackie's Niece

"I was young when Motown left Detroit. I have no memory of Jackie's Motown days and it wasn't widely discussed at home. I knew that she worked for Motown at one time. Now that all the accolades are being showered on The Andantes I am aware of just how talented and how much of an impact they had on the Motown sound. To know that their voices are on hundreds of songs that I heard then, and continue to hear now, is at times hard to comprehend. I am very proud of my aunt and Marlene's accomplishments. I had no idea growing up that I had such great singers and well-known entertainers in my midst. I truly wish I was old enough to remember. It is a wonderful and proud feeling to know my aunt sings on the legendary Motown songs."

Jeanette McKinney
Friend in Detroit

"My favorite is 'My Guy' because you can hear each one of them singing

'My guy'. My other favorite is 'Baby I Need Your Loving' because I was in the studio with them that day. I was snapping my fingers on that record. I was with them in Washington D.C. for Marvin Gaye Day. He gave them credit for singing and the show was really great. Jackie is an excellent dancer and we have a dance that we do called, The Detroit. Jackie loves to shop and would go down to Woodward Avenue to tell the sales ladies to call her when things went on sale and they would call her."

Gwen Cavitt
Friend in Detroit

"I am extremely proud when I hear Jackie on the radio. I absolutely love 'What Does It Take' and I also love 'My Guy'. Jackie collects Hard Rock Café Pins. I went to Philly with her to see The Liberty Bell and we had to look at pins forever."

Clarence Harris
Friend in Detroit

"I was always a part of their family. I went with them when they were young to Hartford Baptist Church. I sang in the choir with them. I'm happy that they're getting their recognition. They have a unique quality in their singing. I knew that Mildred Dobey named them The Andantes. In 1968, I wrote a song called 'Soul Day'. They sing on that with Carl Temple and Jimmy Scott. We recorded it at a studio on Grand River. They are multi-talented ladies."

Paul and Audrey Woods
Friends in Detroit

"We met Jackie when she was a young girl and are friends with her whole family. We loved and thought it was great that she was singing at Motown. We love all of the songs that she sings on. We feel very proud when we hear those songs on the radio. The nostalgia is overwhelming at times."

Eunice Smith
Friend in Atlanta

"To my dear friend Ms. Demps. You were the answer to my prayers. I met Louvain at a train station in 1991 and she smiled at me. She said, "Good morning, Praise The Lord." I then saw her a second time and we started talking and have been talking ever since. She is a legend and a true friend. The first time I heard her singing in church she was phenomenal. My favorite song is "I

Can't Help Myself, Sugar Pie Honey Bunch"

Janie Bradford
Friend and Motown songwriter

"During the magical days of Motown Records, The Andantes background vocals contribution was equivalent to Holland Dozier Holland's songwriting and productions impact on Motown's music history. Jackie Hicks always had a smile and a joke for everyone. Marlene Barrow was the more reserved one, while Louvain Demps was the cute one. Louvain joined the company at the very beginning singing with the Rayber Voices, whose other members were Brian Holland, Robert Bateman, and Raynoma Liles (who later became Raynoma Gordy). With the Rayber Voices, Louvain sang background on the company's first mega hit, MONEY (That's What I Want), of which I also co-wrote with Berry Gordy. One day while shopping at Crowlelys Department Store, I saw this dress that I wanted but realized that my lunch hour was over and I had to get back to Motown. Louvain was in the lobby and I told her about the dress. After about an hour of fulfilling my receptionist duties Louvain came back with the dress and handed it to me. Remembering this now, I don't think that I ever paid her and the more that I think about it I am sure that I didn't. However, I baby sat her son, Little Max enough in the reception area while she was in the recording studio making 'money' to pay for the dress. So we're even."

The Andantes' Memories

A small collection of their thoughts and memories

The Originals:
A great group of guys and fabulous singers.

Freddy Gorman:
A real friend and a great guy. We miss him terribly.

Jr. Walker:
Nice to work with.

Levi Stubbs:
Fantastic in every way; a fabulous singer and a genuinely nice person to work with.

Richard 'Popcorn' Wylie:
That's our guy. He's our truest friend. He wrote a song titled 'Marlene' and recorded it.

Mary Wells:
Mary was very nice to us and enjoyed us singing on her records. She was the first big star.

Obie Benson:
A class act! A beautiful big smile and always happy!

Lamont Dozier:
A very talented man and fun loving person.

Martha Reeves:
A nice and fun person, Martha accepted us. We are still friends with her today.

Brenda Holloway:
She was a nice person and a great singer. She is still a friend.

Patrice Holloway:
A lovely and nice person and great singer.

Paul Williams:
A clown, fun loving and joking around kind of guy.

Earl Van Dyke:
Talent personified.

Valerie Simpson:
A great visionary and professional.

Eddie Holland:
A very, very, nice man; a great talent with lyrics.

Frank Wilson:
A great talent. He knew what he wanted. He produced everyone just about and was very busy.

Eddie Kendrick:
He was always so nice and polite and so quiet.

Kim Weston:
A jewel of a friend. She wanted us on her records and wanted us on stage with her. She was a stand up lady for us.

Johnny Bristol:
A very great personality.

The Four Tops:
The best male singers!

Dennis Edwards:
A real fun guy.

Liz Lands:
She was from Atlanta, a marvelous voice, great singer.

Brian Holland:
A wonderful talent.

Bobby Rogers:
He is a nice, fun guy.

Smokey Robinson:
A fabulous songwriter and a really genuine and nice person.

Syreeta:
A nice person and wonderful singer. We miss you.

Lawrence Payton:
A true talent. He could hear tones that others could not hear; perfect pitch. The average person could not hear what he heard in his head. He was such an encouragement.

Frances Nero:
A lovely girl with a lot of determination. A big voice!

Clarence Paul:
He was a great stand-up guy; true talent.

Ronnie White:
He was always a gentleman. We miss you.

Marvin Gaye:
Multi-talented with great vision. On 'What's Going On', that's everyone in there just talking. Marvin had a lot of people stopping by and a lot of friends. Never can say goodbye.

Lois Reeves:
A nice girl.

Jimmy Ruffin:
Nice and a quiet, gentle soul and so talented. He was quiet and kept to himself. He was never caught up in what was going on or the gossip. He was always respectful and never talked about

people. He was an observer and never complained. He was a great guy and a great singer.

Hank Cosby:

He was a stand up guy and very helpful and insightful and father-like to us.

Stevie Wonder:

Silly, crazy, and fun-loving guy; a gentle giant.

Tammi Terrell:

What a voice! What a talent!

Mary Wilson:

A very honest person and she will tell it like it is.

Paul Williams:

Has a very soulful voice, he was a balladeer. You are missed.

Deke Richards:

He was a really nice man and a great, great, songwriter.

Paul Riser:

Such a talented man with what he did with the string arrangements. He was young with that talent. He came right out of high school to Motown and did very well.

The Supremes:

You are Supremely wonderful. Thank you!

Uriel Jones:

He was always a very friendly person and a supportive friend to us.

The Marvelettes:

Fantastic women! Thank you Wanda!

Cal Street:

Another lady who was always very friendly and loving, kind, and warm. She's still the same girl. The group was always friendly to us.

Edwin Starr:

We sang on 'War'. He was a very nice guy. We also sing on 'Twenty-Five Miles'.

The Velvelettes:

They were very nice girls. They deserved more recognition too, more promotion. They didn't get into the politics of the time.

James Jamerson:

He was just a genius.

The Funk Brothers:

True talents and unsung heroes.

The Vandellas:

Fantastic women!

Resources, Viewing, and Listening Materials

Further Reading

Berry, Me, and Motown
Raynoma Gordy Singleton
The Publishing Mills

Dreamgirl
My Life As A Supreme
Written by Mary Wilson
with Patricia Romanowski and Ahrgus Juilliard
St. Martin's Press - New York

The Detroit Almanac
Detroit Free Press
By Peter Gavrilovich and Bill MgGraw

To Be Loved
The Music, The Magic,
The Memories of Motown
An Autobiography
written by Berry Gordy
Warner Books

The Supremes
Florence Ballard, Forever Faithful
written by
Randall Wilson
Renaissance Sound and Publications

Divided Soul - The Life of Marvin Gaye
written by David Ritz
PaperJacks Ltd .
McGraw-Hill

Trouble Man
The Life and Death of Marvin Gaye
written by Steve Turner
ECCO Harper Collins

Marvin Gaye
I Heard It Through The Grapevine
written by Sharon Davis
Mainstream Publishing

Secrets of a Sparrow
written by Diana Ross
Villard Book - Random House

Between Each Line of
Pain and Glory
My Life Story
written by Gladys Knight
G.K. Hall & Co.
Thorndike, Maine

Motown: The View From The Bottom
written by Jack Ashford with Charlene Ashford
Bank House Books

My Sister Tommie, The Real Tammi Terrell
Bank House Books 2005
Ludie Montgomery
Vickie Wright

Audio

The Complete Motown Singles (all volumes)
Universal Music Group – Motown

The Motown Story CD Volume 1
Universal Music Group - Motown

Motown Master Recordings Original
Artists Karaoke
Universal Music Company-Motown
www.thesingingmachine.com

Lost in Meditation: Meditative Gregorian Chants on Amazon.com

Suggested Viewing

Marvin Gaye Live in Montreux 1980 - DVD
Eagle Rock Entertainment

Standing In The Shadows Of Motown - DVD
Artisan Home Entertainment

TJ Lubinsky's PBS Specials

Marvin Gaye in performance 1964-1981
The Real Thing DVD
Universal Music - Motown

Lyrics Credits
My Guy
written by William "Smokey" Robinson

THANKYOUS

From The Andantes

We wish to thank all of our Motown, Vee Jay, Brunswick, Chicago, and Detroit record label colleagues and very special friends, some who are no longer with us…

Thank you: The Originals, Marvin Gaye, Sonny Sanders, Popcorn Wylie, Claudette Robinson, Smokey Robinson, The Miracles, Janie Bradford, Singing Sammy Ward, Kim Weston, William Witherspoon, Sylvia Moy, Carl Davis and Brunswick, Paul Riser, Joe Hunter, Stevie Wonder, Beans Bowles, Benny Benjamin, Ivy Joe Hunter, R Dean Taylor, Gloria R. Jones, Shorty Long, Pam Sawyer, Brenda Holloway, Mickey Stevenson, Pat Cosby, Hank Cosby, Caldin Gill-Street, Martha Reeves, Freddy Gorman, Richard Morris, Holland Dozier Holland, Duke Fakir, Levi Stubbs, Lawrence Payton, Obie Benson, Little Willie John, Mabel John, Raynoma Gordy Singleton, Martha Reeves, Jerry Butler, Marv Johnson, Chris Clark, Otis Williams, The Temptations, Frank Wilson, Steve Major, Bobby Rogers, Frances Nero, The Four Tops, Lawrence Horn, Gil Askey, Meatloaf, Berry Gordy, Maurice King, Deke Richards, Ann Bogan, Clarence Paul, Pat Lewis, Clay McMurray and Karen Pree, The Marvelettes, The Funk Brothers, James Jamerson, Uriel Jones, Richard Street, The Contours, Earl Van Dyke, The Vandellas, The Velvelettes, The Elgins, Saundra Edwards, Sylvester Potts, George Fowler, David Van dePitte, Mike McLean, Barrett Strong, Norman Whitfield, Don Davis, Al Cleveland, Harvey Fuqua, The Supremes, Barbara McNair, Jr. Walker, Joe Hinton, Willie Tyler, Johnny Bristol, Morris Broadnax, Joyce and Pam Vincent, Telma Hopkins, Nick Ashford and Valerie Simpson, Marv Tarplin, Cornelius Grant, Harry Balk, Cholly Atkins, Johnny Allen, Isley Brothers, Amos Milburn, Soupy Sales, Gladys Knight and The Pips, John Lee Hooker, Bobby Blue Bland,

We want to thank the numerous friends and colleagues who contributed to this book. Thank you for being honest and helping us to tell our story.

Special thanks to Clarence Harris, Jeanette McKinney, Gwen Cavitt, Candace Wolfe, Gloria Hinton, Carl Lyons, Patricia A. Scott, Bertha Swain, Edith and Delbert Fails, Addie Moses, Mildred Harris, Carolyn Crawford, Ken Woods, Jacqueline Baker, Sheryl Mendoza, Toni J. Weems, Ulysses Council, Vicky Jackson, William Dorsey, Paul and Audrey Woods, Mary Lofton, Randy Amaker, Michael Amaker.

From Marlene Barrow-Tate

Thank you: My family, Lawrence Barrow, Marlene and Racing, Pearl Reid, Mr. Mrs. Thomas Barrow Sr., Harold Tate, Yvonne Rashida Harbin, Mildred Dobey, Pat Lewis, Etolia White, Ronald Rice, Rita Lumpkin-Daily, Vickie Dorsey.

From Jackie Hicks

Thank you: My family, Emory and Doris Hicks, Kevin Miller, Bridgett Jackson, William Brooks, Gloria, Darryl and Carryl Hicks, and all of my nieces and nephews.

From Louvain Demps

Thank you: My Lord and Savoir, Jesus Christ, my parents Alfred and Louvain Moore, Michael and Janece Demps, Max Demps Jr, Tony and Twinnette Demps, Max Demps Sr., Mattie Jean-Fawcett, Connie Dent, Joe and Coleman Castro, Ruthie, Ella, and Martina Satterfield, Alice Carter, John Szegedi, San Carmen, The Campbell-Gitomer Family, Meg, Richard, Austin and Campbell, The Boltz Family, Sarah, Adam, Bob and Christine, all of my children I have taught over the years, The Love Family, Marva, Josie, Youlanda, The Fierer Family, Bishop Alvin Andrews Sr., John Clemente, Henry and Susan Deluka, Pastor Joel Adams, Blenda Walker, Unice Smith, Apryl Berney, Dr. Neil Cooper, Michelle Jackson, Helen Taylor, Rocci Fissh, Charlie Dorch, Evangelist Vivian Evans, Sam Gilford, Harry Goodall, James Brey, Gregory Green, Julian Kent, Brenda Shirley, Joe Rivera, Lavern Washington, Elder Lee Ross and Shekina, Theresa Robinson, Rick Spirling and Mosaic Youth Theatre and cast of

Now That I Can Dance, Ester Edwards, Dr. Linda Cuture, Crawford Long Hospital, Pastor Alberta Lewis, Ministers Katherine Richardson, Lucy Heath, Tina Quinn, Gwen Hambrick, Barbra and Roland McLaurin, Ora and Peter Garel, Pastor Ann Avery, Ruby Martin, Bill Dahl, Dr. Erroll Effatt, Ralph Echols, Levetia Howard, Bill and Dawn Randell, Robert Taxlier, Janece and Martina Spencer, Steve Turner, Professor David Bell, Vence Kerney, Therisa Davis, Dianne Madison, Jeff Chrzcozn of Ideal Entertainment, Julie Demps Tucker, Prestatyn North Wales, John Pool, Mark Fletcher, Bernie O'Brien, Rob Wigley, Harry and Diana Grundy, The Midnight Hour Band singers Clair and Joe.

Special thanks to Raynoma Gordy, very special thanks to the following people; Marlene Barrow-Tate and Jackie Hicks for allowing Karen and Lolita to fill in when we performed in Wales, I love you both very much, I appreciate your graciousness and support; Karen Pree and Lolita, Clay McMurray, Jeanne Sorenson, Mike Critchley and Romeo, Tim, Dave Tidswell for his wonderfulness, Ian Curtis, for giving me the shirt off his back, Rhoda Collins, Tata Vega, for the prayer that we had together, Paul Barker, Steve Holsey, Oreal Taylor, Jackie and Marlene Harper, Norman Middlton, Maxine Sullivan, Harold Stone, Hal Lamar, Richard and Mary Law, Mike Thevis, Ed McQueen, Charles and Anita Russ, Bohannon, Harry Weinger, Andy Skurow, Universal Music Group, Janie Bradford, Charlotte Dudley, Susaye Green, Frances Nero, My family at Light of The World Church, Archbishop Jimmy Smith, and Pastor Ruth Smith, The Fountain of Praise Church, Bishop Gregory Bryant and First Lady Yvonnde Bryant, The PBS Family and TJ Lubinsky, Pattic Grober, Brenda Purcell, the Soulfood Gourmet, Jeanne Whitlow-Mosley, Julian Kent, Darlene Gist, Francine Owens, Marilyn Stewart, Louis and Jean Burton, Mary Andrews, Richard Anderson, Georgia Brock, Avivah, Lou Amaker, Steve Major. Rhythm and Blues Foundation, Timothy Websters, Donald Glenn, The Doctors at Emory Crawford Hospital. Thank you to all of the Motown and music fans worldwide, E.H thank you always. To Vickie Wright, thank you for taking on the project and for your time, talent, laughter, tears, and yes, monies – forever Louvain Demps.

THANKYOUS

This book is in loving memory of all of our colleagues who are no longer with us.

We also want to thank the following people for their generous outpouring of support and understanding during the process of this work.

The wonderful people of Detroit; there are hundreds and too many to mention. We thank you all. The Motown Museum, Robin Terry, Josephine Dare, The St. Regis Hotel, The Inn on Ferry Street, The Michigan Chronicle, Detroit Free Press, everyone at Sixties Detroit and Soulful Detroit, Kinkos in Detroit, for helping under the deadline. The wonderful Yahoo Group, Women of Motown, our friends at TammiTerrell.com, The Tammi Terrell Yahoo Group, thank you Collins Crapo, Walter at the Yahoo Groups,

From Vickie Wright

We had great support from all over. I am eternally grateful to everyone. I enjoy staying in touch with the fans and friends of Tammi and The Andantes, thank you so much. I answer every email I get and I appreciate all of you so much.

Very secial thanks to my family: Mother, my sisters Brenda, Linda, Teresa, Inette, my brother Dennis. My nieces and nephews Nick, Jessica, Brandi, Tommy, Sabrina, Tabitha, Jack, Billy Joe, Lilly, Willy and Aunt Helen Bailey. All of my super great cousins, and my great nieces and nephews too.

Thank you to my friends and associates: Phil Miller, Dorian Jones, Mary Sanchez, Vil Towers, Serge Crawford, Tina McLauren, Amanda Lewis , Mae E. Campbell, Albert and Alissa Haro, Andrea Nelson-Meigs, Beyonce Knowles (our muse), Julian Riley, Ritchie Hardin, John Lester, David Meikle, Lowell Boileau, Carl Dixon, Sis Detroit, Cool Ju, Keith Summers, Dave Leedham, Graham Finch, Andy Rix, Randi Russi, Nish, Soul Sister and Jimmy, Bobby and Vonnie Eli, Ian Melia "Mel and Then Some" for the wonderful scans, Chris "Uptight", Julie Dugan, Dave Randall K-Earth 101, Nicole Gutierrez, Kathy Buckley, Vivian

Porter K-Earth 101, Jameen Haynes, Cheryl A. West in The Fisher Building, Vanessa Wilson,Tom and Ann Ferranti, Rick Bueche, Laura Wright, Dr, Nicki Monti, Maryanne and Jenna Johnson, Martha Wash, Ray Gibson,Walter in the Yahoo Groups, Sharon Benson, Linda Sherlin, Talya Meldy for all of the advice on health, nutrition, love, and cleansing, Miguel Herrera, Michelle Mercado at Meesh Designs, David Rubin, Sue and Michael Egenolf, Jackie Jefferson, Mia Moser, Bruce Johnson RN, Noelle Blockson, James Hinton and Portrait in Black Films for your continued support, Mr. Dan Gross, Sonya Bernard Hollis in Battle Creek, Sharon Davis, John Brank, Lars Nilsson, Tammi Terrell-Dixon, Tammie Terrell Thompson, John Rajca, Shana Garrett, Sean Chapman, Dan Verona, Mary Gordon, Jillian Barberie at Fox, Keith Covington, Belita Moreno, Constance Marie, Sarah Mastey, Loralie Hernandez, Karen Samfilipo, Kelly Diaz, Sam Rahbari, Victoria Strauss and Writer Beware, Harry Weinger and Andy Skurow, Paul Barker, Sonny Sanders for coming in at the 11th hour, and Mr. Popcorn Wylie, we'll never forget the legend that you are. David Goodyear and Terry Dennison, Christopher Columbus, a very special angel when we needed one, Beth Swofford, Danielle Sisk, Patti Greany, Bob Giraldi, more angels when we needed them, Dinelle Watson, Keith Clarke, BIG BIG thanks to all of the motivational speakers I enjoy, Jim Rohn, Bob Proctor, Zig Ziglar, Vic Johnson, Guy Finley, Wayne Dyer, Maryanne Williamson, Louise Hay, you all help me more than you will ever know. Berry Gordy, The Supremes; Diana, Mary, and Flo, (my favorites), Dionne Warwick, Carol Williams, Jennifer Polston and Spencer, Susaye Green, Darlene Gist, a special remembrance for Renee Diggs. My family at Warner Bros Television: Deborah Oppenheimer, Bari Halle, Jamie Barton, Geriann McIntosh, Jeri Gray, Judy Bennett, Jeff Nagler, Myrna Cannon, Janie, Meneses, Lisa Haskins, Donnie Banks, Henry Johnson, Tonie Palermo, Bob Pincus, Emily Oshiro, Mr. Jon Gilbert, Frances Stevens, Esperanza Perez, Wendy Ward, Monalo Monteras, Kevin Fortson, John Stamos, Marc Alexander.

Contact the authors at AndantesBio@aol.com
and VickieandFriends.com
We look forward to hearing from you.

The Andantes receiving The Distinguished Achievement Award at The Detroit Music Awards.

Photo credit: Courtesy of The Paul Barker Collection

Louvain on stage in Wales with Karen Pree and Lolita.

Photo credit: Mike Critchley

Louvain belts out her signature high note on stage in Wales.

Photo credit: Mike Critchley

Louvain, Bobby Taylor and Jackie at The Heroes and Legends Awards in Los Angeles.

Photo credit: Mike Critchley

Louvain with Brenda Holloway.

Photo credit: Mike Critchley

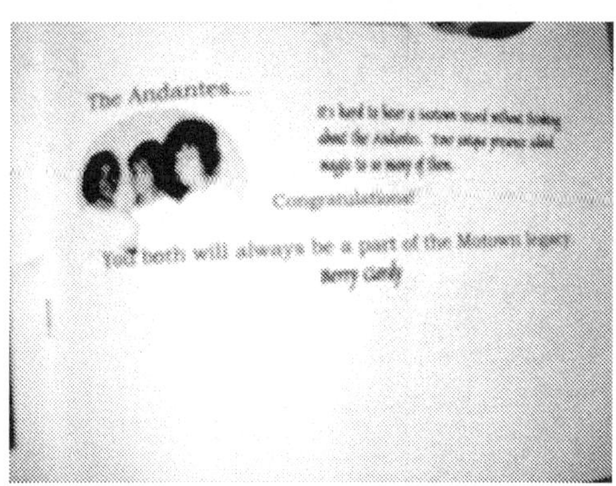

Accolades from Berry Gordy, taken from The Hal Awards Program.

"It's hard to hear a Motown record without thinking about The Andantes.
Your unique presence added magic to so many of them.
Congratulations!
You will always be a part of the Motown legacy."

Brian Holland, Martha Reeves, Jackie, and Eddie Holland on the right.

Photo credit: Jakcie Hicks Collection

Our friends, Sonny Sanders and Singing Sammy Ward

Photo credit: Jackie Hicks Collection

Our friends Bobby Rogers, Marv Johnson, and Johnny Bristol

Photo credit: Marlene Barrow-Tate Collection

Our friends, The Originals

Photo credit: Marlene Barrow-Tate Collection

Jackie, Duke of The Four Tops, Louvain, and Marlene

Photo Credit The Louvain Demps Collection

This was the first day I met Marlene and Jackie in person in Detroit.

Photo credit: Lynette Turner

Louvain and Berry Gordy Junior at the HAL Awards

Photo credit: Lynette Turner

Louvain's class

Photo credt: Louvain Demps Collection

Katherine Schaffner with Louvain at Now That I Can Dance

The Louvain Demps Collection

Louvain with original Supreme, Mary Wilson.
Photo credit
The Louvain Demps Collection

Louvain with Mable John

Photo credit: Lynette Turner

With the Holland brothers

Photo credit: Lynette Turner

Gil Askey and Louis Bellson at the HAL awards

Photo credit: Lynette Turner

The Andantes with dear and loyal friend Paul Barker for the grand reopening of Hitsville USA in 1995. From what Louvain said, this was their first time together since Motown left Detroit.

Photo credit: Courtesy of The Paul Barker Collection

Louvain, Marlene, and Jackie in Studio A.

Photo credit: Lynette Turner

The Andantes, the group that made Motown's records even better

By Steve Holsey

In all probability, the names Marlene Barrow, Jackie Hicks and Louvain Demps are unfamiliar to you. But you have heard them sing many, many times. Known collectively as the Andantes, these ladies, whose voices blend so well that one can only assume that it was ordained for it to be so, were Motown's foremost background singers.

One would be hard-pressed to name a Motown artist who has not had their recordings enhanced by the tight harmonies of the Andantes. The Four Tops, the Supremes, Kim Weston, Martha Reeves & the Vandellas, Stevie Wonder, Marvin Gaye...just about everybody. And especially the Marvelettes (more on that later).

The Andantes were formed in the early '60s, and right away Motown realized what a treasure it had in these ladies. One of their earliest assignments was providing background vocals for "Jamie," a Top 10 hit for Eddie Holland in the first quarter of 1962. From that time they were seldom not busy.

THE ANDANTES at the recent Motown Historical Museum "A Celebration of the Women of Motown" tribute/fundraiser. From left are Jackie Hicks, Marlene Barrow and Louvain Demps.

Studio A at 2648 West Grand Blvd. ("Hitsville U.S.A.") became, in many ways, like a second home for the Andantes. Demps, Hicks and Barrow became almost as essential to the sound and success of Motown recordings as the company's musicians, led by Earl Van Dyke.

To clearly hear the Andantes, one need only tune in to recordings like the Four Tops' "Ask the Lonely," Brenda Holloway's "When I'm Gone," Diana Ross & the Supremes' "Love Child," Marvin Gaye's "Ain't That Peculiar" and Mary Wells' "My Guy."

In 1964, the Andantes had a release of their own, "Like a Nightmare," which did not, unfortunately, become a hit but is said to be worth well over $1 thousand on the collectors market.

This is where there is another Marvelettes connection. Anne Bogan, who was recruited by the Marvelettes when one of their lead singer, Gladys Horton, left the group, was hired to do the lead vocal on "Like a Nightmare." (One would assume that Barrow, Hicks and Demps were not happy with this arrangement.)

Much to Motown's displeasure, the Andantes would occasionally leave Detroit to do backup sessions for non-Motown artists, most notably on Jackie Wilson's No. 1 classic from 1967, "(Your Love Keeps Lifting Me) Higher and Higher."

From the mid '60s onward, to expedite the recording process and to improve the sound of its "girl group" records, Motown took a giant step beyond merely having the Andantes sing *along with* the background singers on, say, records by Diana Ross & the Supremes and Martha Reeves & the Vandellas. Now the Andantes were sometimes singing *in place of* the other members of the group.

The lead singer and the Andantes — that's how it sometimes went. This was especially true with the Marvelettes. That's Wanda Rogers with the Andantes on, among others, "The Hunter Gets Captured by the Game," "When You're Young and in Love," "My Baby Must Be a Magician" and "Don't Mess With Bill." (It was the Marvelettes alone on earlier songs like "Please Mr. Postman" and "Too Many Fish in the Sea.")

It's Diana Ross with the Andantes on "Love Child" rather than Mary Wilson and Cindy Birdsong. Martha Reeves with the Andantes on "In and Out of My Life" instead of the Vandellas. Carolyn Gill Street with the Andantes on "These Things Will Keep Me Loving You" rather than the other Velvelettes, etc.

Louvain Demps says that she, Jackie Hicks and Marlene Barrow simply considered this doing the job they were hired to do as highly skilled session singers. There was, understandably, no sense of wrongdoing.

Incidentally, Barrow had to frequently stand in for Florence Ballard in the studio when Ballard began having the problems that would eventually result in her being asked to leave the group. It has been reported that on at least one occasion, Barrow went on stage with Mary Wilson and Diana Ross in Ballard's place (before Cindy Birdsong was hired).

Today, Jackie Hicks and Marlene Barrow still live in Detroit. They sing now and then. Louvain Demps lives in Atlanta. She, too, still sings but not on a full-time basis.

Though not pleased when Motown left Detroit in 1972 and did not ask them to go with them, after all they had contributed, the Andantes have a treasure chest of golden memories. On those rare occasions when they reunite, the harmonics fall right back in place.

The Andantes are stars in their own right.